Group Care
Practice with Children

Group Care
Practice with Children

Edited by

Leon C. Fulcher and
Frank Ainsworth

Tavistock Publications
London and New York

First published in 1985 by
Tavistock Publications Ltd
11 New Fetter Lane, London EC4P 4EE

Published in the USA by
Tavistock Publications
in association with Methuen, Inc.
29 West 35th Street, New York 10001

Printed in Great Britain by
Richard Clay (The Chaucer Press)
Bungay, Suffolk

British Library Cataloguing in Publication Data

Group care practice with children.
1. Children – Institutional care
I. Fulcher, Leon C.   II. Ainsworth, Frank
362.7′32   HV862

ISBN 0–422–78190–8
ISBN 0–422–78200–9 Pbk

Library of Congress Cataloging in Publication Data
Main entry under title:

Group care practice with children.

Bibliography: p.
Includes indexes.
1. Social work with children – Addresses, essays, lectures. 2. Social group work – Addresses,
essays, lectures. 3. Children – Institutional care – Addresses, essays, lectures. I. Fulcher, Leon
C. II. Ainsworth, Frank.
HV713.G763 1985   362.7   86–8641

ISBN 0–422–78190–8
ISBN 0–422–78200–9 (pbk.)

For our children
Katie, Mark, Helen, and Ewen

Contents

Acknowledgements

As editors we are greatly indebted to Gale Burford, Stephen Casson, Jon Conte, Angela Hopkinson, Henry Maier, Richard Small, and Karen VanderVen, the contributors to this volume. We are grateful to them for their endeavours on our behalf and their tolerance in waiting for this manuscript finally to reach publication. In the process of putting this volume together, delays were encountered because of life events neither editor anticipated.

We would both like to record our appreciation to the many people – students, teaching colleagues, agency personnel, and members of group care programmes – with whom we have had associations over the past few years. Through discussion and direct involvement, they have made us think again and again about particular features of practice.

Leon Fulcher would like to record his appreciation to the University of Stirling, Departments of Sociology and Continuing Education, for supporting initiatives which led to the development of group care training and research. He would also like to acknowledge the support of training personnel, managers, and practitioners from the Aberlour Child Care Trust, Dr Barnardo's Scottish Division, National Children's Home, Scottish Region, the Province of Newfoundland and Labrador Department of Social Services, the Royal Scottish Society for the Prevention of Cruelty to Children, and Strathclyde Region Social Work Department, Ayr Division, for providing opportunities to test out ideas about group care practice. The University of Haifa, School of Social

Work, and the Northern Ireland Certificate in Social Service Scheme have also contributed to the development of a cross-cultural perspective. Finally, he would like to convey his appreciation to Jane, Mark, and Katie for their support and encouragement, especially during the final stages of the volume's preparation.

Frank Ainsworth would like to acknowledge Middlesex Polytechnic, School of Social Work, which provided a testing ground for many of the ideas contained in this volume. Equally, he would like to acknowledge support from the British Council which enabled him to travel to Israel on two occasions, latterly to a joint University of Haifa, School of Social Work/University of Minnesota, Centre for Youth Development and Research symposium, facilitating the further development of a cross-systems and cross-cultural perspective. Additionally, the University of Western Australia, Department of Social Work and Social Administration in Perth is acknowledged for providing a visiting position on two consecutive summers (but Australian winters), offering time to think in a new environment and thereby enriching his cross-cultural perspective. At a personal level, Patricia Hansen of the Perth department is thanked for being a sensitive guide, alerting him to many of the subtle differences between British and Australian services and practices. Last, but not least, he would like to record his thanks to immediate family members.

Finally, we would like to acknowledge the technical support offered by staff at the Information Technology Unit at the University of Stirling without whose assistance the volume would have been delayed even longer. The editorial support and secretarial wizardry provided by Jane Fulcher is richly appreciated and we hope she will accept our warmest thanks in this regard.

Preface

Since publication of our first volume, *Group Care for Children: Concept and Issues*, the editors have travelled far. The distance travelled is both in regard to ideas about group care practice as well as land miles. We are fortunate to have been invited to take the material contained in the last volume to many audiences, either individually or in partnership. Most of these audiences have contained direct care practitioners as well as supervisory or service planning personnel who have received these contributions with enthusiasm. Confirmation was obtained for views articulated about the positive aspects of group care services for children, and this allowed some of the inaccurate and harmful myths about this area of practice to be challenged, if not dispelled. Such confirmation has come not only from British and American audiences, but from those in some of the remoter parts of Canada, Denmark, Israel, and more recently Australia.

Throughout these endeavours, support has also been obtained for our view that a cross-system analysis of group care services is useful in enabling understanding of the field to grow. Certainly practitioners from all four major resource systems – health care, education, social welfare, and criminal justice – have responded to our material with enthusiasm. Our travels have also re-affirmed the importance of maintaining a comparative perspective, both cross-cultural and cross-national, to ensure that theoretical and practical materials have a wider application and are not restricted to local interpretations.

This testing out of our material, with many audiences and in many places, has also pushed us to think still further about group care practice with children and other populations, most notably handicapped adults and elderly people. This second volume is a by-product of that thinking. We have endeavoured, along with our contributors, to write more directly about practice issues. This has proved to be a very demanding task and our success, or otherwise, will no doubt be judged by the readers. We have sought to provide materials that can be easily understood and used in practice. At the same time, we have selected materials based on established knowledge rather than simply anecdotal musings.

We are aware that the notion of 'de-institutionalization' has continued to receive extensive publicity since the publication of our last volume. This attractive ideological initiative – described as such because it lacks clear empirical support – deserves both praise and criticism. Clearly, any child who can be assisted with their difficulties, while living in their natural home, should be supported in this way. The criticism of 'de-institutionalization' is that it represents more than simply good professional practice based on the idea of 'least restrictive' care and treatment options. 'De-institutionalization' is supported by an alliance of those who oppose all forms of group living *per se* and financial administrators whose only interest is the reduction of service costs. This simply reduces the range of service options available to children and families, especially those who for sound reasons warrant a period of care and treatment in a group care programme. 'De-institutionalization' draws support from a limited number of studies – now dated – that point to the dysfunctional nature of some institutional contexts. We hope that our first volume and this one will go some way towards challenging that literature.

A final note is required with regard to the use of terms and spelling. As before, we were faced with problems of terminology and consistency of presentation when drawing chapters together from both sides of the Atlantic. We have again used the convention of allowing each chapter to reflect national differences, such as in the spelling of 'programme' and 'program'. We hope that our readers will not find this approach too distracting. Lastly, we have chosen to use the term 'children' throughout, even though we are well aware of the fact that many practitioners who read this book will be engaged in work with older children. Thus, our use of the term 'children' should be taken to refer to both children and young people. We hope that our readers will find this decision acceptable.

1 Group care practice with children

Frank Ainsworth and
Leon C. Fulcher[1]

Introduction

Our aims in this volume – although somewhat ambitious – have been to draw together, from both sides of the Atlantic, contributions which make use of concepts and issues outlined in our earlier volume *Group Care for Children* (1981). We asked two of our former contributors and five new ones to address specific themes which highlight group care practice with children in each of society's four major resource networks, including health care, education, social welfare, and criminal justice. We remain committed to the idea that comparative methods of enquiry are fundamental to the continuing development of services for children. In carrying out their tasks, our contributors have considered practice themes from a range of theoretical perspectives, giving added substance to the comparative aims established at the beginning.

By way of introduction, we outline the concept of group care as developed in our earlier volume, re-establishing the claims for viewing group care as a field of study, an occupational focus, and a discrete area of practice. This is followed by a discussion on the purpose of group care, focusing on developmental enhancement and the promotion of competence in children. Next, the methods which underlie group care practice with children are explored, calling attention to both direct care and indirect care methods and skills outlined in our original volume. Finally, the contributions offered in this new volume are introduced and discussed, highlighting the context of practice and ways in which direct and indirect care are related in group care practice with children.

Group care as a field of study

In our earlier work, a number of means were used to draw attention to group care as a field of study. Initially we noted how group care facilities are to be found in each of society's major resource systems of health care, education, social welfare, and criminal justice. This was done by highlighting the presence in each of these systems of comparable large institutions, namely mental hospitals in health care, boarding schools in education, former workhouses in social welfare, and prisons or reformatories in criminal justice. The extent to which these institutions reflect the historical development of the field of group care was also acknowledged, as was the manner in which the client populations in each of the various institutions may overlap. A diagram was used to underscore the presence of different types of institution in each system and this is repeated in *Figure 1.1* (Ainsworth and Fulcher 1981: 4).

Figure 1.1 Large institutions across systems

Health care	Education	Social welfare	Criminal justice
Asylums	Day and boarding	Orphanages	Prisons
Mental hospitals	schools, incl.	Lodging houses	Reformatories
Hospitals for the	normal,	Emergency care	Detention centres
mentally retarded	maladjusted, and	centres	Training schools
General hospitals	emotionally	Community	
	disturbed	homes	
	children		

We then commented on the emergence in each of the four resource systems of a range of smaller group living situations, which developed often in response to criticisms of the debilitating nature of life in large institutions. These smaller group living situations were identified as residential nurseries, family group homes, peer group residences, hostels, refuges, shelters, or semi-independent grouped living units. Finally, attention was drawn to the apparently simultaneous growth in all four resource systems of various types of day service. This was also underscored by the use of a further diagram, as shown in *Figure 1.2* (Ainsworth and Fulcher 1981: 8).

Figure 1.2 Types of day service across systems

Health care	Education	Social welfare	Criminal justice
Day hospitals Day clinics Health centres Day nurseries	Youth and community centres Recreation and leisure centres Day nurseries Day schools Intermediate treatment units Alternative schools	Day care/play groups Activity programmes Intermediate treatment units	Community service centres Day and project centres Intermediate treatment units

In this way, it was possible to present a composite picture of the field of group care as it incorporates institutional care, residential group living, and day services across the four resource systems, a picture which is encapsulated in *Figure 1.3*, also drawn from our earlier work (Ainsworth and Fulcher 1981: 8).

Figure 1.3 The field of group care across systems

Health care — Institutional care — Residential — Day care,
Education group living treatment,
Social welfare learning
Criminal justice activity,
recreation, or
leisure
service

Excluded: Other community-based services, i.e. general practice, community nursing, classroom teaching, clinical social work, or probation.

As a result of the foregoing explanations, it was possible to offer a statement setting out the extent of the field of group care. The field was said to

> 'incorporate those area of service – institutional care, residential group living (including, but not necessarily requiring, twenty-four hour, seven day per week care) and other community-based day services (covering lesser time periods) – that supply a range of developmentally enhancing services for groups of consumers. The location of a service in the Group Care field results from identifying how each pattern of service places emphasis on shared living and learning arrangements in a specified centre of activity.' (1981: 8)

In making such a statement, it can be seen that we resist the superficial dichotomy that currently prevails in the human services, where institutional care is located at one end of the 'continuum of care' and day services at the other extreme (Jones and Fowles 1984). Such a dichotomy between institutional and community care services is to be resisted in that it is based primarily on a social policy perspective and fails to acknowledge the other structural and organizational commonalities we choose to emphasize (Glaser and Strauss 1967). All forms of institutional care, residential group living, and day services operate with a group focus, using the physical and social characteristics of a service centre to produce a shared life-space (Lewin 1952) between those in receipt of care and those who give it. By identifying the field of group care as it spans each of society's four major resource systems, and by calling attention to the common characteristics of programmes in this field, it is therefore possible to consider group care as a discrete area of practice. As such, group care practice needs to take its place alongside other services that offer benefits to children and families.

Group care as an occupational focus

Having delineated the field in this way, and noting the characteristics of institutional care, residential group living and day services that result in a centre being located in the group care field, consideration was then given to ways in which a distinct occupational focus is created for practitioners. It was noted how group care personnel in each of the four resource systems are given diverse occupational titles and the children with whom they work were also labelled differently. In health care, for example, group care practitioners are usually called nurses and the children are referred to as patients. In education practitioners are generally identified as teachers and the children as students or pupils. Social welfare offers even greater diversity with group care practitioners being referred to as child care workers (in North America), for example, or social workers (usually residential social workers in Britain), while children are identified as clients or residents. Finally, in the justice system titles may vary widely from officer, warden, warder, or guard to correctional counsellor, and children may be referred to as detainees or inmates. Each occupational title given to practitioners or ascribed to the children reflects the changing emphasis found in each system, be this a treatment, teaching, nurturing, or control function. It was acknowledged that some of the broad generic titles, like nurse, teacher, or social worker, applied to broader categories of personnel who would not be referred to as group care practitioners, since they can be found working in services that would not qualify for inclusion in the group care field.

A brief review of the training orientation adopted for group care practitioners within the four resource systems also highlighted some important issues. It was noted how in current training endeavours for nurses, teachers, social workers, and those in the area of penal practice scant attention is given to core issues for group care practitioners. These issues involve such features as group composition, life-space counselling, and environmental characteristics of the centre from which services are provided. Comment was also made on the general absence of attempts in training efforts to blend material that supports the broad orientations of education, recreation, counselling, and care. It was suggested that this was a matter of serious concern since these diverse orientations provide the methodological basis from which group care practice is developed.

Delineation of the field and identification of common character-istics at the heart of all group care programmes inevitably led to other considerations. In the earlier writings an attempt was made to construct a curriculum statement that outlined the training requirements of group care practitioners. This reflected an awareness of deficiencies in training that inevitably grew out of the considerations referred to above. Thus, support was found for the argument that group care practice is not simply an extension of other occupations such as nursing, teaching, or social work but is a separate occupation which warrants, indeed demands, training that focuses on specific material that is omitted from the training of particular occupational groups.

The purpose of group care for children

Before examining the methodological basis of group care practice with children, some comment is necessary on the purpose of group care. We have already shown how group care facilities are to be found in each of society's major resource systems, including health care, education, social welfare, and criminal justice. Each of these resource systems is, of course, much broader in conception than the field of group care as we have defined it. In fact, each system has evolved at various points in time in response to widely held notions of human need. It is in this respect worth clarifying the central notion or purpose which underpins each of the systems in question. As shown in *Figure 1.4*, the major purpose for health care is to treat, for education to teach, for social welfare to nurture, and for justice to control.

Figure 1.4 Systems and underlying purposes

Health care	Education	Social welfare	Criminal justice
Treat	Teach	Nurture	Control

All of these systems, therefore, embody value preferences, organizational features, and occupational characteristics that reflect these purposes. As far as group care services for children are concerned, this creates a dilemma, irrespective of the sponsoring resource system. The dilemma is that, in seeking to provide developmentally enhancing services for children, group care needs to blend all of these purposes and to blend them in such a way that they result in the provision of nurturing care, socialization experiences and, if necessary, offer specific therapeutic intervention (Maier 1979). This means that any group care centre has in various ways to incorporate aspects of treatment, teaching, nurturance, and control, according to the specific needs of children referred there. Yet experience has shown that the ethos of most group care centres is heavily dominated by the single, yet simplistic purpose that underpins the resource system sponsoring a centre. This often results in the overall developmental needs of children being overwhelmed by a single purpose, which although important, is an incomplete response at best. *Figure 1.5* enables us to convey some of these issues more clearly.

Figure 1.5 Resource system, underlying purpose, and areas of overlap in group care

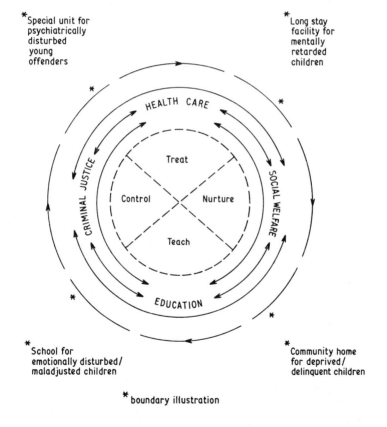

This diagram can be viewed in several ways. First, it offers a

purely static picture of the way in which each resource system reflects a single purpose and how a group care centre contained within that system will emphasize that purpose. By including illustrations of group care services which combine more than one purpose, or which seek to transcend the boundaries between systems, it is our intention to give the diagram a more dynamic or interactive perspective. It is worth noting, however, that facilities which seek to transcend or overlap boundaries, and in that respect respond to a broader conception of children's developmental needs, are invariably the most controversial programmes. Public debate frequently surrounds the operation of these programmes, with strong pressure being exerted from many sources for these group care services to concentrate on a single purpose rather than operating from a multiple-purpose orientation. This is the case even when a multiple focus or a blending of purposes is obviously in the best interests of children and their developmental progress.

Having made the point that resource systems are reluctant to incorporate a broader perspective on the developmental needs of children (although specific personnel working within systems may not be so constrained in their thinking), it is worth giving further consideration to the notion of developmental enhancement. The notion of developmental enhancement can be seen to have links with other notions, such as those based on the promotion of competence (Maluccio 1981) which are evolving in other areas of human service. The life model of social work practice, for example, which incorporates a competency perspective and conceives of people 'as active, purposeful and having potential for growth and development' (Germain and Gitterman 1980: 370) is remarkably similar to the notion of developmental enhancement we have used here. The competency approach places emphasis on practitioners 'identifying, supporting and mobilising adoptive processes through the use of meaningful life experiences and the provision of opportunities that enhance mutual fit between persons and environments' (Maluccio 1981: 10–11).

This description about the function of social work practitioners is similar to that noted in our earlier volume about group care personnel. There, it was said that

'practitioners take as the theatre for their work the actual living situation as shared and experienced by the child. This is because it is through events that occur and experiences that are acquired in this life space that developmental opportunities are either reduced or enlarged. The group care practitioner therefore seeks to use the natural opportunities provided by daily life events within the group care programme (such as the provision of food, clothing, play opportunities) as foci for interventive acts that raise a child's level of personal functioning.'

(Ainsworth and Fulcher 1981: 234)

It can be seen that both sets of practitioners must apparently give attention to the use of life experiences and the provision of growth-enhancing opportunities. It was further pointed out that: 'Planned interventions are also arranged which exploit the total environment of a programme ... involving the disciplined use of time, space, objects, events, activities, and exchanges between children and significant others, be they staff or children' (Ainsworth and Fulcher 1981: 234).

In this way, attention was drawn to the importance of person–environment interactions, which are an integral part of the life model of social work practice articulated by Germain and Gitterman (1980).

Central to the life model of social work, and the notion of developmental enhancement used here, is the notion of competence. This notion, which implies 'effective functioning within one's environment' (Goldfield and D'Zurilla 1969: 156), has a rather chequered history, involving both an internal psychodynamic perspective and a behavioural approach. Recently a more overtly ecological dimension has been expounded (Sundberg, Snowdon, and Reynolds 1978) which takes note of differences in capacity and skills, variations in motivation and recognizes environmental features that impinge on personal functioning. This particular approach to competence is thought to be especially relevant for social work practice (Maluccio 1981) and in our view has similar value for group care practitioners. Maluccio suggests that in association with the life model, the concept of ecological competence leads to an approach which views the promotion of competence in human beings (adults and children) as a significant function of social work intervention! We would argue that this is a comparable function to that performed by group care practitioners when they promote developmental enhancement for children. According to Maluccio, this approach to promoting competence is characterized by eight special features (1981: 11). For our purposes these features have been adapted to refer to child populations only.

- A *humanistic* perspective towards children.
- A re-definition of children's problems in *transactional* terms.
- A re-formulation of assessment procedures as *competence clarification*.
- A re-definition of child and practitioner roles, with children viewed primarily as *resources* and practitioners as *enabling agents*.
- A re-definition of the child–practitioner relationship in terms of *mutuality* and *authenticity*.
- A focus on life *processes* and life *experiences*.
- An emphasis on using the *environment*.
- Regular use of *feedback to children*.

Noticeably these features do not refer to the purposes which underlie the resource systems of health care, education, social welfare, or criminal justice we have outlined. Instead, these features require a blending of the principal functions performed by each of the four systems and find application in every group care centre.

The emphasis on person–environment transactions, on the use of normal life events, and on the positive exploitation of environmental influences to support developmental processes is, of course, entirely compatible with recent contributions on the ecology of human development (Bronfenbrenner 1979). Interestingly enough, it also emphasizes the 'triggering function' group care practitioners perform in their relations with children. Practitioners perform this function by seeking to 'set in motion, or mobilize [a child's] coping capacities, natural life processes and striving towards growth' (Maluccio 1981: 22). In our view, this describes what group care practitioners seek to do whenever they engage with children in a group care centre, using a variety of educational, recreational, counselling, and nurturing interventions to promote development. It is to these types of intervention, and the methods and skills used in practice with children, that our attention turns.

Group care methods and skills

We suggested earlier (Ainsworth and Fulcher 1981) that methods and skills in group care practice can be classified in relation to *direct care* or *indirect care*. Direct care involves work carried out directly with children, while indirect care involves work carried out for and on behalf of children, but not necessarily with them directly. Such a distinction can be used to clarify the tasks carried out by different practitioners and the range of activities which take place in any group care programme. Whilst providing an initial overview of the functions of group care with children, it is still necessary to identify methods and skills that are essential components of practice in this field. McMaster (1982a, 1982b) has gone some way towards clarifying the methods and skills associated with group care practice, but we remain unconvinced by the simplistic distinctions this writer has used. We think it is more helpful to distinguish between a range of direct and indirect care methods and skills, as referred to in *Figure 1.6* (Ainsworth and Fulcher 1981: 240).

It is the aim of this new volume to consider a range of methods and skills that are available to group care practitioners seeking to offer developmentally enhancing services for children and families. In the chapters that follow – loosely in some instances and more directly in others – attempts are made to elaborate on some of the methods and skills identified above. We think this will assist the development of a wider framework within which to understand group care practice with children. It is our view that the absence of such an agreed framework has had adverse effects on practice in the field, by limiting the ability of practitioners to communicate with others about their work and by confusing the focus of training initiatives.

Before introducing the contents of this volume, we think it will be helpful to clarify further the direct–indirect methods and skills framework outlined above. While such clarification is offered primarily in relation to the direct care areas, we are of course conscious of the need to extend this to a clarification of indirect care areas as well. However, we make no apology for concentrating our efforts in this instance on direct care methods and skills. This is because face-to-face encounters between workers and children

Figure 1.6 Group care methods and skills in direct and indirect care

Direct care (work with children)	Indirect care (work for and on behalf of children)
Provision of everyday personal care (food, clothes, warmth)	Environmental planning (fabric maintenance, improvement, modification, or extension and purchase of personal care essentials and equipment)
Formulation of individual care and treatment plans	Design implementation and evaluation of unit programme
Developmental scheduling (individual and group) play and activity based	Administration and management of programme budgets, data collection, and resource acquisition exercises
Activity programming (individual and group) play, recreation, and informal education	External relations with media, local community, kindred systems and significant others
Group work (educational, activity, and therapeutic formats)	Programme leadership and team development
Life-space counselling (individual and group)	Selection, training, and assessment of performance of practitioners
Programme planning, unit level	Supervision and monitoring of practitioners' work and programme achievements

can be said to offer the most powerful influences available to those who spend time in a group care centre.

To provide a more detailed assessment of the methods and skills framework, two analytic views of practice in a group care programme will be used. These analytic devices, one referred to as a side elevation and the other as a cross-section, were developed through participation in teaching and consultation exercises with group care practitioners (CCETSW 1983).[2] Both diagrams have helped us to convey our ideas and to engage practitioners in exploring the implications of our framework in direct care work with children and other populations. We hope the material will be of similar benefit to the reader. For analytic purposes, a side elevation of group care practice can be illustrated as shown in *Figure 1.7*.

This diagram allows us to emphasize the view expressed in

Figure 1.7 A group care programme – side elevation analysis

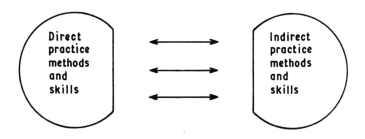

our first volume, that direct and indirect methods and skills have to interact with each other in a dynamic, yet ordered manner. We acknowledged then and confirm again that this presentational device is useful only to the extent that it allows one to 'freeze' for analytic purposes the complex elements of practice interacting in any group care programme. One must guard against the static picture which *Figure 1.7* can convey, for we in no way wish to reduce a complex set of relationships to an unrealistic level of simplicity. Direct and indirect methods and skills are both interacting and interlocking in the operational life of a group care centre. However, in order to understand these features of practice and to be able to converse about them as well as assist practitioners in learning how to use them, a still analytic picture is necessary. This allows one to identify the component parts of practice and provides the opportunity for studying and understanding processes by which the parts are assembled and become an interacting entity. We think that such a visual representation will assist practitioners to comprehend the framework and endorse its relevance in their work with children.

To extend the analysis of direct care methods and skills, it is possible to take both halves of this side elevation and, so to speak, convert them into a cross-sectional view of group care practice, as illustrated in *Figure 1.8*.

Here our efforts are focused on the direct care portion of this side elevation, detailing the analysis as shown in *Figure 1.9*.

In developing this analytic and presentational device, we faced the problem of order once again. Whilst we are certain that each method and skill area has to be accommodated in every group

Figure 1.8 A group care programme – cross-sectional analysis

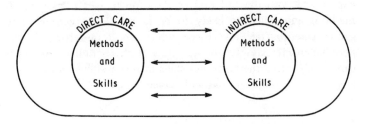

Figure 1.9 A group care programme – side elevation analysis (direct care only)

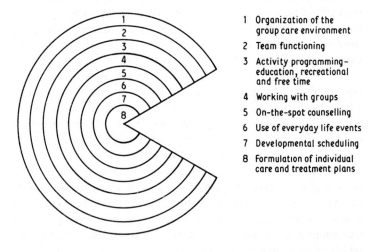

1 Organization of the group care environment
2 Team functioning
3 Activity programming – education, recreational and free time
4 Working with groups
5 On-the-spot counselling
6 Use of everyday life events
7 Developmental scheduling
8 Formulation of individual care and treatment plans

care centre seeking to provide developmental opportunities, we are aware that differences in emphasis or priority may be found in the use of these methods and skills in practice. We are also aware that each method and skill area is in dynamic interaction with the others. In this respect the order implied in *Figure 1.9* may be open to question. For this reason, the point is again made that we are not presenting a static model. Rather we are seeking to hold still or 'freeze' a set of variables in order to facilitate closer examination of each. For this reason a somewhat arbitrary presentation is inevitable. Readers should, therefore, feel free to experiment with the ordering of these areas, to consider which methods and skills are likely to be found at the very core of group care practice and those which are found towards the periphery. Interestingly enough, it is at the periphery of direct care practice that methods and skills in this and the indirect care area are most often blurred and subject to overlap.

Group care practice with children

This volume is divided into four main sections which develop from the foregoing discussion. The first section, focusing on the context of practice, is introduced with a paper by Henry Maier which explores the inherent strains that exist when trying to provide primary care in secondary settings. Drawing from his knowledge of child development, Professor Maier draws upon the contributions of social systems theory to consider how group care practice is influenced by the organizational structures which sponsor them. Next, we explore the culture of group care practice with children. Attention is drawn to the developmental conditions which are available in a centre, issues of organizational design, the physical environment, team functioning, and group development – all of which contribute to the culture of practice found in any centre.

Consideration then turns to a section on direct care practice with children. Stephen Casson introduces this section with a chapter emphasizing the importance of a shared language and practice. Addressing the issue of programme planning at unit level, this chapter outlines an Action Plan approach to practice which should be of particular interest to managers and team leaders as well as members of group care teams working in the social welfare and social services sector. Next, Gale Burford provides a discussion on personal care and treatment planning, drawing primarily from work carried out in the criminal justice sector with children and young people. This chapter offers a detailed review of the research and practice literature, giving special attention to the assessment of interpersonal maturity and the importance of differential care and treatment planning. Richard Small and Leon Fulcher then consider practice themes developing out of the educational sector. These writers note how teachers and group care workers can work co-operatively to teach competence skills and thereby assist children with special learning needs to engage their social world more effectively. Finally, Karen VanderVen explores the developmental and therapeutic role of activity programming in group care. Drawing from an ego psychology perspective, this chapter addresses a range of issues which apply to younger children as well as those in the older age range.

The third section is concerned with indirect care practice carried out on behalf of children. The first chapter in this section, written by Gale Burford and Leon Fulcher, explores the extent to which resident group composition influences the functioning of group care teams. Reporting on practice research carried out over a three-year period, this material is unique in terms of both its research design and the confirmation it provides for practice wisdom which assumes that different residents influence group care workers in very significant ways. Next, Angela Hopkinson addresses the problem of working across boundaries in group care practice. Writing from a background of practice in the health care sector, this chapter focuses on the complexities of group care and treatment in a multi-disciplinary child psychiatric unit. Finally, Jon Conte provides a challenging argument in support of group care workers engaging with parents to teach them how to manage their children's behaviour problems more effectively. This chapter offers a detailed review of the literature on parent training interventions and addresses a number of practical questions associated with the relative advantages of different approaches to parent training activity.

In conclusion, we return to the question of future directions for group care. Building from a comparative perspective, we briefly summarize conclusions drawn from more than a decade of travel throughout Britain, the United States and Canada, many European countries, Israel, and Australia. The need for new training initiatives is highlighted; initiatives which are not limited to a particular occupational grouping, client grouping, or limited to practice in a particular type of setting. Finally, consideration is given to the application of concepts, methods, and skills outlined in this and our earlier volume, emphasizing the need for practice teaching units and centres for group care training and research.

As before, this volume is not intended to provide a total statement about group care practice with children. Rather, it gathers together current thinking from both sides of the Atlantic and addresses a number of practice concerns which confront workers in this field, whether they be nurses, teachers, child care workers, social workers, or personnel working in the juvenile justice system. In this respect, we hope that the volume will be added to an expanding literature which seeks to enhance our understanding of group care practice and promotes interest in the positive contributions services in this field can offer children and families in the decades ahead.

Notes

1 Frank Ainsworth is Head of the School of Social Work at Phillip Institute of Technology in Melbourne, Australia. Leon C. Fulcher is Director of Social Work Education at the University of Stirling in Scotland.
2 We are indebted to members of a workshop held at Green Park, Aylesbury, Buckinghamshire, in September 1981, under the sponsorship of the London and South East Office of the Central Council for Education and Training in Social Work, for assistance in the development of this material.

References

Ainsworth, F. and Fulcher, L. C. (eds) (1981) *Group Care for Children: Concept and Issues.* London: Tavistock.

Bronfenbrenner, U. (1979) *The Ecology of Human Development.* Cambridge, Massachusetts: Harvard University Press.

Central Council for Education and Training in Social Work (1983) *A Practice Curriculum for Group Care.* London: Staff Development in Social Services, Paper 14.2.

Germain, C. B. and Gitterman, A. (1980) *The Life Model of Social Work Practice.* New York: Columbia University Press.

Glaser, B. G. and Strauss, A. L. (1967) *The Discovery of Grounded Theory: Strategies for Qualitative Research.* New York: Aldine.

Goldfield, M. R. and D'Zurilla, T. J. (1969) A Behavioural Analytic Model of Assessing Competence. In C. H. Spielberger (ed.) *Current Topics in Clinical and Community Psychology,* vol. 1. New York: Academic Press, 151–96.

Jones, K. and Fowles, A. J. (1984) *Ideas on Institutions: Analysing the Literature on Long-Term Care and Custody.* London: Routledge & Kegan Paul.

Lewin, K. (1952) *Field Theory in Social Sciences.* London: Tavistock.

McMaster, J. M. (ed.) (1982a) *Methods in Social and Educational Caring.* Aldershot, England: Gower Publishing.

—— (1982b) *Skills in Social and Educational Caring.* Aldershot, England: Gower Publishing.

Maier, H. W. (1979) The Core of Care: Essential Ingredients for the Development of Children at Home or Away from Home. *Child Care Quarterly* 8 (3): 161–73.

Maluccio, A. N. (ed.) (1981) *Promoting Competence in Clients: A New/Old Approach to Social Work Practice.* New York: Free Press.

Redl, F. (1959) Strategy and Technique of Life Space Interview. *American Journal of Orthopsychiatry* 29 (1): 1–18.

Sundberg, N. D., Snowdon, L. R., and Reynolds, W. M. (1978) Towards Assessment of Personal Competence and Incompetence in Life Situations. *Annual Review of Psychology* 29: 179–211.

Section I

The context of practice

2 Primary care in secondary settings: inherent strains

Henry W. Maier[1]

Introduction

The ever present struggle of reconciling *primary* care requirements of children[2] living in group care facilities with the programs *secondary* organizational demands, finds its expression and potential balance in the daily work of the child care staff. Actually, workers seem to be serving two masters. The following account of a staff meeting at a prestigious child care agency serving forty severely disturbed elementary and high-school age youngsters has all the symptoms of the aforementioned strain. I submit that the underlying themes[3] are inherent in staff deliberations almost anywhere.

Let us look in on a typical one-and-a-half-hour staff meeting. Forty minutes have been taken up with general announcements, enquiries, administrative admonitions, and 'success proclamations'. Finally, the main topic of the particular staff session was raised: in which ways can we strengthen the group care components of the residential program? This topic was introduced and interpreted by the group life supervisor expressing the need for more precisely tailored individual approaches to the residents' therapeutic requirements. One worker immediately elaborated on her idea that she could do more for the children if she were to work solely on weekdays. It seemed that the children with whom she was the most involved tended to be away on weekends. Additionally, she pointed out, on Mondays and Tuesdays these children were apt to have their difficult days, coinciding with the time she was off-duty. Numerous other valid suggestions were brought up, each one involving potential alterations in each worker's investment in time or personal energy. Workers also volunteered specific program suggestions for selected children and recommended different care practices for a particular sub-unit. These latter suggestions created both excitement and frustrations. A member of the administrative staff, in the midst of this lively discussion, wondered with serious concern whether or not these valid suggestions may not lead to a kaleidoscope of practices and potentially a separate group care program for each resident! Another worker quickly added that the administrator was right; the suggestions would result in a unit with extremely poor organization. Someone else added ironically: 'These kids could then get up at any hour of the day. Maybe then the evening shift can see how it is to get the youngsters to straighten out their rooms rather than always creating a mess.' At this point, other workers voiced in turn their readiness for more personal involvement with the children. Several questioned with sincerity whether they could muster the energy for added personal care engagement − particularly with the difficult children under discussion. Somehow the perennial request surfaced about keeping the children's play areas free of office staff cars so that the children and care workers could play unhampered. This concern was pushed aside with embarrassed laughter and the meeting continued as before, by more or less acknowledging all input but dealing with none.

Towards the end of the allotted meeting time, a residential worker recommended a trade-off in more time with the kids in exchange for less paperwork. This suggestion, which received an affirmative sigh from many workers, reminded the agency director (who chaired the session) that he was about to take up the issue of recording with the care staff. He wanted their assistance in finding ways the agency could more effectively manage their recordings and to verify the residents' progress. He regretted that time had run out too quickly for this 'lively and productive' staff meeting. The issue of alternative ways of recording was recommended as the major topic for next month's staff meeting.

What happened in this staff session seems to be merely an echo of what happens on the front lines of group care practice. In the treatment planning for each child, in the daily care activities, in the co-operation and stress of group care work, in programme planning, and in the scheduling of staff, an inherent struggle exists between provisions of personalized care and institutionalized demands for organizational accountability. We also noted that the primary care issues, though central to service delivery and the agenda of this particular staff meeting, still remained sandwiched between organizational concerns. The scenario offered above articulates the major thesis of this chapter, which is that provision of *primary* (personal) care within a *secondary* (organizational) care context always presents a difficult course but it can also offer challenging opportunities.

Primary care within a secondary care context

Care in everyday life

The care received by children growing up in their own families is directly impacted by the quality of care rendered to their immediate care-givers. Infants have their parent(s) 'at their command, families to protect the mothers or alternate caregivers, societies to support the structure of families and traditions to give a cultural continuity to systems of tending and training' (Erikson, as quoted in Maier 1978: 89–90). It is common knowledge that the quality of care and training of children is directly related to the sense of well-being experienced by their care-givers. Emlen's reminder, 'if you care for children, then care for parents' (Gabarino 1982: 234), can be broadened and applied to all types of primary care-givers: grandparents, babysitters, foster parents, day care and, of course, residential care workers. In fact, a decisive factor in group care work is whether there is or is not 'ample care for the caring' (Maier 1979: 172). Bronfenbrenner pointedly asks, 'Who cares for those who care?' (in Gabarino and Stocking 1980: 3).

An ecological perspective about care

Validation of the above notion has recently been elaborated by Bronfenbrenner in his empirically grounded ecological formulations

(Bronfenbrenner 1979). An ecological system perspective applies not only to interpersonal interactions but also to the mutually reinforcing processes and events between larger and smaller systems. Interconnectedness is part of the nature and pattern of life (Bronfenbrenner 1979). In particular, we note that events in larger systems impact as much, if not more so, the nature of events in the relevant subordinate systems. In everyday life, for example, to cite Bronfenbrenner, 'a person's development is profoundly affected by events occurring in settings in which the person is not even present ... Among the most powerful influences affecting the development of young children in modern industrialized societies are the conditions of parental employment' (Bronfenbrenner 1979: 3–4). The degree of work satisfaction, working hours, and take-home pay more strongly affect the degree of each parent's active and psychological availability and the nature of parent–child interactions than his or her personal qualifications for parenthood.

We note that much of a child's life is determined by secondary life systems which involve neither the developing persons as active participants nor the young persons' care-givers in their role as the children's nurturers. Significant events occur that affect what happens in the setting which contains the developing person (Bronfenbrenner 1979: 25). It is important to note that members of the subordinate settings have little power to influence the very events which tend to influence strongly their own as well as the lives of care-receivers (Bronfenbrenner 1979: 255–56). As illustrated, working hours, salaries or wages, and to an extent, work satisfaction, are beyond the control of the recipients. The labour market, policy makers, and other *settings of power* 'control the allocation of resources and make decisions affecting what happens in other settings in the community or in the society at large' (Bronfenbrenner 1979: 255). These decisions also reach into the lives of almost all individuals within their spheres – and subsequently impact the course of each family.

Applied to our immediate concerns, the nature of primary care in any children's centre is strongly coloured by the employment policy and the institution's pronouncements on the workers' roles within the total scheme. Such factors operate quite independently of the workers' personal and professional qualifications or the staff members' personal commitments to daily work tasks.

The ecological impact of secondary systems upon primary relationships is applicable to group care situations, regardless of whether the children are in care for part of, most of, or continuous 24-hour services. We noted in the staff meeting described above that a worker's personal readiness to adapt her/his working periods to the requirements of a particular group of children hinged on the program's readiness to adapt to particular working arrangements. One can assume with relative certainty that the decision would ultimately be made on the basis of how feasible it was for scheduling changes to be instituted within administrative considerations, in other words 'making the least waves'. It is unlikely that such a decision would be made on the basis of children's and workers' urgent need for each other.

At another point in the foregoing meeting, a clinical recommendation for greater individualization was immediately counteracted with the fear that increased attention to individual children's differential requirements would lead to a lack of clarity in oversight and would result in organizational 'shambles'. It is true that individualism in its extremes becomes the antithesis to organizational order, yet the reverse is also the case: organizational rigidity negates individuality, which is apt to receive less emphasis on organizational deliberations. Finally, we noted that a staff meeting, with an agenda focused upon the children's welfare, started and ended with organizational concerns. Service factors, such as whether recording for communication between staff would allow more intense therapeutic involvement, were easily overridden by administrative concerns. The professional dilemma of increased direct versus indirect service time became reframed into an organizational dilemma; the urgency of translating service gains into measurable standards of reporting. There is an ever-present pressure to account for the program's efficacy to the next *larger* systems, namely the sponsoring and controlling systems. Altogether the issue before us is that primary, individualized care concerns tend to give way to those of secondary, organizational power.

The dominance of administrative over immediate child care concerns is not necessarily a peculiarity of the foregoing staff meeting. Rather it is inherent in the exchanges between two systems where the super-system or the organizational system substantially influences the norms, pace, limits, and flow of communication of its sub-systems. The sub-systems are those of the client, staff, group care, and physical domain systems. Each of the sub-systems, in turn, from time to time attempts to impact the organization. Only when persons associated with any one of the sub-systems marshall sufficient thrust to counteract organizational 'necessities' do such sub-system efforts prevail. For instance, care workers could have jointly and in a determined manner insisted upon a more flexible waking-up time for children going to a school some distance away. They might have their breakfast ahead of the children attending the local school. The latter could proceed more leisurely, as they were also typically children who required more flexible time demands. It is possible that the straightening up of rooms could occur at varying points of the day. For some youngsters it is more important to start the day and get off to school with as little hassle as possible, whether their room is sufficiently tidied up or not. Such a thrust from the care staff might have led to an organizational change where workers were employed and supported for their flexibility and adaptiveness to situational demands rather than for allegiance and conformity to institutional practices. Moreover, such a thrust from a sub-unit could bolster administrative adaptiveness and readiness to justify to its own workers and the outside that children's centres are for adaptive living rather than providing a showpiece in housekeeping. Unmade beds at noon can represent sure signs that certain children and staff are working actively on other issues vital in the developmental lives of these particular children. (No apologies or regrets are necessary, if such conditions are part of acceptable agency standards.)

In general, the tendency is for organizational requirements to modify special individual care requirements. Such a dilemma can be witnessed when plans for children who are ready to engage in a wider range of activities are throttled when an *agency* does not perceive itself as being ready to branch out. Many activities beyond the perimeter of a group care centre are prematurely curtailed for fear of unfavourable public relations. Other activities within the walls, such as appropriate exceptions for some children, variations in procedures, and programmes for separate living units are discouraged, or, worse, not even considered due to fear of de-stabilizing the programme's overall efficiency. The submergence of exceptions, special considerations, or a thrust towards greater diversity, all have a slight ring of truthful imperative. Where would the children, the staff, and the service be, if the stability of the agency or programme were endangered? But is it really such an either/or dichotomy?

The very struggle between individual freedom for personal initiative and adherence to organizational norms, the desire to serve individual children, and to remain mindful of what others would say; and above all, the strain to become fully involved in child care activities while remaining a faithful peer to one's fellow workers, represent mind-boggling and organizational nightmares. It is not unlike the everyday struggle of being a 'good' parent as well as a full marriage partner; or a 'good' sales person who fully meets a customer's interests as well as her/his own, as a business person. All these activities elicit conflicting requirements, a notion considered more fully below.

In group care practice it is a common occurrence that an intense involvement with one child readily creates a demand by other children for equal time. The result may be a rivalrous frown by co-workers with a possible warning against over-involvement or at least a curt reminder that not every staff member can afford such a heavy investment. Similarly, the impulse to deal with children according to the situation, viewing rules as being flexible or not applicable at a particular time, can easily be interpreted as a worker operating without standards or denying support to her/his fellow workers. It is also true that a search for common guidelines in the care of children may be continuously disrupted by the awareness that such common rules cannot apply logically to a number of children, or will not be carried out by some 'notorious' care worker. In another instance, the hope that a token economy can provide a reliable and objective approach, rendering personal involvement unnecessary, is somewhat marred by recent data revealing that private, interpersonal negotiations over the allotment of a token may be more important than the token system *per se* (Maier 1981: 49–50).

The complexities just described spell out the interactional conflict between the individual's worker role and her/his larger system – the work group. Actually, this inter-system strain exists between all individual and organizationally oriented processes and systems. Individual and peer group needs, situational and organizational procedures, clinical and bureaucratic considerations are in continuous interaction, meaning that one cannot deny the other. All are part and partners within the same larger whole. While this is so, in this struggle it is a fact of life that the supra-system largely determines the eventual outcome (Resnick 1980). The credence which is ultimately given to work with each child, to staff co-ordination, and to the creation of specific care procedures is not so much decided by the children's and staff's ongoing requirements, as by the *organization's* capability and status to deal with these vexing issues. Child care issues, clinical considerations, and staff investments decline or flourish in the arms of the bureaucratic organization.

Bureaucratic and clinical issues

It is taken for granted that much or most of an administrator's time (director, superintendent, principal, chief, or others) is necessarily absorbed with organizational concerns and the representation of her/his organization to the outside world (its respective supra-system). It is not surprising that much of her/his time is consequently spent separated from the day-to-day concerns of the service. When she/he does devote time to any particular feature of the programme, the impact of that agency administrator will be keenly felt and how she/he chooses to assess a particular programme segment will also influence the direction and quality of care delivery of the centre's staff. In a visit to one centre, for instance, is the administrator, with concerns about the number of children in service, likely to focus on whether things are 'going smoothly', whether the hot water supply is sufficient, or the reasons why two window panes are broken again? In another example, the administrator's interests might focus upon the residents' progress, and, in particular, upon the difficulties and problems encountered by the staff, especially in the most recently emerging trouble spots. The former scenario of *administrative* emphasis is more common. That is understandable because this dimension relates to an administrator's working spheres. The latter foci of enquiry dip into the domain of care systems, also appropriate but more removed from the group care manager's view. It is no wonder then that care workers sense administrators' preoccupation with the 'agency's' major management;

consequently administrators' preoccupations readily become part of the operational norms of a staff team.

The clinical aspect of group care work

Practice in group care entails clinical work — that is, care provided on the basis of actual *observation of specific individuals' (child's) requirements* in contrast to a provision of group care on the basis of generalized expectations for members of a circumscribed group — a class of people.[4] *Clinical* means selected care for a specific individual in terms of her/his idiosyncratic situation on the basis of the group care worker's best professional understanding and skills.

The bureaucratic aspects of group care work

Practice in group care also entails bureaucratic performance. This framework inherently requires that a worker fulfils and enhances the service obligations of a particular organization, simultaneously delivering such service efficiently, regularly and impartially. Child care, when it is bureaucratically couched, means providing care of equal quality to all residents, without regard to personal discriminatory differences or personal whims. Bureaucratic service means performance by established norms, applicable as decreed or agreed, regardless of individual reservations or inconveniences. Both clinical and bureaucratic perspectives, that is *primary* and *secondary* care, have their legitimate claims for existence. Both systems seem to be diametrically opposing forces. Both exist within the same interactive field in group care practice with children. A closer look at this interlocking of primary and secondary care (or clinical and bureaucratic) systems may be helpful.

A conceptual look at primary (clinical) and secondary (bureaucratic) care systems

The individual and organizational strains and dilemmas mentioned above may be understood and explained through reference to system analysis (Parsons 1964) and, in particular, Herman Resnick's explication (1980).

Historical vestiges

Group care centres, in many ways, possess some stark vestiges of pre-industrial economic society where kinship controlled the occupational system. Members of the kinship system virtually owed their lives to their place of work, with its intense face-to-face encounters, strong authority structure, and close kinship alliances. By contrast, modern society assures economic success through mobility, loyalty to the task rather than persons, and entails de-personalization of face-to-face contacts (Litwak and Szelenyi 1969).[5]

The interpersonal linking functions of the former kinship system are, in general, currently maintained by the family, but also by other modern primary systems: friendship, club, community or group, and group care centres. The ecological, economic, and political functions of kinship systems are now distributed over many modern structures such as government, worlds of business, the trades, and professions. This professional realm also includes the service delivery aspects of group care. The two contemporary spheres of everyday social functioning – the *interpersonal* and the *economic/political* spheres of group care practice – can be likened to a kinship economy.

Sociological manifestations

Parsons (1964) and Resnick (1980) establish that nowadays we are confronted with two distinctly separate *group* systems and system patterns of interactions. *Primary systems* comprise face-to-face small groups in close association like teams, cliques, and gangs as well as socially engineered primary systems. Such socially engineered systems might include communes, educational classes, military platoons, therapy and encounter groups, as well as day care or around-the-clock-care groups. *Secondary systems*, on the other hand, are organizational, usually large impersonal systems, for example: business, religious, professional, military, industrial, recreational, and other societal organizations, including group care service organizations.

Primary social systems are noted for their face-to-face association and co-operation among the members. They serve individuals and, at the same time, these individuals are fused into a common whole. Means and ends become intimately tied to one another within a primary system.

Secondary systems, by contrast, stand out as opposite but also complementary to primary group systems. Secondary group systems represent a larger whole, with an emphasis upon contractual, formal, and rational convenient relationships. People are linked with each other; nevertheless their involvement remains specialized and limited. Most striking, these systems function separately and apart from the individuals involved. Secondary settings, in contrast to primary ones, are not an end in themselves, but represent means to other ends (Resnick 1980: 29).

Secondary orientations – such as formality, rationality, and structural emphases – find less favour in primary systems. In secondary systems, correspondingly, primary orientations – such as spontaneity, informality, and personalization – cause strain and are a sign of dysfunctioning. It is essential then to identify and discriminate between the respective variables and demands of primary and secondary groups.

Variations in emotional demands
The expression of emotions in primary systems is expected and encouraged. Group members are expected to convey affect and to be emotionally supportive of each other. In secondary groups, a different norm is operative: emotional neutrality. The latter requires a withholding of personal emotions and relies upon an inconsequential acceptance of others. Emotional expression may deplete energy and lead to a diminishing involvement, or it may be transformed into obstacles for necessary co-operation. The norms of both systems create potential complications. In organizational settings, the demand for emotional neutrality is easily experienced as coolness or disinterest. The latter may lead to a reduction of energy input and to 'merely attending to one's work'.

It is no wonder that workers deeply involved in the care of children find much personal satisfaction in their practice; but they are simultaneously pulled by the need for neutrality and some may even consider deep emotional involvement as 'improper professional' behaviour. Other workers with greater emotional restraints are astonished to find children in care being less personally responsive to their semi-neutral behaviours, even though such workers seemingly attend to all details of group living. The administration is never apt to question the performance of the latter workers' practice; but emotionally expressive *co*-workers may criticize this care-giving performance as being 'cold' and 'uncaring'. We observe that some workers attend *personally* and *affectively* to the children, deeming that fulfilling *care* requirements is central to group care practice; others conscientiously attend most judiciously to *service* demands, expressing harmonious caring within the organization. These competing expectations create an ever-present strain in primary systems which have an organizational mission. These factors have been pointed out emphatically by Wolins and Wozner: 'The logistic requirements of the well-oiled bureaucracy negated the demands of close, intimate interactions — the essence of people-changing activity ... The recipients of care become objects of the bureaucrat's manipulations and are denied control or participation in decisions that affect reclaiming and activity' (1982: 54). As Goffman (1961) contends, the bureaucratic model is antithetical to reclaiming.

Standardization in opposite directions

Primary group systems depend essentially upon *particularistic* standards. Only the person within each situation will know in which way a rule is applicable. It all depends upon the particular circumstances and the individuals involved. These notions are applicable to face-to-face interactions. In contrast, secondary group systems build upon *universalistic* standards. Rules apply to all in order to be fair to each. Uniformity in standards assures clarity, order, and authority of standards. Either standard — particularism or universalism — may lead to complications for its respective system. Standards purely adaptable to each situation may eventually obviate all standards, while an insistence upon general standards will deny individual requirements. This may be carried to the extent where uniform rules may eventually have little relevance for the person involved, rendering uniform regulations ridiculous.

In organizational life, particularistic considerations are immediately perceived as a threat to law and order, or favouritism unbecoming to an organization. In primary group life, universal rules are quickly resented as obstacles to individual initiative and differences. In group care practice, much energy is invested in working out applicable rules or standards for each living unit and child. These struggles, whether or not a set of rules is actually fair and applicable, can be understood by Parsonian concepts. Arguments for uniform getting-up time, for instance, are supported for their fairness, orderliness, and universal clarity for *all*. Counter-arguments could justify adaptive wake-up procedures citing fairness to particular children's circumstances or individual worker's preferences.

Scope of interest

Primary group systems like their forerunners, the kinship systems, serve *manifold* interests. This multi-dimensional interest or preoccupation with many details, forges a homogeneous group prototype (i.e. a family, a commune, a friendship association, or a congenial living unit). Secondary systems, in comparison, concentrate upon *specific* interests in well-defined areas while serving a wide spectrum of purposes. It is not surprising that, in a case presentation for example, the organization-oriented workers can explain her/his *typical* work with specificity and technical detail. On the other hand, clinically oriented persons will likely preface their remarks with the explanation that their account is 'atypical'. They are apt to lose their audience with their mixture of details spiked with generalizations, unless their clinical accounting establishes a profile or constellation – that is a viable case report. A valid case presentation, by the way, evolves out of an interlinking of details into a generalized explanatory whole.

In another area of practice, we note that diffusion of worker or agency interests is frequently augmented by specific interests, such as an all-out push for greater physical order, for individual tutoring, or for a reliance upon group meetings. Each push tends to distort the program towards the selected, more narrowly specified area. In addition, while undergoing these 'purges', workers and children tend to become classified according to their performance in the selected sphere of interest. It is no wonder that group care programs blossom or shrivel under specialized program reforms. Much depends upon whether such program alterations include both inherent group care realities: primary and secondary system demands.

Status alignment

A preference for *ascription* – the qualities owned by persons according to their positions in life – adds stability to primary group life. This is true so long as these qualities actually define the nature of face-to-face interactions. The following instances are a few of many variations: older and experienced staff are more competent; younger or new members require added guidance. Sex, ethnic, and other genuine differences are significant so long as they do not perpetuate stereotypes but represent affirmative differences instead. In organizational and primary systems, achievement or accountable competence defines status. Definition of status and change of status for organizational and primary systems have relevance in relation to system strains (Resnick 1980) and contemporary struggles over changing societal norms (Maier 1969, 1974). In group care practice, a continuous internal conflict exists as to how members' status is to be measured in their *ascribed* roles within their primary group position. For children, an example would be eldest, youngest, leader; or for workers, seniority, job classification, or personal achievements may apply. Competence requirements seem to encroach more and more upon primary as well as secondary group demands (Maier 1974). Then, too, the recent awareness of sexism and racism in traditional primary group life − where reliance upon ascriptive values also perpetuated discriminatory practices − has furthered a shift to secondary system practices. To put it another way, there is a shift to award status by actual competence and achievements. This leaning towards competence rating in primary settings brings with it the danger of 'hollow existence' for staff and residents alike. Are children and workers appreciated because they are familiar in one's life experience, because they are part of one's heritage, or because of their accomplishments and deeds (Resnick 1980: 40–2)?

A study of the foregoing variables highlights dynamic tension which is inevitable in both types of system, primary or secondary. Tension and repeated requirements of adaptation are particularly germane to group care settings, where the organizational service demands basically rely upon face-to-face interactions. System stresses, then, call attention to either adaptation towards organizational maintenance or clearer emphases upon children's and workers' primary care requirements. In either event, system strains can be viewed as dynamic rather than stultifying forces.

Two orders of primary group systems

Children and workers are frequently admonished to adhere to group norms 'for the sake of everyone' or 'for the sake of the group'. Frequently, it is not clear whether 'everyone' pertains to the group members or refers to the persons associated with the group's sponsorship, the group's supra-system. On the other hand, 'for the sake of the group' might be a shorthand expression used for the wellbeing of the individual group members as persons. Another possibility could be 'for the sake of the maintenance of a group' as a sub-unit of a larger system (Maier 1978: 202–05). Each of these appeals serves different demands and different masters. Group care workers have to be clear in knowing with which primary group they are aligned at various points of their 'practice'.

If the group focus and concern of the moment pertain directly and personally to the individuals making up the group, then the interactions serve essentially the individuals' capabilities, enhancing interpersonal relations and self-verification. Care workers then have to deal with the group members' effectiveness in communication, interpersonal negotiations, and power juggling. Workers' group building efforts serve, essentially, as a source of individual identity formation. In practice, this would mean that a group planning session for an evening of fun would have to include an opportunity for *all* group members to share their wishes and expectations, searching for common denominators and give-and-take negotiations with regard to expectations which cannot be accommodated on that particular evening. Above all, the evening of fun has to stand as a joint group accomplishment so that members may verify that 'I had a part in our having fun'. In short, 'for the sake of the group' in this context reflects individual group members' investment as well as a sense of group achievement.

In contrast, when concerns revolve around group building tasks which seek to maintain and to enhance the group as part of a larger whole, then efforts serve primarily a supra-system of which the immediate group is a part. An example would be care workers and children engaged in establishing their 'citizenship' credibility, posing their group as a viable unit within a larger group care centre. Concerns will typically reflect the mechanisms of control, establishment of norms, and value aspirations which are in tune with the larger system's expectations. Adaptation occurs not so much in tune with individual members' readiness but instead to the degree that everyone can stretch in adapting to the group's standards. Workers and children are challenged to find a fit. The group forgoes personal whims, shaping up in order that *the group* can gain or maintain a favourable place within a larger scheme.

Care workers' strains

The foregoing discussion of natural system uncertainties and differential but interlocking group-building factors may explain the many worlds in which group care workers operate. Yet an explanation never resolves day-to-day practice dilemmas. A *care* worker within an organizational context exists always in a dual world – in two contradictory systems. No wonder that 'burn-out' is a rather common occurrence (Mattingly 1977). Burn-out, rapid staff turnover, a high degree of personal frustration, perplexing diffusion in job descriptions as well as expectations can be traced to these contradictory work conditions. The work circumstances have inherent systemic difficulties; they have to be surveyed for their organizational facets rather than for signs of human frailties (Mattingly 1977; Pines and Maslach 1980). These complications emerge for all human service workers who are *employed* or *engaged* voluntarily to help individuals within the context of a service organization. In everyday family life, a parent comes close to such a dilemma when she/he shares in a child's discouragement or delight over school requirements. Is the parent subsequently to respond as a partner and spokesperson for the child and her/his family or the school system? Moreover, the group care worker is continuously required to function as the clinical (*individual*-care oriented) worker *and* as the agency's (organizational *service*-oriented – bureaucratic) worker. Nevertheless, solutions for some of these vexing situations may potentially be possible.

Potential solutions to the strains between clinical and organizational service delivery

Child care within an organizational context does not necessarily have to lurch in different directions, frustrating both clinical or organizational operations. Clinical and organizational requirements do demand different efforts. They can be conceived as dialectic rather than counter-productive forces at the point where either system's pull constitutes a partial investment rather than a negation of the other system. In other words, clinical demands for continuous flexibility and basic care decisions in the hands of the group care workers can be recognized and carried out as basic organizational procedures. Organizational uniformity is established through decentralization of power and responsibility. Management and organizational supervision are called upon to oversee that care workers fulfil their *clinical* obligations to their clientele. At the same time the care workers can operate among themselves with a high degree of variation in style within the agreed care and treatment plans.

Parallel to such a clinical/organizational conceptual shift is the organizational stance which demands a universal program policy and which requires care workers and others to formulate concrete and communicable care and treatment programs. Such programs have to define both the definite outcomes expected (objectives) and also the actual care and treatment activities to be pursued with the children and their respective families. Care workers and their supervisory staff have then the opportunity and challenge of defining their territory and operations *within* these spheres of work (Bakker and Bakker-Radbau 1973). Many instances of organizational interference with child care decisions can be traced to the absence of clarity about the nature and boundaries of group care practice, in addition to the tendency of organizational requirements to permeate uniformly all parts of the service. Clear enunciation of care and treatment objectives and procedures could establish the extent to which group care works as a vital part of the organizational machinery.

The above suggestion to define primary care or clinical work within a secondary system or bureaucratic operation is consistent with an organizational perspective which views the parts as a dialectic whole. But the purpose here is not to give greater credence to bureaucratic considerations but rather to call attention to the organizational context which constitutes the *supra*-system within which clinical work proceeds. Group care workers may feel even greater commitment to their work with the children and, hopefully, a true identification with practice rather than yielding unnecessarily to bureaucratic demands. In reality it *is* the larger context — the organizational factors — which ultimately shape and determine the nature of group care practice. Consequently, group care work has to be formulated, operated, and evaluated from an organizational perspective. It is within such a perspective that personal (clinical) care and treatment can fully proceed and flourish within a well-organized agency programme.

Responses to children's emotional demands
We postulated earlier that quality practice in group care demands close intimate interactions — the essence of people-changing activity — while bureaucratic practices are antithetical to care and treatment efforts (Wolins and Wozner 1982: 54). Group care workers tend to be caught between these opposing demands such as being fully engaged with *all* children and being especially attentive to children who require individual adult involvement. The daily worker's dilemma is well known: provide a very personal 'good night' to all and also provide quality involvement with a few individuals. These difficult time-chores are inherent in all caring care and do not represent an inadequacy in the organization or staff. The organizational issue is: in which way can staff be assisted to assure more quality time with the children or young people *plus* added time with some. Simultaneously, one needs to recognize as appropriate the children's wish for more attention and the workers' disappointment in not being able to deliver to everyone's satisfaction. Organizationally and clinically, caring efforts have to be objectively reviewed for the possibility of additional or alternative opportunities for personal, intimate interactions between the children and their daily care-givers. Clinically and organizationally, efforts have to be directed towards finding new opportunities for intimate and varied interaction between children and workers. For the latter, this kind of searching may lead to such practices as provision for intimate conversations before bedtime, rather than a mere get-together snack period; reading a story rather than a TV hour; a quick tussle, or other special quality time with workers. Another example would be the worker being available in the morning as a person for protests or laughter rather than as an organizer of chores and a manager of the long day ahead.

Bureaucratically, *individualized nurturing care* has to be conceived as the central ingredient of group care work with children who have experienced many separations and disruptions in their lives. Nurturing is not only required out of compassion and a humanistic belief that children and young people need love and affection, it is also based on scientific knowledge that children and young people want and will learn to care for and to love others when they have experienced genuine care themselves (Kobak 1979; Maier 1982). Organizationally, then, emotional involvement has to be defined as part and parcel of the work commitment for care workers. It has to be explicitly specified in each job description as an integral part of the daily ingredients of group care practice.

Another practice dilemma stems from the continuous personal and emotional demands placed upon workers in the face of administrative expectations that they must not get too deeply involved emotionally in their work. This admonition seems to originate from the organizational demand for objectivity. Emotional involvement, at the same time, is the group care worker's speciality (Barnes and Kelman 1974; Maier 1984). In many ways, group care workers find themselves in the same situation as parents who are overtaxed by children's never-ending and frequently incomprehensible demands. In fact, care workers, in a different way, find themselves akin to 'abusive parents', who, as Durkin observes, 'are chronically overstressed and under-supported, have incompatible demands made on them, and are alienated and relatively powerless to control their fate' (Durkin 1982a: 5).

In tune with Durkin's pointed analysis, desired change cannot be accomplished by a frontal attack on the quality of a worker's involvement. Instead, personal stress can be reduced through institutional support and the establishment of manageable working conditions. In concrete terms, this would mean established working hours with periodic rest breaks in a location which assures separation from the work place. Also, it is essential to work out concrete, achievable care objectives rather than vague care expectations. A vague objective like 'to help the children to manage well throughout the day' is absurd when these same youngsters can actually barely manage sufficient concentration to lace up their shoes. Above all, it means providing care workers with support and supervision for their *care* work rather than their managerial work *per se* so that their emotional involvement enhances rather than deters nurturing care. Such practices are psychologically sound, make clinical sense, and can be logically as well as bureaucratically arranged, managed, and appraised.

Standardization in apparently opposite directions
Clinical processes and organizational processes, as has been recounted earlier, proceed in opposite directions as if the two should never meet. Maybe a conceptual shift can link the clinical necessity to deal with individuals and small primary units in terms of their requirements with the organizational mandate for *universality*.

In group care practice, workers tend to stress vehemently the special needs of individuals and their separate living units, as if these needs were so unusual. Actually, individual requirements of people within their particular primary groups are derived not special, they represent merely the facts of life. Our difficulties are not so much from the children's special needs as from our inability effectively to formulate, communicate, and organize these requirements. Teachers have lesson plans and curricula. Nurses have charts and nursing procedures (Krueger 1981: 4). Social workers, psychologists, and psychiatrists have case summaries, assessments and treatment plans with step-by-step interventive objectives and evaluations. What do other group care workers have? They have, at best, generalized statements, specifying acts of close control, unending patience, or the mandate of providing loving care. In some settings, they do have precise directions about how to award points and tokens for specific behaviours, but workers are left on their own to decide how they deal with the children and their group in general. These widely varied expectations are topped by the organizational expectation to maintain an orderly, smoothly run, contented group care centre. The fact remains that from a clinical point of view there is no doubt that group care workers must have a *program* for each child in care and for the management of their unit-as-a-whole.

To augment general schemes, workers and their supervisors have to set up *personal care programs* akin to curricula in education. Such undertakings must be the *universal* practice of the service. The organization has to see to it that this kind of framework is maintained in order to assure fair and consistent care objectives for all. At the same time, the collective of children in care will be guaranteed, in principle, life-fulfilling activities according to idiosyncratic requirements. *Personal care* programs would then take up plans in the way educational plans specify the events of the day as a curriculum. In so doing,

> 'the entire nature of present definitions of childcare work in a residential programme ... the grind of supervising kids ends. We are with them both individually and as they mesh together in the group. Control issues vanish and are replaced with content issues, highly relevant pieces of the total curriculum.'
> (Barnes and Kelman 1974: 19)

Bureaucratic verification of individualized care and treatment can be further refined by the very fact that every service receiver has individual requirements. The service deals with ordinary growth and developmental phenomena which for all children is anchored in the *interpersonal* interactions between care-givers and care-receivers (Maier 1984). Children are children, regardless of whether they receive family care or not. This truism is particularly relevant for the transmission of macro-systems values. 'Children learn particular cultural values and particular moral systems only from those people with whom they have close contact and who exhibit that culture in frequent relationships with them' (Washington 1982: 105).

Moreover, an extensive study of children successfully and unsuccessfully treated highlights that the most salutary change occurred when consistency existed in meeting clients according to their particular situations and their current understanding. Such results can be obtained even though it creates for the casual onlooker situations of uneven, inconsistent behavioural handling (Division of Youth and Family Service of the State of New Jersey 1978).

Interests on different ends of the continuum
As outlined earlier, clinical considerations encompass a wide spectrum of the residents' lives. In fact, the more diffused the styles of workers interacting in a child's life, the more efficiently workers carry out their care obligations. It is also true, however, that organizationally a group care service has to be clear about its exact service mission and its use of resources. However, rigid adherence to a bureaucratic service mission, in turn, tends to stifle

all those responses which seem appropriate in a creative clinical care and treatment programme for children.

There seems to be a pull in two opposite directions. In one direction there is an effort to expand and deal with more when more is needed, in the other there is a gravitation towards holding the line within the province of the available resources, that is, to manage with that which is actually at hand. In holding to their respective directions both group care workers and organizational administrators are doing their respective jobs. In fact, at times, the workers in the group care centre themselves become administrators and they themselves are apt to limit the use of resources in order to have enough to go around. But whatever the circumstances this struggle will be evoked between human and humane desires for an abundance of life and the bureaucratic necessity to control and to make do with that which is given in an economy of scarcity.

The organizational managers have the actual knowledge and control over the boundaries (just as in the living units, the group care workers have their sway). The organizational team are the 'gatekeepers' and the ultimate controls are without question in their hands. Having made a realistic acknowledgement of these factors, it is then important that group care workers relate themselves to the requirements of their practice and see to it that provision is made for those things they deem necessary for the children's development and enriched living experience. They are the ones who know what is needed. Organizational limitations, never-ending demands, public relations, and limited budgets are all legitimate pressures, and clearly enunciated reminders of them may be offered at periodic intervals, yet the necessity for additional resources, unexpected requirements, alterations and expansion in activities, as well as unforeseen circumstances, are also legitimate reasons for service delivery. All these demands would remain unnoticed and unattended by the service unless clearly articulated by care personnel.

Group care workers have to operate foremost and throughout as the representatives of care, ever ready to interpret the care requirements of children. Organizational wishes and restraints will always become readily known, due to indigenous power contained in supra-system demands. Workers' faithful and unchallenged acceptance of this power renders them 'good servants' of the organization but diminishes their value as group care workers. The workers' pronouncements on the necessities for 'their' children, including apparent luxuries, make them into responsible child care workers, and thereby into effective members of the organization. The distance between management and care practitioners must be shortened in order to make known and to secure what is needed for a life similar to that afforded to children in their own homes. Moreover, workers on the front lines, to follow Pina's poignant assessment, are the ones who discover innovative solutions. Their concerns can no longer be treated as exceptions when, in reality, they are a continuing feature demanding novel and urgent solutions (Pina 1983: 3).

Status alignment

Employment on the basis of ascribed or achieved qualifications presents a dilemma either way. Group care as a profession or as a craft (Eisikovitz and Beker 1983; Maier 1983) demands training and competency achievement in terms of clinical *and* organizational work. The ascribed value of 'being part of the children's lives' is another essential feature. The care-givers' role as vital participants in the residents' life development – to be the children's or young people's primary care persons in their everyday life – becomes a decisive variable in terms of staff selection, work, or time-off scheduling, and the workers' place within the centre. Ascriptively, care staff *own* their place in the organization while the quality of their work has to be prescribed and appraised on the basis of actual achievement in providing interpersonal care services. This achievement is colourfully described by Durkin: 'one of the greatest joys of being a child care worker is that what you are as a unique configuration of personality traits, interests, skills, hobbies and how you have fun, etc. – that is, what you are as a person – gets full use on the job' (Durkin 1982b: 16). And it can be added that such personal qualities are used to meet the life requirements of the children as developing persons and members of a residential living-unit group. Then the group care worker will be a full professional within a bureaucratic organization: she/he can find personal satisfaction, using her/his own creativity as a professional.

Closing comments

Provision of individualized (clinical) child care work within a group care (organizational) setting has been reviewed using a Parsons/Resnick 'thinking screen'. The latter explains the counter-pulls of primary and secondary system variables and processes. Resnick's conceptual analysis (1980) has been employed to understand some of the strains inherent in group care practice pursued as a clinical endeavour and, by contrast, as an organizational model.

Our purpose has been to conceive of group care practice as primary care or a clinical enterprise. *Primary care* is the essence of a group care worker's activities, implementing the children's developmental requirements (Maier 1984), to obtain a close attachment with the children in care, and lastly, in order to foster a sense of permanency in the children's lives (Maier 1982). The care-givers' work is defined as *clinical*, because their focus has to proceed on the basis of each child's individual requirements rather than to deal sociologically with the children as a class or group. At the same time, we must be mindful of the fact that such care is not being provided within a primary group system – the family, commune, or kinship network. Instead, it occurs in a socially engineered group care setting – a secondary organizational group. Organizational features place primary care in a different context and bring organizational demands in conflict with clinical realities.

In the second half of this chapter we have attempted to seek out potential ways and possible solutions for accepting inter-system strains as necessary ingredients of nurturing care within an organization. In fact, for many of these inter-system strains we neither have a solution nor want to provide solutions. The system strains seem to be part and parcel of the nature of contemporary living in modern, technological societies. Moreover, while the mutual 'system wheels' turn, the partial intermeshing can be conceived as dialectical control processes which 'grind' out a viable whole of ill-meshing but salutary encounters. Organizational demands may offer their own legitimate character-istics, such as minimizing or guarding against depletion of workers' own individual energies by yielding to children's endless personal requirements. The introduction of interpersonal neutrality within an organizational context may assist staff to maintain satisfactory work relationships with co-workers and supervisors while they are intensely involved with the youngsters in care. An ancient proverb can be paraphrased here: Give to the children what *is* the children's and to the organization what *is* the organization's!

In the spheres of standard setting and diversity of interests, the strains of the system or dialectic envelopment might include a scenario which can neither be accounted for nor resolved by workers or the organization. Indeed, this kind of tension may be representative of future life experiences anywhere. It is important for workers to deal with these events as part of a child's life experience. It is to be hoped that workers can transmit skills to children which allow them to reframe their experiences or at times to adapt to them, rather than by-pass or flatly accept restraints. This can be powerful intervention in group care practice.

Finally, this chapter brings together two spheres of life experience and two disciplines of knowledge that are rarely studied, viewed, and dealt with as one joint enterprise. This way of thinking requires that separate system-partners, by virtue of their division of labour and allegiances, become co-operators in their naturally conflict-ridden joint enterprise. These highly distinctive work approaches necessitate additional working orientations in order to incorporate the other system's realities (Resnick 1983). In other words, personal care work within an organizational context demands more than appreciating and co-operating with other systems' demands. Viable group care practice may also require an evaluation and expansion of one's own theoretical stance and practice procedures. The next step is to find bridging concepts and linking practices with the immediate and wider worlds of which every child, young person or staff, every living-unit, however securely fenced off, and each service organization and their respective communities, are a part.

Notes

1 Henry Maier was formerly Professor of Social Work at the School of Social Work, University of Washington, Seattle, USA.
2 For simplicity, the terms 'children' or 'child' will refer to children as well as to adolescents or young people.
3 The major ideas underlying this chapter build upon Talcott Parson's formulation on 'Pattern Variables' (1964), and in particular, Professor Resnick's lucid development of Parson's formulation (1980). I am personally indebted

to my colleague, Professor Herman Resnick, for teaching me this rich material on primary/secondary system strains.
4 'A class of people' is here used sociologically – an empirically defined category of people as a distinct unit which is separate from other classes.
5 This factor is clearly visible in a number of highly applauded and well-known residential treatment programmes which are operated akin to the norms of former feudal societies. We can list among others, Bettelheim's Orthogenic School (Bettelheim 1950 and 1955; Neil, 1960; Mayer 1960; Phillips, Phillips, Fixsen, and Wolf 1973).

References

Bakker, C. and Bakker-Radbau, M. K. (1973) *No Trespassing: Explorations in Human Territoriality.* San Francisco: Chandler and Sharp.

Barnes, F. H. and Kelman, S. M. (1974) From Slogans to Concepts: A Basis for Change in Child Care Work. *Child Care Quarterly* 3 (1): 7–23.

Bettelheim, B. (1950) *Love Is Not Enough.* New York: Free Press.

—— (1955) *Truants from Life.* New York: Free Press.

Bronfenbrenner, U. (1979) *The Ecology of Human Development.* Cambridge, Mass.: Harvard University Press.

Division of Youth and Family Service of the State of New Jersey (1978) *The Impact of Residential Treatment.* New Brunswick, NJ: Institute for Criminology Research, Rutgers University.

Durkin, R. (1982a) *The Crisis in Children's Services: The Dangers and Opportunities for Child Care Workers.* Banff, Alberta: 2nd National Child Care Workers' Conference. Mimeographed paper.

—— (1982b) Institutional Child Abuse from a Family Systems Perspective: A Working Paper. *Child and Youth Services Review* 4 (1): 15–22.

—— (1982c) No One Will Thank You: First Thoughts on Reporting Institutional Abuse. *Child and Youth Services Review* 4 (1): 109–13.

Eisikovitz, K. and Beker, J. (1983) Beyond Professionalism, the Child and Youth Care Workers as Craftsmen. *Child Care Quarterly* 12 (2): 93–112.

Gabarino, J. (ed.) (1982) *Children and Families in the Social Environment.* New York: Aldine.

Gabarino, J. and Stocking, S. M. (1980) *Protecting Children from Abuse and Neglect.* San Francisco: Jossey-Bass.

Goffman, E. (1961) *Asylums.* New York: Doubleday.

Kobak, D. (1979) Teaching Children to Care. *Children Today* 8 (2): 6–7, 34–5.

Krueger, M. (1981) Some Thoughts on Research and the Education of Child Care Personnel. Milwaukee: University of Wisconsin. Unpublished paper.

Litwak, E. and Szelenyi, I. (1969) Primary Group Structures and their Functions: Kin, Neighbors and Friends. *American Sociological Review* 34 (4): 465–81.

Maier, H. W. (1969) When Father Is no Longer the Father. *Journal of Applied Social Studies* 1 (1): 13–20.

—— (1974) A Sidewards Look at Change and What Comes into View. In *Social Work in Transition: Issues, Dilemmas and Choices.* Seattle, Washington: School of Social Work, University of Washington.

—— (1977) The Child Care Worker. In J. B. Turner (ed.) *Encyclopedia of Social Work*. New York: National Association of Social Workers.

—— (1978) *Three Theories of Child Development*, 3rd edition. New York: Harper & Row.

—— (1979) The Core of Care. *Child Care Quarterly* 8 (3): 161–73.

—— (1981) Essential Components in Care and Treatment Environments for Children and Youth. In F. Ainsworth and L. C. Fulcher (eds) *Group Care for Children: Concepts and Issues*. New York: Methuen/Tavistock.

—— (1982) To Be Attached and Free: The Challenge of Child Development. *Child Welfare* 61 (2): 67–76.

—— (1983) Should Child and Youth Care Go the Craft or the Professional Route? *Child Care Quarterly* 12 (2): 113–18.

—— (1984) Developmental Foundations of Residential Care and Youth Care. In Z. Eisikovitz and J. Beker (eds) *Knowledge Utilization in Residential Care Practice: The Child and Youth Care Worker as Knowledge Implementor and Generator*.

Mattingly, M. A. (1977) Sources of Stress and Burn-out in Professional Child Care Work. *Child Care Quarterly* 6 (2): 127–37.

Mayer, M. F. (1960) The Parental Figures in Residential Treatment. *Social Services Review* 34 (3): 273–85.

Neil, A. S. (1960) *Summerhill: A Radical Approach to Child Rearing*. New York: Hart Publishing.

Parsons, T. (1964) *The Social System*. New York: Free Press.

Phillips, E. L., Phillips, E. A., Fixsen, D. L., and Wolf, M. M. (1973) Achievement Place: Behavior Shaping Works for Delinquents. *Psychology Today* 7 (1): 74–80.

Pina, V. (1983) Comment: Isolationism is Dead: Survival Mandates Flexible Systems. *Newsletter of the Child Care Learning Center* 5 (2): 3.

Pines, A. and Maslach, C. (1980) Combating Staff Burnout in a Day Care Center: A Case Study. *Child Care Quarterly* 9 (1): 5–16.

Redl, F. and Wineman, D. (1957) *The Aggressive Child*. New York: Free Press.

Resnick, H. (1980) A Social System View of Strain. In H. Resnick and R. J. Patti *Change from Within*. Philadelphia: Temple University Press.

Resnick, H. (1983) The Political Dimension in Social Welfare Organizations: The Missing Ingredient in Social Work Education. Seattle: School of Social Work, University of Washington. Unpublished mimeographed paper.

VanderVen, K. (1982) Principles and Guidelines for Child Care Personnel Preparation Programs. *Child Care Quarterly* 11 (3): 221–49.

Washington, R. O. (1982) Social Development: A Focus for Practice and Education. *Social Work* 27 (1): 104–09.

Whittaker, J. K. (1979) *Caring for Troubled Children*. San Francisco: Jossey-Bass.

Wolf, M. M., Phillips, E. L., Fixsen, D. L., Braukmann, C. T., Kirigin, K. A., Wither, A. G., and Schumaker, J. (1976) Achievement Place: The Teaching-Family Model. *Child Care Quarterly* 5 (2): 92–103.

Wolins, M. and Wozner, Y. (1982) *Revitalizing Residential Settings*. San Francisco: Jossey-Bass.

3   The culture of group care for children

Frank Ainsworth and
Leon C. Fulcher

Introduction

Group care centres – namely institutional care, residential group living, and day services – exist to provide a range of 'living, learning and treatment opportunities' (Ainsworth 1981: 223) for children who, for a variety of reasons, need alternative, supplementary, or substitute provision (Davis 1981) of a type usually available within the context of family life. This is the *raison d'être* for the existence of group care. It is important, therefore, for group care centres to provide an ethos or culture that is consistent with the above objectives. This is accomplished through reference to a centre's internal organizational design, its administrative routines, its physical environment, and characteristics of staff team functioning in the programme, including reference to specific work methods. Such factors are influential in shaping the culture of a centre, irrespective of whether it is located within the health care system, education, social welfare, or the criminal justice system.

When considering all of the factors which influence the culture of group care, due account has also to be taken of knowledge from studies about how children learn and develop. It is argued that knowledge such as this should always guide decisions about events in the life of a group care centre, rather than being subservient to decisions. It is suggested that the cultural integrity of a centre can only be achieved by a constant monitoring of decisions related to the organization and physical environment of a centre, and an evaluation of whether these decisions support growth and development for children. Only in this way can practitioners confirm whether the culture of group care in a centre provides living, learning, and treatment opportunities which reinforce growth-enhancing processes for children. It is all too easy for these processes to be disrupted, if well-intentioned group care personnel – be they nurses, teachers, child care workers, social workers, or staff in penal establishments – fail to consider the implications of particular actions carried out with children in their care. Growth-diminishing, as compared with growth-enabling, experiences are unfortunately common features of group care practice with children.

Developmental conditions

Few authors have written about child development in a manner that allows contemporary research findings to be immediately useful to group care practitioners. Because this knowledge needs to retain a central place in group care practice, it is worth reviewing the conditions which provide the most favourable opportunities for children to learn and develop. The focus will be on interpersonal structures (Bronfenbrenner 1979) and processes (Maier 1981) which make up the developmental conditions of group care, but which have not until recent years been grounded sufficiently in an understanding of contextual influences.

In attempting to move towards a clearer appreciation of these matters, Bronfenbrenner (1979) has provided a series of core definitions and hypotheses that seek to spell out the optimal conditions in which learning and development take place. These definitions are associated with the ecology of human development and refer to various elements in settings including activities, roles, and interpersonal relations. Attention is particularly drawn to those definitions and hypotheses which clarify the contributions made by interpersonal relations in developmental processes with children. Such a narrowing of focus here should not be taken to imply a downgrading of the other elements, nor a failure to recognize how all the elements interact.

Bronfenbrenner defined a *relation* as that which 'obtains whenever one person in a setting pays attention to, or participates in the activities of another' (1979: 56). Three different types of relation were identified, each of which applies to group care practice with children. The first of these involves situations where someone engages with a child to *observe* a particular activity, such as when a worker and child pay attention to each other's activities during the first days of placement in a centre. By acknowledging the part that each plays in such an observational process, the minimal conditions for learning are enacted and the stage is set for a second type of child–adult relations. Here, the focus is on *shared participation* in related but not necessarily identical tasks, such as when a worker and child wash the dishes after a meal. The emphasis in this type of relation is the reciprocal nature of the activity, through which the emotional dimension of a relationship develops. This leads to a third type of child–adult relations where *enduring feelings develop* between one and the other which influence the thoughts and behaviours of the parties involved. In such instances, a relationship can be said to exist even when the parties are no longer together.

These formulations may help one to understand better the influence of interpersonal relations in life-long learning. For group care practitioners working with children, they offer special possibilities, taking as 'the theatre for their work the actual living situation as shared and experienced by the child' (Ainsworth 1981: 234). As a result, group care practitioners are in an ideal position to engage continuously and deliberately in relations of the type described above, and in so doing provide contexts for learning. Throughout every hour of every day, group care practitioners are presented with valuable opportunities in which they can engage in all three types of relation and thereby help children to grow and develop. Bronfenbrenner hypothesized that maximum achievable impact occurs when a practitioner and child engage in all three types of relation simultaneously (1979: 60). If a relation is characterized by mutual antagonism then it is disruptive of learning, emphasizing the point that learning and development are most likely to be achieved when a close relationship exists between practitioners and children.

While Bronfenbrenner has helped to clarify the types of relation practitioners need to create in their work with children, Maier (1981) has highlighted the importance of attachment and the experience of dependency which are part of the intimate process of forming relationships. Maier noted how temperamental differences – even amongst very young children – can influence the rhythms of interaction which develop with those who provide care. It is important for practitioners to understand these facts, so as to respond to any antagonism which may enter into and disrupt their relationships with children, thereby restricting learning opportunities. Group care practice involves sensitive engagement with children in a manner that is compatible with each child's needs and avoids the disruptive pitfalls which limit development.

Maier (1981) addresses the importance of establishing vital attachments between practitioners and children which offer opportunities for a good experience of dependency, the pursuit of which may be clouded by difficult and demanding behaviours. Maier allows the group care practitioner to view these phenomena afresh by placing these aspects of development in a normal sequence of daily life events. Dependency need not be viewed as a sign of weakness or psychopathology. Through attachment relationships, children obtain the necessary prerequisites for learning and development. Rather than being fearful of the implied demands associated with attachment relationships, group care practitioners need to encourage these processes so that children will eventually 'be free' (Maier 1982a) to assume responsibility for themselves in later life. Such freedom cannot, however, be forced into existence. It develops instead through the experience of a secure attachment to another person and safe dependence on them.

Better than most writers, Bronfenbrenner and Maier help group care practitioners to see how to engage in the task of encouraging developmental processes with children. Bronfenbrenner does this by clarifying the type of interpersonal relations which have to develop, while Maier provides a detailed understanding of the events which facilitate these relations. In so doing, these writers also highlight how dysfunctional institutions – so often referred to in the literature (Jones and Fowles 1984) – need not exist provided that they are restructured to allow practices outlined above. Wolins and Wozner (1982) echo this view, highlighting the extent to which 'theoretical and ideological determinants' influence the culture of a group care centre (Fulcher and Ainsworth 1981: 83). In this respect, it may be helpful to pose a number of questions which practitioners can ask about their own group care centres.

Questions

- To what extent is recognition given to the importance of all three types of interpersonal relations in your centre, including observational relations, shared activity relations, and emotional attachments?
- How does your centre acknowledge the importance of and facilitate opportunities for children to experience dependency, or is this frowned upon and seen only as a negative feature of relationships which develop between practitioners and children?
- In what ways can it be said that your centre accepts the need for practitioners and children to develop attachment relationships, or is attachment viewed with suspicion?
- To what extent does your centre allow for differences in the temperament of children and the different patterns of interaction which are required as a consequence?

The culture of practice

Before considering some of the other structural features of practice in group care referred to earlier (Fulcher and Ainsworth 1981), it is perhaps helpful to clarify the notion of culture used here. This notion highlights the way in which all participants in a group care centre − children and practitioners alike − interact within a system that contains a language, values, norms, and social structure of its own (Eisikovitz 1980). Culture therefore takes account of the totality of experience in a centre, enabling one to consider whether some aspects of a centre's culture may be at variance with the wider culture which exists in the surrounding community. In this respect, the culture of a group care centre warrants careful examination because variance between the internal cultures may be evidence that the original learning and development goals have been compromised and the centre's integrity has been undermined. Such a situation can emerge as the result of concerns in the wider service system, or because of unrealistic community expectations imposed by way of a confused 'social policy mandate' (Fulcher and Ainsworth 1981: 78).

Much has been written, although not necessarily in the children's field, about efforts in therapeutic communities to create an internal culture which facilitates personal growth and change amongst members (Hinslelwood and Manning 1979; Jansen 1980; Kennard 1983). In such instances, variance between the culture of a group care centre and that of the wider community may be justified. On the other hand, purely institutional cultures must be evaluated critically, given the negative evaluations which have come from the health care (mental health and mental handicap) and criminal justice (prison and reformatory) systems. These studies have provided support for the notion of institutional dysfunction (Jones 1967), seriously questioning the integrity of some of the oldest and now least attractive group care centres. Indeed, much of the thrust towards normalization of resident experiences (Wolfensberger 1972) is stimulated by attempts to reduce differences between group care cultures and promote more culturally normative conditions.

The culture of practice is, of course, the product of a multiplicity of factors, some of which are to be found in interactions between children and practitioners within the centre and some with those outside it. Other interactions are also influential in shaping services in the group care field and the culture of practice can only be fully understood through consideration of both 'interpersonal dynamics and organizational contexts' (Ainsworth and Fulcher 1981: 2). Eleven structural variables associated with group care programmes were identified earlier (1981: 77–85), two of which – theoretical and ideological determinants and social policy mandate – have already been noted here. Other variables, such as siting and physical design of a centre, personnel complement and deployment, and recurring patterns in the use of time and activity, are considered below as important influences on the culture of practice in group care. Other variables, such as social customs and sanctions, social climate of the centre, links with family, school, and community, criteria for reviewing and evaluating performance, and cost factors, also influence the culture of practice, but receive only limited reference here. With the addition of a twelfth variable (Fulcher 1983) – the external organization environment – it is worth noting that all the structural variables can be clustered under the four themes of social structure, language, norms, and values which make up the culture of practice in a centre (*Figure 3.1*).

Figure 3.1 Structural features which shape the culture of practice in group care

Social structure	*Norms*
Siting and physical design of centre	Admission and discharge practices
Personnel complement and	Social customs and sanctions
deployment	Links with family, school, and
External organization environment	community
Language	*Values*
Patterns in the use of time and activity	Social policy mandate and focus
Social climate of the centre	Theoretical and ideological
Criteria used for reviewing and	determinants
evaluating performance	Cost factors

The task of mapping interactions between all these variables, the interpersonal dynamics, and the organizational contexts over time remains to be done, to see how each feature is influenced by the others. Anthropological research methods offer some possibilities in regard to this complex task. An anthropological perspective is compatible with the social ecology orientation (Apter 1982; Whittaker 1975) and to some extent that of a systems perspective (Hunter and Ainsworth 1973; Polsky 1963). Each of these frameworks encourages one to view group care centres as dynamic entities and to think of the constituent parts of a whole being in constant interaction and change. As one part changes, so it interacts with other parts, resulting in a new equilibrium.

These perspectives have immediate relevance for supervisory, service monitoring, service planning, or group care management personnel, both within group care centres and in the broader service system. This is because many of these personnel are in the business of holding boundaries (Miller and Gwynne 1972) between the constituent parts of a centre and the wider service system and this includes attempting to balance conflicting demands. Because the cultural perspective enables group care practitioners at all levels to see how an action at one point affects events in other parts of a centre, it also has immediate relevance for children. This is because it allows practitioners of various standing to think of a wider range of interventions which can be used to achieve learning and development outcomes. Interventions cannot therefore focus solely on interactions with children. Interventions at some point in the physical environment and organizational or administrative systems may also be required, so as to improve learning and developmental opportunities for children. Of course, this does not in any way limit the importance of work undertaken directly with children or the importance of direct practice skills which this entails. A further set of questions which practitioners can use to check out the validity of arrangements established in the centre they know best are:

Questions

- How far is the culture of your centre in keeping with that of the community which immediately surrounds it?
- Do any variations – list them – assist or limit the growth and development opportunities available in your centre?
- If this is not already happening, what would have to be changed so that children acquire normative cultural experiences?
- Is there any valid reason for the special cultural features found in your centre, or are these merely for the convenience of staff or the wider service system?

It is expected that answers to these questions will vary depending on the occupational identity of those asking the questions, be they nurses, teachers, child care workers, social workers, or staff in penal establishments. The location of the centre within its wider service system – health care, education, social welfare, or criminal justice – will also influence the answers to each question. This comment underscores the extent to which language, as an aspect of culture, differs across each of the four systems where different terminology is used to address practice issues. This holds, even though all four systems provide group care services for children and practitioners in all four systems provide opportunities which are intended to result in similar, if not the same learning and development practices with children.

Issues of organizational design

A supportive organizational design and a sympathetic administrative ethos are necessary prerequisites of a group care centre for practitioners to create and exploit the interpersonal processes which promote learning for children. This applies to the internal organization of a centre as well as the broad service system within which a centre is located. Regrettably, there is evidence to suggest that the conventions of large organizations often take over and inhibit far-sighted therapeutic environments (Canter and Canter 1979). There is also evidence which shows that senior administrators, who are prone to making elegant policy statements, may do very little to translate these statements into organizational systems which protect the developmental aims of group care centres (Raynes, Pratt, and Roses 1979).

A partial explanation for this ambiguous situation can be found in the way that large organizations, whether public or private, are controlled by external sources (Pfeffer and Salancik 1978). For example, it is suggested that paid managers carry functions which are largely symbolic and that interest groups – public, professional, and private – ultimately determine the resources available to an organization and are actually able to control the way it functions. If correct, this view has many implications for group care practitioners since, in order to survive, centres have to obtain resources and support from the controllers of social policy, whoever they may be.

Some consequences of inappropriate organizational design and administrative structures have been illustrated in a comparative study of residential facilities for the adult mentally handicapped in the health care system (Raynes, Pratt, and Roses 1979). This study, which is of interest to group care practitioners working with children, has shown how a complex and inappropriate division of responsibility results in a reduced quality of service and limits the developmental opportunities available in a centre. Resource and non-resource factors appear to be critical influences on a centre's capacity to provide services (Davies and Knapp 1981; Fulcher 1983), including factors such as personnel, physical environment, equipment, food and consumables, staff attitudes, characteristics of the social environment which surrounds the centre, experience of residents prior to admission, and so on.

Raynes, Pratt, and Roses (1979) found that the inappropriate division of responsibility limited the authority of the unit leader, making it impossible to control resource and non-resource issues. This, in turn, prevented unit leaders from delegating authority to direct care practitioners who were in continuous contact with residents, preventing them from executing their caring tasks in a manner that was compatible with residents' needs.

If group care practitioners working directly with children are to make maximum use of the interpersonal relations and processes which enable learning and development to take place, then it is important that they possess sufficient authority to ensure that such opportunities are made available. As noted earlier, Bronfenbrenner indicated that learning and development are facilitated when children engage in increasingly complex activities with someone towards whom they have established a strong emotional attachment, and 'when the balance of power shifts in favour of the developing person' (1979: 61). This implies that a unit leader has to be able to guarantee protection of and support for individual practitioners whilst struggling to create developmental conditions for children. It also implies that a unit leader has to be able to delegate authority – a basic essential for practitioners to accomplish their tasks. This may involve allowing a shift in power and responsibility for certain actions from practitioners to children, whenever this is appropriate. However, this transfer of authority needs to occur when children are ready for enhanced responsibility, and not simply because it is administratively convenient or organizationally safe. Having said this, it should be noted that human service organizations find it difficult to tolerate such flexibility, since it runs counter to the managerial control and formality of procedures adopted by most social service bodies (Kakabadse 1982).

The search for models of organization which are in keeping with views about how children learn and develop is not entirely without hope. It is worth examining a systems model that was developed as the result of an action research study of residential institutions for the physically handicapped and young chronic sick (Miller and Gwynne 1972). This model places great store on providing opportunities for residents and practitioners to engage in the type of reciprocal activities and power sharing which are critical to child development. In addition to an overall centre management function, this model identifies three internal systems, as shown in *Figure 3.2,* which cater respectively for the needs of residents and practitioners to have psychological and physical dependence, independence, and support (Miller and Gwynne 1972: 190). The centre management function was conceived in terms of giving a centre legitimacy with the external community, exercising control over admission and discharge practices, and maintaining the integrity of and balance between the three internal systems.

Figure 3.2 Systems of activities and of management roles in group care centres[1]

Centre management		
System management Dependence system	*System management* Independence system	*System management* Support system

In an interesting discussion of this model, Miller and Gwynne (1972) suggested that it differs substantially from that which is normally found in group care centres, drawing attention to concerns which have been expressed earlier in this chapter. They pointed out the need for clarity in the aims of group care centres and also noted that a dependent culture was prominent whenever unit leaders had insufficient authority to control the external boundary between the centre and other parts of the larger organization. In those centres where the unit leader had significantly more authority to control the external boundary, and to limit or enhance resources moving between the centre and the wider organization, it was far more likely that an independence culture was found between residents and practitioners. In other words, the culture of a centre supported learning and development for residents and practitioners alike.

Whilst lacking in detailed work concerning its implementation, the model offered by Miller and Gwynne (1972) provides important insights into issues that concern group care practitioners working with children. It offers an organizational framework which permits them to remain child-centred in their practice. Links can also be made between this model and material contained in the literature on therapeutic communities which emphasizes the importance of participatory styles of decision-making and power sharing, involving all residents and practitioners (Hinslelwood and Manning 1979; Jansen 1980; Kennard 1983). This literature also draws attention to therapeutic communities which failed to survive in the formal resource systems of health care, education, social welfare, and criminal justice which offer group care services for children. Generally speaking, the practical implications associated with implementing therapeutic communities were found to be overwhelming in traditional and hierarchically structured systems where control of resources and decision-making are expected to remain in the hands of senior personnel.

The search is likely to continue whereby those working in group care services can find ways of making organizational structures and administrative routines reflect the need for appropriate levels of participative decision-making and power sharing between practitioners and children. Until such time as clearer solutions are available, practitioners may have to continue using techniques of internal advocacy and change designed to make service systems more human and humane (Brager and Holloway 1978; Resnick and Patti 1980; Weisman 1973). Indeed, it may be that these methods of practice need to be given more concerted attention by group care practitioners wishing to improve the learning and development opportunities available for children in their centres. Given the way that issues of organizational design influence the culture of practice in group care centres, practitioners may find it helpful to consider a further set of questions.

Questions

- In what ways can it be said that the organizational structure of your centre influences the work which is undertaken directly with children?
- What administrative routines can be found within the centre which are designed to support practitioners to initiate activities when these are in children's best interests?
- What systems of accountability can be identified in the centre which respect the need for practitioners and children to engage in joint activity and power sharing?
- In what ways can it be said that the organizational structure

and the administrative routines in the centre promote a culture which encourages learning and development opportunities for practitioners and children?

The physical environment

At first glance it may seem that moving to a focus on the physical environment of a centre detracts attention from the interactional elements which shape the culture of practice in a centre. Unfortunately, there is a commonly held view that, given sufficient imagination, practitioners will be able to overcome poor siting and physical design features in their centres. Regrettably, such a view has even been promoted by an influential government publication on care and treatment environments for children (HMSO 1970). The publication claimed that 'unsuitable buildings may affect adversely the easy workings of a community home even though they do not prevent good staff from operating well' (1970: 41). This statement of belief, unsupported by research evidence, implies that poor siting and physical design characteristics can be overcome by a committed and well-trained workforce who are carefully organized in their work. Of course this is contrary to the experience of many group care practitioners, who know only too well that important limitations are imposed on their practice by the physical environment in which they work.

Yet surprisingly, little has been written directly about designing group care centres and the importance of the physical environment of care. Bettelheim (1974) wrote about a 'Home for the Heart', giving testimony to the importance of environmental symbolism, spatial messages, and territoriality. Redl and Wineman are credited with the familiar statement that group care practice with children requires 'a home that smiles, props that invite and space which allows' (1957: 42). Fortunately, in recent years more attention has been given to the importance of physical environments (Canter and Canter 1979). Environmental psychologists such as Sommer (1969), Proshansky, Ittleson, and Rivlin (1979) and Hayduk (1983) have given increasing attention to the importance of personal space and the physical environment. Germain (1981) has attempted to address this issue as it relates to social work practice, while Maier (1982b) has discussed how 'the space we create controls us' in group care practice.

The views expressed by each of the foregoing writers serve to emphasize the extent to which the culture of group care is heavily influenced by the siting and physical design of a centre. While it is possible for practitioners to influence and adapt to some physical design limitations, countless other design features remain untouched. The siting and physical design of a centre may represent in bricks and mortar the ideas of earlier generations of practice. This architectural history serves to inhibit the development of new and more contemporary approaches. Many practitioners have referred to their facility as a 'purpose-built unit with the wrong purpose built in', even when their centres are comparatively new. The location of a centre can reduce the opportunities for practitioners and children to engage in ordinary life tasks through which learning by observation and shared activity might be achieved (Rivlin and Wolfe 1979). The uninviting external appearance of a centre, possibly the fortress-like image of an institution, can make valuable contacts with adults and children in the immediate neighbourhood more difficult to achieve.

Slater and Lipman (1980) identified several concerns associated with caring through design in group care practice. First, the amount of *choice* which a building allows for practitioners and children is worthy of consideration. Second, attention needs to be given to the question of whether the building *encourages independence*. The extent to which centre design is based on *convenience* provides a third consideration which practitioners should address. A fourth concern involves the way in which *privacy* is allowed for in the centre. Finally, practitioners will benefit from considering the extent to which the design of a centre is *comprehensible*, in terms of quickly finding one's way around the building and feeling safe there. In so far as resources for group care centres are likely to remain limited in the foreseeable future, practitioners are advised to consider a range of potential pressure points in their work which are aggravated by poor design features. It is ironic that practitioners may need to call in builders rather than employing new care staff, since it may be a more effective means of using resources.

The recent development of comprehensive assessment schedules for sheltered care environments (Moos and Lemke 1979) enables group care practitioners to evaluate their centres along a number of dimensions, including physical and architectural features, staff–

resident characteristics, policy and programme resources, and social environments. Such measures offer those with responsibility for group care centres the possibility of pinpointing key items which put added stress on practitioners and restrict their effectiveness in direct work with children. At the very least, practitioners need to recognize the importance of space and physical arrangements, if they are to make the best possible use of space that is available. The protection of limited private space, or concern about the physical condition of furnishings, can do much to make an unsympathetic environment more welcoming and comfortable to live in. Often, very basic issues such as whether children have access to all parts of a centre, whether they have space allocated to them which is theirs alone, and whether children can retreat into a private space have a profound impact on the culture of a group care centre.

Writing about group care centres for the elderly, Davies and Knapp (1981) called attention to a number of *indicators of centre design*. These features also apply to living and learning environments for children where the language of space and physical arrangements are especially powerful (Maier 1981). Ownership and original function of the centre are worthy of consideration, as is size, general centre design, and the internal scale or relations between rooms. Bedrooms, sitting rooms or sitting spaces, dining rooms, bathrooms, and toilets: their location and the number they serve are all worthy of attention. Corridors, halls, or passageways should not be ignored, since a rich variety of social interactions take place in these 'spaces between the rooms'. Space for parties, games, or meetings are important considerations, as are general resources such as stereo, snooker table, or minibus. Micro design features, such as lighting, full-length mirrors, and lockers are design indicators which can be easily ignored. Availability of accommodation for practitioners, its location and size relative to space occupied by children represents another important consideration. Finally, in addition to the siting of a centre, its age, general state of repair, and decor are all influential in the culture of practice which develops there.

All of these issues were highlighted in one particular centre which did not have a room large enough to contain seating for all the members – practitioners and children – who lived and worked there. This had a profound impact on the culture of the centre. A total community meeting could not be held, with the consequence that opportunities for shared decision-making were restricted. In evaluating the effectiveness of the centre's work with children, this physical constraint was not even considered. Instead, the centre's limited effectiveness was attributed entirely to lack of skill on the part of the unit leader and to inadequate training on the part of other practitioners. This example illustrates how 'the space we create controls us' (Maier 1982b) and how evaluations of group care practice may ignore the influence which physical environments have on care and treatment outcomes with children.

Once again, it is possible to construct a set of questions which practitioners may legitimately ask, irrespective of where they work. These questions will hopefully assist practitioners to think about how the physical environment of their centre supports a culture which is compatible with learning and development objectives.

Questions

- To what extent does the geographic location of your centre reduce or enhance opportunities for children to learn and develop?
- In what ways can it be said that the internal layout of the centre facilitates interactions between children and practitioners?
- To what parts of the centre can children have access and where do they have personal space which is allocated to them into which they can retreat at all times?
- To what extent does the physical design of your centre support practitioners in the task of creating developmental opportunities for children?

Team functioning and group development

Group care practice with children is pre-eminently team practice. Since group care services are provided from a physically defined centre of activity, primarily (although not exclusively) through the medium of a group, so there is created a life-space in which daily life events are shared between practitioners and children collectively (Ainsworth and Fulcher 1981). A group culture is also reinforced as practitioners operate in a public arena and share responsibility with others for the growth and development of individual children. Most exchanges are open to observation by others, and over the course of weeks (up to 168 hours in duration every week) or months, it is inevitable that work with individual children or groups will be shared by several practitioners. Such is the case, even when a system of key worker responsibilities is operating in a centre, where direct work with individual children is assigned to a specific practitioner (Elliot 1980). Implementation of personal care and treatment plans can only be achieved through co-operation with others.

As members of a team, group care practitioners are required to engage in work with individual children and a group of many children simultaneously. This often requires changing focus very quickly from the needs of one child to the needs of another, whilst at the same time ensuring that the needs of the total group of children are not neglected. This is a particularly difficult aspect of group care practice and highlights the complex task which practitioners are expected to perform. Success or failure is shared between a number of different people. It is rarely possible in group care practice for one person to claim responsibility for successful interventions with children. In the same way, individual practitioners are rarely to blame for a centre's failure with a child. The occupational stresses associated with group care practice are not unrelated to the complexities of work in this field, nor to the fact that personal practice is almost always observed by others of similar status (Mattingly 1981). Further stresses are associated with the inevitable closeness which develops between practitioners and children, a theme which is examined more closely by Burford and Fulcher later in this volume.

The literature on these features of practice, and teamwork in particular, is not extensive. More often than not, when teamwork has been addressed, it has been examined from a managerial perspective (Payne 1982; Payne and Scott 1982). Less attention has been given to the occupational focus of group care which underpins a team approach to practice. In our earlier volume, Fulcher identified six issues which are worthy of consideration when addressing the problem of team functioning in group care practice (1981: 194–95). These issues involve: who the team members are; how the team carries out its work; where team members are assigned for duty; when team members are expected to work; what orientations different members have in the team; and for what reasons teamwork objectives receive support.

In this analysis of team functioning in group care some attention was also given to certain aspects of leadership and decision-making. These issues are invariably addressed by writers about group processes (Douglas 1979) from outside the field of group care. This is because there is agreement that these matters are of central importance in team or group development strategies, namely identity formation and group cohesion. Moreover leadership styles that involve open discussion and shared decision-making are more supportive of group development than authoritarian styles. Most writers on group or team development, therefore, seem to favour a style of leadership which encourages reciprocity, mutuality of positive feelings, and shared decision-making amongst the members of a group. In essence, this parallels the type of developmental conditions outlined by Bronfenbrenner (1979) in which children have optimal opportunities for learning.

In highlighting the parallels between conditions which optimally promote team or group development and those which promote individual learning and development, a cautionary note is indicated. Whilst having a responsibility for its own development and that of its members, a group care team has the primary task of providing learning and development opportunities for children placed in its centre. A careful balancing of needs and responsibilities has therefore to occur if practitioners and children alike are to achieve satisfactory experiences during their involvement in a group care centre. A balance must be found between task performance with children and the maintenance of team cohesion and collaboration between team members. Without this balance, the primary task cannot be performed and team morale is likely to suffer (Adair 1983).

This problem conveniently illustrates the relationship between individual and group-oriented objectives, drawing attention to an issue that is very real for those engaged in group care practice. Practitioners are regularly faced with the dilemma of needing to assist an individual child with personal learning and development issues, when at the same time having to give attention to a group of children. In this respect, it is worth noting the relationship which Maier (1978: 205) has drawn between individual and group-oriented objectives, as shown in *Figure 3.3*.

Figure 3.3 Relations between developmental objectives for individual and group intervention

Individual objectives	Group objectives
Self-realization	Clarity in group norms and values
Personal competence	Tolerance of individual differences
Competence in relating to and identifying with others	Group cohesion
Competence in problem solving	Division of labour and clarification of group roles
Meeting cultural role expectations	Shared decision-making and group continuity

It can be seen how the individual and group objectives noted by Maier (1978) might refer to both children and practitioners in a group care centre. Whichever the case, it shows how individual and group needs must be accommodated simultaneously. In this respect a dilemma is addressed which group care practitioners often feel is at the heart of their practice. It also emphasizes the culture of practice by identifying aspects of group development that are associated with social structure, language, norms, and values. It underlines the socialization influence offered by a centre's culture, assisting individual children to enhance their social competence and engage in acceptable cultural roles. As before, issues associated with team functioning and group development pose a further set of questions which practitioners can ask about their own centres.

Questions

– What do you mean by the notion of 'team' and in what sort of team are you involved?
– How does the style of leadership used in your team affect the way the team works?
– By whom are decisions made in your team?
– What sort of messages do children get when they look at the way your team works?
– Are there any parallel processes which can be recognized in

comparing the functioning of your team and that of the children's group?
- To what extent does the group culture in your centre assist children with individual learning and developmental needs?

The individual practitioner

This chapter has been concerned throughout with a consideration of interpersonal relations and processes which are essential for learning and development in children. As such, the focus on interactions between individual children and group care practitioners was inevitable. We have adopted the position that a strong culture, pervading and consistently reinforcing the work carried out in a group care centre, is essential if learning and development for children in these contexts is to be achieved. Factors which were thought to influence the culture of practice in group care have included organization design, administrative routines, the physical environment, team functioning, and group development, along with the roles carried out by individual practitioners.

The roles played by individual practitioners have been explored elsewhere (Ainsworth 1981) emphasizing the importance of mentoring relationships, a construct based on work in the field of adult development (Levinson *et al.* 1978). Mentoring which focuses on group care practice with children includes the following roles:

- to act as a teacher to enhance a child's skills and intellectual development;
- to serve as a sponsor and use influence to facilitate a child's advancement;
- to be host and guide who welcomes a child into new situations and the social world, acquainting a child with the values, customs, resources, and cast of characters;
- to act as a role model through demonstrating virtues, achievement, and ways of living that a child can admire and seek to emulate;
- to provide counsel and moral support in times of stress;
- to support and facilitate a child's development and realization of personal goals.

All of the roles referred to above can be said to reinforce the culture of practice in group care for children. As our understanding of child development increases, it may be possible to identify additional dimensions of the mentoring role which group care practitioners fulfil with children. This is especially important given that reciprocal activity and mutuality of feeling between child and practitioner is necessary, if a gradual transfer of power from one to the other is to be achieved.

In the various systems that contain group care centres, practitioners are referred to by a range of titles, whether nurses, teachers, child care workers, social workers, or staff in penal establishments. Because of their training backgrounds and occupational allegiance, group care practitioners may not see or describe their primary task in developmental terms and may use a different language to describe their work. The nurse may think primarily of 'treating', the teacher of 'teaching', the child care worker or social worker may think of 'caring', while the correctional or prison officer may think in terms of 'controlling'. This all implies, to a greater or lesser extent, the unequal status which exists between practitioners and children rather than reciprocal interaction, mutuality of feeling and shared decision-making. This is likely to result in increased social distance rather than encouraging closeness where practitioners and children are side by side observing each other, doing things together and jointly influencing each other's thinking and behaviour.

This developmental focus and the mentoring roles which group care practitioners fulfil with children need to be supported by the culture of practice in a centre. Some further questions may be posed to enable practitioners to assess the extent to which this is available in their own centre.

Questions

- How is the group care practitioner's role described in your centre?
- To what extent are practitioners encouraged to get closely involved with a child, or is some other position adopted?
- To what extent does the formal language of your centre – for example job titles or descriptions of daily tasks – emphasize learning and development for children?
- In what ways can it be said that closeness between practitioners and particular children is protected or disrupted?

Summary
In this chapter, we have explored various aspects associated with the culture of practice in group care for children. First, the

developmental conditions in which children learn and develop most effectively were outlined. Next, the culture of practice in group care was considered, emphasizing the social structure, language, norms, and values associated with practice in a centre. Third, issues of organizational design were addressed, highlighting the relationships which exist between interpersonal dynamics and organizational contexts in group care practice. Attention then turned to a consideration of the physical environment and to ways in which the siting and physical design of a centre influences the culture of practice which develops there. This led on to a consideration of team functioning and group development, since group dynamics are an integral part of practice in the group care field. Finally, we returned to the role of the individual practitioner, exploring the extent to which individuals can support development and learning for individual children. Throughout the chapter, questions have been posed which may assist group care practitioners, supervisors, managers, and service planners to evaluate the culture of practice in centres with which they are primarily concerned. Whether referring to the culture of practice in health care settings, educational settings, social welfare settings, or criminal justice settings, group care practice is likely to require treatment, teaching, nurture, and control to assist children towards learning and development objectives.

Notes

1 Miller and Gwynne have noted how the diagrammatic presentation of organizational systems was developed by A. K. Rice (1963: 16–25) and Miller and Rice (1967: 32–42).

References

Adair, J. (1983) *Effective Leadership*. London: Pan Books.

Ainsworth, F. (1981) The Training of Personnel for Group Care with Children. In F. Ainsworth and L. C. Fulcher (eds) *Group Care for Children: Concept and Issues*. London: Tavistock.

Ainsworth, F. and Fulcher, L. C. (eds) (1981) *Group Care for Children, Concept and Issues*. London: Tavistock.

Apter, S. (1982) *Troubled Children Troubled Systems*. Oxford: Pergamon Press.

Bettelheim, B. (1974) *A Home for the Heart*. London: Thames & Hudson.

Brager, G. and Holloway, S. (1978) *Changing Human Service Organisations, Politics and Practice*. San Francisco: Free Press.

Bronfenbrenner, U. (1979) *The Ecology of Human Development*. Cambridge, Mass.: Harvard University Press.

Canter, D. and Canter, S. (1979) *Designing for Therapeutic Environments*. Chichester, England: Wiley.

Davis, A. (1981) *The Residential Solution*. London: Tavistock.

Davies, B. and Knapp, M. (1981) *Old People's Homes and the Production of Welfare*. London: Routledge & Kegan Paul.

Douglas, T. (1979) *Group Processes in Social Work*. Chichester, England: Wiley.

Eisikovitz, R. (1980) The Cultural Scene of a Juvenile Treatment Center for Girls: Another Look. *Child Care Quarterly* 9 (3): 158–74.

Elliot, D. (1980) Some Current Issues in Residential Work: Implications for the Social Work Task. In R. Walton and D. Elliot (eds) *Residential Care, a Reader in Current Theory and Practice*. Oxford: Pergamon Press.

Fulcher, L. C. (1981) Team Functioning in Group Care. In F. Ainsworth and L. C. Fulcher (eds) *Group Care for Children: Concept and Issues*. London: Tavistock.

—— (1983) *Who Cares for the Caregivers? A Comparative Study of Residential and Day Care Teams Working with Children*. PhD Thesis. Stirling, Scotland: University of Stirling.

Fulcher, L. C. and Ainsworth, F. (1981) Planned Care and Treatment: The Notion of Programme. In F. Ainsworth and L. C. Fulcher (eds) *Group Care for Children: Concept and Issues*. London: Tavistock.

Germain, C. B. (1981) The Physical Environment and Social Work Practice. In A. N. Maluccio (ed.) *Promoting Competence in Clients, a New/Old Approach to Social Work Practice*. New York: Free Press.

Hayduk, L. A. (1983) Personal Space: Where We Now Stand. *Psychological Bulletin* 94 (2): 293–335.

Her Majesty's Stationery Office (1970) *Care and Treatment in a Planned Environment*. London: Home Office Advisory Council on Child Care.

Hinslelwood, R. D. and Manning, N. (eds) (1979) *Therapeutic Communities: Reflections and Progress*. London: Routledge & Kegan Paul.

Hunter, J. and Ainsworth, F. (eds) (1973) *Residential Establishments, the Evolving of Caring Systems*. Dundee, Scotland: Dundee University, School of Social Administration.

Jansen, E. (1980) *Therapeutic Communities*. London: Croom Helm.

Jones, K. (1967) *New Thinking about Institutional Care*. London: Association of Social Workers.

Jones, K. and Fowles, A. J. (1984) *Ideas on Institutions*. London: Routledge & Kegan Paul.

Kakabadse, A. (1982) *Culture of the Social Services*. Aldershot, Hampshire: Gower Publishing.

Kennard, D. (1983) *An Introduction to Therapeutic Communities*. London: Routledge & Kegan Paul.

Levinson, D. J., Darrow, C. N., Klein, E. G., Levinson, M. H., and McKee, B. (1978) *The Seasons of a Man's Life*. New York: Alfred Knopf.

Maier, H. W. (1978) *Three Theories of Child Development*, 3rd edition. New York: Harper & Row.

—— (1981) Essential Components in Care and Treatment Environments for Children. In F. Ainsworth and L. C. Fulcher (eds) *Group Care for Children: Concept and Issues*. London: Tavistock.

—— (1982a) To be Attached and Free: The Challenge of Child Development in the Eighties *Child Welfare* 61 (2): 67–76.

—— (1982b) The Space We Create Controls Us *Residential Group Care and Treatment* 1 (1): 51–9.

Maluccio, A. N. (ed.) (1981) *Promoting Competence in Clients. A New/Old Approach to Social Work Practice.* New York: Free Press.

Mattingly, M. (1981) Occupational Stress for Group Care Personnel. In F. Ainsworth and L. C. Fulcher (eds) *Group Care for Children: Concept and Issues.* London: Tavistock.

Miller, E. J. and Gwynne, E. G. (1972) *A Life Apart.* London: Tavistock.

Miller, E. J. and Rice, A. K. (1967) *Systems of Organization.* London: Tavistock.

Moos, R. and Lemke, S. (1979) *The Multi-phasic Environmental Assessment Procedure, Preliminary Manual.* Palo Alto, California: Stanford University Social Ecology Laboratory.

Payne, C. and Scott, T. (1982) Developing Supervision of Teams in Field and Residential Social Work. Paper No. 12. London: National Institute for Social Work.

Payne, M. (1982) *Working in Teams.* London: Macmillan.

Pfeffer, J. and Salancik, G. R. (1978) *The External Control of Organisations, A Resource Dependence Perspective.* New York: Harper & Row.

Polsky, H. W. (1963) *Cottage Six – The Social System of Delinquent Boys in Residential Treatment.* New York: John Wiley.

Proshansky, H. M., Ittleson, W. H., and Rivlin, L. G. (eds) (1979) *Environmental Psychology: Man and His Physical Space.* New York: Holt, Rinehart & Winston.

Raynes, N. V., Pratt, M. W., and Roses S. (1979) *Organisational Structure and the Care of the Mentally Retarded.* London: Croom Helm.

Redl, F. and Wineman, D. (1957) *The Aggressive Child.* New York: Free Press.

Resnick, H. and Patti, R. J. (1980) *Change from Within, Humanizing Social Welfare Organisations.* Philadelphia: Temple University Press.

Rice, A. K. (1963) *The Enterprise and the Environment.* London: Tavistock.

Rivlin, L. G. and Wolfe, M. (1979) Understanding and Evaluating Therapeutic Environments for Children. In D. Canter and S. Canter (eds) *Designing for Therapeutic Environments.* Chichester, England: Wiley.

Slater, R. and Lipman, A. (1980) Towards Caring Through Design. In R. Walton and D. Elliott (eds) *Residential Care: A Reader in Current Theory and Practice.* Oxford: Pergamon Press.

Sommer, R. (1969) *Personal Space, the Behavioural Basis of Design.* Englewood Cliffs, NJ: Prentice-Hall.

—— (1977) *The End of Imprisonment.* Oxford: Oxford University Press.

Weismann, H. W. (1973) *Overcoming Mismanagement in the Human Service Professions.* San Francisco: Jossey-Bass.

Whittaker, J. K. (1975) The Ecology of Child Treatment: A Developmental Educational Approach to the Therapeutic Milieu. *Journal of Autism and Child Schizophrenia* 5 (3): 223–37.

Wolfensberger, E. (ed.) (1972) *The Principle of Normalisation in Human Services.* Toronto: National Institute on Mental Retardation.

Wolins, M. and Wozner, Y. (1982) *Revitalizing Residential Settings.* San Francisco: Jossey-Bass.

Section II

Working directly with children

4   Developing a shared language and practice

Stephen F. Casson[1]

More than a job – a pound of flesh

It is 3.45 p.m. Jerry, a group home worker, is responsible for twelve adolescent boys and girls, ranging in age from fifteen to eighteen, who are returning from work or school. His colleague who should have been on duty has just called in sick. This colleague predicts she will be away from her work for seven days. Two residents are preparing a sandwich, another is watching television, one is getting ready to go out and two of the others are doing nothing in particular. Jerry knows he has to take care of all that happens until two other group home workers arrive at 8 a.m. the next day. He calculates that there are $16\frac{1}{4}$ hours left as the minutes start ticking by interminably slowly. Jerry keeps his fingers crossed that tonight the residents will behave themselves, perhaps watch television, go out to a disco or just do anything that interests them. If all goes well, he will write up some case records, bring some financial accounts up to date, and generally be helpful. He will make his mark on this shift, so at the staff meeting people will recognize the hard work he has put in to get the paperwork up to date. He might even have time to watch the film on television at 8 p.m. If there are only three or four residents in the building, it might be a pleasantly quiet evening.

Commentary: *What is the purpose of Jerry coming to work? What should he do with the residents until they go to bed? How should Jerry or any group home worker spend his time with a group of adolescents? To what extent does he organize activities for them, arrange transport, and go places? What would be the point of it? Should he go and rent a couple of video films to entertain a sizeable number of boys and girls and thereby probably encourage them to stay in? Should he have a heart-to-heart conversation with the two residents with whom he gets on best, to help them straighten out some of their problems (is this counselling?)? On the other hand, should he do nothing at all, as this would be a good preparation for the residents to learn how to fill up their own time, to work out for themselves how to spend the evening and be a bit realistic about life in the big wide world?*

A social worker for Julie, aged seventeen and four months pregnant, drops in to talk about Julie and her plans for the future. She wants to talk to Jerry privately in the office. Jerry wishes she had more sensitivity about how the establishment works and realized he should be amongst the boys and girls as they return home from school. Perhaps she might telephone next time to make an appointment? What is the point of talking to her anyway — she is not interested and he has got too much to do. At least she might spend an hour with Julie which will keep her quiet.

The phone rings and it is an assertive auditor saying he is coming tomorrow morning to go through the books. The group home worker explains that tomorrow there is a staff meeting. The auditor states that he only needs an hour from the senior worker in the establishment and that will not cause too much disruption to the staff meeting. He will arrive at 10.30 a.m. Jerry feels a surge of anger that this outsider — probably in a suit — takes no notice of him and intends to interfere with an important meeting. There will be less time to discuss four residents due for in-depth discussion. Oh well, the interminable conversations about residents get nowhere, so an hour less might be a good thing.

Commentary: *Where does Jerry stand with an unscheduled visit from a social worker and insensitive high pressure from an auditor? Should he tell them both to come at a time convenient to the establishment, or should the establishment constantly shuffle its operations like a small pack of cards to maintain the good will and co-operation of outsiders?*

Whatever Jerry decides, how will he know whether or not he is doing the 'right thing'? If he means to ensure outsiders come at convenient times, how will he go about influencing the social worker and auditor to co-operate? If what he does succeeds will he be looked upon as a competent and mature person and if there are complaints, what will it be that he has done wrong?

Charles, an aggressive sixteen-year-old who recently left school, throws himself into the office complaining that he will not work an hour longer at the Youth Employment Programme where he has been working. Someone has accused Charles of stealing money. He tells Jerry what he can do with the job, and that what is more, he will not be looking for another one. The group home worker feels embarrassed to be the subject of such an outburst in front of the social worker. He wonders what she is thinking about him, allowing this verbal aggression and all these interruptions, when he is meant to be talking with her. Jerry thinks, 'If only I had more time and there was someone else working with me, then things would be different.'

Jerry nods to the social worker to let her know that he has not forgotten his business with her, while he reassures Charles that he realizes he must have a lot of strong feelings about what has just happened at work. 'However, I will spend time with you later', says Jerry, 'because I am talking to the social worker about an important matter just now.' Charles shouts at Jerry that if that is the way he feels about his being called a liar and a thief then it isn't important to Jerry; he will go out and break into somebody's home and it will all be Jerry's fault. In his own head, Jerry believes he should be talking with Charles, yet why does he receive the blame? He is only doing his job.

Commentary: *What is the optimum approach to working with Charles? What kind of person is he? Can he be described or assessed in such a way that Jerry is given an immediate knowledge of how to deal with this anger and hurt? Should Jerry immediately stop what he is doing with the social worker and turn all his sympathy to Charles? Should he model to Charles the social skill of holding an emotion in check until the 'right time' to let it out? Should he be very matter-of-fact in his approach to Charles? Should he let him know that it is Charles's problem and although he might help Charles work out what to do, the solution rests with Charles? Should he immediately act on*

*Charles's behalf, call the Youth Employment Programme, sort things
out, and try to get him another chance? How can a group home worker
know what response to give Charles apart from an intuitive guess
about what might work, or on the other hand what might not? If his
response does not help, then his competence is undermined in his own
eyes and those of his colleagues.*

At that moment the doorbell rings and in walks a man delivering
numerous food provisions for the next seven days. He comes
into the office to get a signature and to explain why the provisions
delivered are different from what was ordered; how certain missing
items will be delivered next week; and how this will not affect
the bill, as ... Jerry signs the order form and makes a few notes
at the bottom about next week's order. Charles and the delivery
man leave the office.

The social worker talks about Julie's pregnancy with Jerry as
he finishes his note about the provisions. She wants to know
what Julie thinks about adoption. Jerry, who has not seen Julie
for some time and has never talked to her about adoption, shows
his impatience. He has suddenly remembered that the agency's
local maintenance crew have not yet unblocked the drains from
the first-floor kitchen and toilet, although someone telephoned
them five hours ago with an urgent request. Jerry apologizes to
the social worker and excuses himself, suggesting she return when
Julie's key or primary worker is on duty and, together, she and
the social worker can plan the next stage. He inwardly curses the
time and energy he has expended on this irritating woman.

Jerry telephones the maintenance service and finds that there
is no chance that they will arrive before tomorrow afternoon. He
telephones the supervisor but gets no reply. He looks through
the Yellow Pages for emergency drain cleaning numbers and
makes arrangements for one company to visit within the next
two hours. Just as he is congratulating himself on solving the
problem, he hears shouting in the passage. He looks out and finds
Mark being accosted by a middle-aged man and a younger
woman. He has never seen them before. Jerry tries to put his
stamp of authority on the scene. 'What is going on?' he demands.
The older man, smelling of alcohol, says he is Mark's father and
this is his new wife. He is not leaving without Mark, as he is
having to pay a sizeable proportion of his wages to keep his son

in this den of iniquity. 'Look at those two,' he says, as he points at two girls reclining on a settee, one with a dress slid halfway up her thighs and the other with her mouth open and her tongue provocatively aggravating Mark's father. This older man walks up to Jerry, and standing only three feet away from his face, demands that Jerry should tell Mark to pack and that he should hand over all Mark's money, medical card, and so on.

The group home worker's blood is thumping through his body. His mouth is dry. Jerry tells Mark, his father, and the new wife that he is not going to carry on an argument like this in front of everybody. If they want to discuss it then they can come into the office. In the office Mark's father stands over Jerry as he sits in a chair, and shouts belligerently. Mark tells his father to stop it. Jerry informs all three parties that if Mark leaves the building, the police will be called and he will be reported as an absconder. Mark solves the problem by telling his father that he will not go with him. He has never given him any breaks in life and therefore he does not want anything to do with him now. He storms out of the group home. The father blames Jerry and threatens him. Twenty minutes later the father and his new wife leave, telling Jerry that they will be back to get their revenge.

Commentary: *What is the optimum approach this worker could use to reduce the turmoil with Mark, his father, and new wife? Should he be confronting, reflective, directive, or permissive? Is it a matter of chance whether the intervention of this worker causes a belligerent response or reduced tension? Do different workers deal with this sort of situation in a purely idiosyncratic way that reflects their personality? If one approach works, should all workers adopt that approach whether or not the recipe will be as effective for other colleagues? Is it possible to weigh up the characteristics of the children, the characteristics of the group home worker, and the characteristics of the setting to come up with a recipe that will work for everyone in this situation at that time with those particular people? If this does not work, is the solution that one recruits workers solely on the basis that in their own indomitable way, the right personalities can deal with all comers? Does a person who can deal with all comers and all situations do anything other than enforce a spirit of calm, order, and control on an establishment whether or not this has anything to do with development and growth for children? Will one energetic worker operate in a unique and different way from other persevering staff?*

Jerry goes into the main living area to welcome back three residents who have been working. He is about to ask them how their day has gone when the emergency drain cleaners arrive. Jerry shows them what is blocked and leaves them to it. A couple of girls, immaturely and with much noise, follow the workmen around making loud whispers about their looks and how they are not likely to be worthy of their attention because of their menial job as drain cleaners. The two men respond in kind and Jerry attempts to move the girls elsewhere. They are abusive to him, they resist and enjoy being the centre of attention. Jerry gives up, returning to the kitchen, feeling embarrassed that he has so little power and influence on residents that he knows well when they are willing to publicly abuse him. He finds a couple of boys unearthing fruit and biscuits from the boxes of supplies. He reacts angrily as he has not yet checked the produce that has been left. He starts the inventory of those provisions to ensure everything is there. He makes a note that they are 4 lb of butter short. He asks a resident to put the supplies away for him.

It is now 6.30 p.m. The boy and girl responsible for preparing and cooking the evening meal for everybody have not returned from school. Jerry asks Fiona and Marian if they will do it. They refuse. Jerry debates in his mind whether to force the issue and tell them they have got to do it. Instead, he asks another resident, John, who says he might but only if Jerry gives him three cigarettes. They end up in an argument about people only doing things if they are paid for them. Jerry becomes more irate with this non co-operation and starts peeling potatoes and preparing vegetables himself.

Commentary: *Are there some common attributes or strategies which can make an impact on provocative adolescent girls or residents that refuse to help out with the overall functioning of the establishment? If people will not give a hand, is it best to let people go hungry or should the group home worker do it himself? After all, the worker is responsible for the nutritional needs of the adolescents. Is bribery or cajoling people with future reinforcement relevant here? Is it preferable to let the attention-seeking girls work it out with the drain-cleaning crew or is intervening strongly more appropriate? How does a group home worker come up with an answer?*

The two drain cleaners tell Jerry they have finished, get him to sign that the work is complete, and they leave. Jerry checks the toilets and showers and finds them working adequately. At that moment the drain cleaners return and state that a wallet has been taken from a jacket in the van outside. The crime must have been engineered by a resident from the home. Two of the residents immediately start arguing with the cleaners that in no way are they thieves and how dare they blame poor unfortunates who live in residential care. The men shout back and insults are thrown to and fro. Jerry tells the cleaners he has no evidence about who took the wallet and they ought therefore to call the police. The telephone call is made. Forty minutes later two policemen arrive and interview the two men, Jerry, and all the group home residents who were around at the time. Jerry has to sit in on each interview with the residents. The police, no further on, leave at 8.50 p.m. No evening meal has been cooked. The two residents who should have prepared dinner have still not returned. Jerry questions in his mind when to report them as missing.

By this time eight people are hungry and are waiting for a meal. They criticize Jerry for not being a proper child care worker since he has not provided adequate food and nutrition. Jerry calls them all into the lounge. He states he is not prepared to do the work, and unless he has some volunteers who will make the meal, everyone will go hungry. Jerry questions in his own mind whether he is doing the right thing or not, and whether it is his duty to get adequate food prepared for each person.

Three residents volunteer to do the cooking. Jerry sits down to discuss with the two girls the provoking of the drain cleaners. He asks them what they were trying to achieve. They laugh. He tells them in strong, cutting terms that their behaviour is unacceptable and that they have given the home a bad name. This could mean that in retaliation service companies may provide only a second-rate service in the future.

Commentary: *Jerry's head is pounding. For five-and-a-half hours there has been turmoil. It will be another eleven hours before he is relieved by other workers. 'All my hard work is merely stopping this place from disintegrating,' he thought. 'Surely this is not why I applied for*

*this type of work.' Jerry feels alone. He has no idea what he will do
if the residents are unco-operative tonight and give him a hard time.
Other jobs and professions suddenly seem more attractive.*

Reflection on the foregoing incident with Jerry, the apocryphal
and yet surprisingly real group home worker, leaves one with a
sense of chaos, a state of affairs characteristic of this line of work
now that the so-called profession of residential and day care has
come into its own. The profession's foundations have been built
on shifting sands of change. Until the last decade or so, many
child care establishments were run on the notion of a husband or
wife, or both, managing a group of children virtually singlehanded
as house-parents, with the assistance of cleaning staff, laundry
maids and the occasional relief worker. The philosophies, ideologies, and values of child care were integrated within that husband
and wife as house-parents, or in some particular individual who
worked virtually every hour of the week. Thus, while the
philosophies, ideologies, and values used by the house-parents
might be judged by others to be right or wrong, simple or
complex, rigid or flexible, the essential merit in this arrangement
was that each resident was confronted with a single set of attitudes
and values that were both consistent and enduring. When these
particular philosophies and attitudes were in tune with and
matched the needs and characteristics of a particular child, then
progress was likely to be seen; where there was a mismatch, the
successes were less common and transfers to other centres were
a frequent result. Group home facilities such as these were
advocated in the United Kingdom in 1946 by the Curtis Committee
which envisaged the establishment of family group homes,
preferably run by a married couple, where children could be
closely in touch with the experiences of everyday life. The woman
was expected to 'play the part of a mother to the children, while
the man must play the father ... [pursuing] out of door recreational
activities rather than physical care of the child' (Cmd 6922).

Today with the vast increase in numbers of child care staff and
supervisors working in group care settings, there is some comfort
in knowing that somewhere amongst the differing philosophies
and attitudes of staff, a child is likely to find someone who
understands him and who is on his wavelength. On the other
hand the provision of a coherent 'parenting', 'teaching', and

'developmental' programme is a complex undertaking as with, for instance, twelve children and six child care staff. The exercise becomes an organizational, managerial, and therapeutic nightmare! More often than not, what happens is that a collection of different types of worker, with marked differences in personality and values, become responsible for a collection of different types of children with a variety of problems. Together these two groups interact in an environment where all too frequently the philosophies, assumptions, approaches, and styles have not been clearly determined. This problem is the curse of residential and day care services for children; and indeed the curse of the helping professions when several different persons have to work together to provide therapeutic interventions for a child and his family.

Disparity amongst workers

Senior managers in residential and day care services frequently comment on the number of people who apply to them for employment in settings for children, elderly, mentally handicapped, or mentally ill people, even when no vacancies have been advertised. At interview these job applicants will emphasize that what has motivated them is their interest in working with people; they have something to offer to residents; they have always got on well with children, adolescents, elderly, or handicapped people; and they want to do something meaningful with their lives. In the main, the majority of these people are untrained.

As the interview progresses, it is common practice to ask for specific information about how the applicant would view a particular situation and what his/her response might be. A typical answer is, 'It depends on the circumstances, and what I find to be best at that particular moment of time. It will depend on who is involved, what is the background to the problem and what is expected in that particular establishment.' A response such as this suggests that the applicant is interested in using personality, beliefs, attitudes, and intuition to help persons less fortunate than himself/herself. Personality and beliefs are in their own right a product of personal background, upbringing, and experience. It may be that the applicant wants to apply his/her own skills and knowledge, his/her own relationship abilities, and his/her own uniqueness to work intensively with a particular group of children, using the programme elements available at the centre in which she/he could be working. But, in more sophisticated language, the applicant will be expected to use personality – still the product of genetic make-up and upbringing – in interactions with children, whether these have an impact or not.

When recruiting and employing staff for group care settings, what is the hirer looking for? Consideration will be given to values, personality, mixture of rigidity and flexibility, dogged control versus negotiation, permissive approaches versus detailed surveillance, and so on. Without a definite profile of the type of person best suited to working in a particular group care centre or agency, then recruitment involves an intuitive and possibly prejudicial approach to hiring staff. Decisions are based more on the characteristics of the hirer than on the traits of the employee. Some hirers' track record for recruitment is excellent, while others' records are abysmal when considering the length of service of those they hire, the candidates being able to manage the job and their ability to work as team members. Some people are good at hiring men but do a poor job with women; some are excellent with basic grade workers but second-rate at employing supervisors.

Thus, in group care settings there will be a range of staff from different backgrounds, with different values, different parenting experiences, different religious principles, different sexual mores, different hygiene habits, dressing and grooming practices, different nutritional ideals, and different eating habits. In summary, an establishment with six workers will tend to be a place where six individual workers come together to work with a group of children, with a spectrum of philosophies, practices, and behaviours that will be varied in at least six different ways.

If one person had been responsible for hiring these six workers, then it may be easier to detect a pattern in their characteristics; it is more likely that one would find people with certain similarities included and those with other traits excluded. The frequent pattern is that several persons have had the responsibility over months or years for hiring staff for a particular establishment or group of establishments. Thus, the differences and heterogeneity will probably be greater and values, ideology, and morals will frequently be in conflict amongst workers at the shop floor and at the level of shop floor supervisors.

It can be argued that the attitudes, energies, and optimism of each staff member is the critical influences for maintaining 'Good Order' in an establishment; for stimulating children to interact with each other, staff, and outsiders in a positive way; and for making definite progress in a planned direction. Based on these unique personality features, the group care worker assesses the crucial elements of treatment, makes decisions about the children's group and specific treatment plans for individual children, and imposes sanctions on behaviour within a given set of procedures. This personality quagmire, the coherence or lack of coherence between staff members, would seem to be the main element which influences the success or failure of routines, intervention methods, and planned activities that surround a child's total working day. Unless staff have organized themselves into a cohesive team, with an integrated climate which absorbs the different ideologies, values, and philosophies, then the energies of workers may go into surviving or just competing with each other, virtually ensuring that no treatment is accomplished.

Taking into account the complexity of practice and the number of personalities involved, let us return to the picture of Jerry doing battle in his group care centre. Immediate questions that are posed include:

- How can a centre deal with a host of unanticipated eventualities, but in a way that is predictable and planned?
- How can a group of staff, working shifts with no more than one or two workers on duty at a time, maintain a particular intervention approach for a particular child — whatever the circumstances?
- Or, to use Henry Maier's (1981) imagery, how can the best or ideal rhythm for a specific child be learned and practised by the group care worker in all interventions, resulting in the unity of rhythm between staff member(s) and child?
- Furthermore, how can a centre draw together a diverse group of workers into a cohesive team which can affect the lives of a diverse group of children?

Some of these questions can be answered by having a clear statement of intentions within a specific group care establishment. The following sections examine a step by step approach to formulating an 'Action Plan' for group care practice.

Developing an action plan: strategic and practical considerations

An Action Plan seeks to define a care and treatment programme with children. It details specific actions and establishes clear boundaries within which certain types of action will take place. It describes the children with whom the centre works and the norms and culture of the staff. Logic first dictates a clear knowledge of the people for whom the programme is intended. Thus, prior to the development of any residential or day care setting, it is essential to know something about the existing children and those anticipated in the future.

When group care workers are asked to describe the residents with whom they work, some of the most frequent responses include: sex, age, criminal offence active/passive, co-operative/un-co-operative, violent/victims, clever/stupid, runaways, impulsive, thieves, cheats, substance abusers, liars, fearful, untrustworthy, people with life scripts about never being close to others, not being successful, not being sane or well, or not being happy. Frequently these descriptions revolve around a child's behaviour. There might be half-a-dozen positive descriptions and a dozen negative descriptions concerning any one child. Psychological, psychiatric, and educational reports produce some other descriptions for the same child. However sophisticated, the labels have little bearing on day-to-day interactions between staff and child. Indeed, with twelve children in a residential unit there would be an overload on any one worker if he were to remember all the assessment statements concerning all the children. Such statements and the implied responses are seldom helpful in a window-smashing episode, a refusal to go to bed, a scapegoat incident, or one involving damage to a staff member's car. At such times the group care worker's natural, intuitive, and personality-induced responses come to the fore. If the problem is resolved then the worker will be looked upon as being competent, whether or not the diagnostic description and implied treatment strategy have been adhered to in any way.

Hoghughi (1980) described the usefulness of a diagnosis and treatment description for problem children. All considerations were thought to be subservient to the usefulness of assessment in order to meet the objective of alleviating a child's problems.

David Hunt (1972) has written about the same problem experienced by teachers in school. Hunt (1966) proposed a set of conditional statements indicating the environmental conditions thought appropriate for a child of a specified state in order to produce a sequence of change which was aimed towards a desired state. The crucial issue involves whether workers are able to make use of such information on most occasions and under most circumstances. This is quite different from the diagnostic approach which a psychotherapist might hold in his mind at a bi-monthly outpatient clinic. Here, the psychotherapist is likely to be in charge and his background, uniqueness, and idiosyncracies are integrated with his approach to treatment, which he alone puts into practice every two weeks. When more than one person is involved in the therapy then approaches need to be understood by each participant, so that each response a worker gives is integrated with shared attitudes, philosophies, and practices.

Brill, using the Conceptual Level Model (1977), demonstrated that in some situations group care environments can be specifically designed to give children differing amounts of 'structure'. Conceptual Level is based on a theory of personality development (Harvey, Hunt, and Schroder 1961), where the stage of development for a person – whether maladjusted, delinquent, or normal – may be assessed. Where a person is located on this developmental continuum indicates his Conceptual Level, made up of cognitive complexity (differentiation, discrimination, and integration) as well as interpersonal maturity (increasing self-responsibility). A person with a higher Conceptual Level is thought to be more structurally complex, more capable of responsible actions, and more capable of adapting to a changing environment than a person at a lower Conceptual Level.

Brill's research was based on the Conceptual Level of each child placed in two different residential units. These units were designed with different amounts of predictability, consistency, staff control, order, and organization, doing tasks alongside children, tangible reinforcements, opportunity for expressiveness, emphasis on personal problems, autonomy, and so on. Children of very low Conceptual Level did better in the higher structured residential facility and had fewer problems in terms of time being spent in detention or absconding from the programme. These results compared favourably with the results of children with very low

Conceptual Level placed in a unit where the environment was less 'structured' and less organized by staff. Those children whose Conceptual Level was low, as compared with very low, did slightly better when the amount of 'structure' was reduced in small quantities. In short, the mismatched, low Conceptual Level boys in residence had more than two times the problem behaviour incidents of those matched to the programme in which they were placed in terms of precision, consistency, directiveness, and structure of that unit. Also the time spent out of 'programme' (in their room or elsewhere) because of unacceptable behaviour or because of absconding was three-and-a-half times greater for the mismatched children than for those matched.

Brill and Reitsma (1978) further discovered that if the Conceptual Level of the primary worker (the key person in charge of co-ordinating the care and treatment plan for a child and providing most counselling time with him) is one stage above that of the child in Conceptual Level terms then development was apparently heightened, and change in a positive direction was most obvious. In addition, Brill and Reitsma found that according to another differential treatment model – that based on Interpersonal Maturity Level (Grant, Grant, and Sullivan 1957) – if the primary worker was matched by his personality to the needs and characteristics of the child, then progress in a residential establishment was significantly greater than for those children not matched or completely mismatched (Palmer 1967, 1968, 1972).

In short, Brill and Reitsma found that when there was an optimum match between the resident and the key or primary worker, using the Conceptual Level Model, then residents spent one-third less time in residential care and had one-half the rate of problem incidents than when there was a mismatch between resident and primary worker. Yet again, when the primary worker was matched to the child, according to Palmer's I-Level matching criteria, these residents had one-eighth of the problem incidents and only 2 per cent of their time in residence was spent out of programme. This is compared favourably with the mismatched primary worker where residents had eight times as many problem incidents and 25 per cent of their time in residence was spent out of programme. The importance of this is that both the Interpersonal Maturity (I-Level) and Conceptual Level Models provide typologies from which to develop differential treatment environments for different children. A great deal is known about which type of staff member will work best with which type of children and in what type of programme. There is also a good deal known about what basic techniques are best used with different children.

In summary, our starting point was the chaotic set of crises encountered by Jerry the care worker. It is possible for Jerry to achieve greater clarity as to how he should try and deal with each situation that confronts him. It is possible to know more clearly what type of residents are normally placed in his unit, with the obvious implication this has for any type of intervention. Appropriate recipe(s) for particular groups of children can help maintain Jerry's sanity and motivation, while assisting the children themselves to progress on to more complex and responsible behaviour. Then the 'dynamic' characteristics of practice in a unit necessitates the monitoring of children's progress to keep track of what developmental changes take place over their period of placement in group care. As the make-up of the resident group alters over time, so the Action Plan of the care establishment will change in fairly precise ways, because of the characteristic patterns of interaction between particular children and particular environments to produce planned results. Hunt stated, 'The issue is not which environment is best, but rather which environment is best for a particular person to produce a specific effect' (1972: 17).

In the same way that a child's developmental stage is regularly assessed, so it is equally important to monitor what is happening between staff and children, and between different children. It is necessary to assess whether the action plan is really being put into practice or whether aberrations and numerous exceptions are the order of the day. Finally, the tasks of monitoring child and centre characteristics should be balanced against an evaluation of the programme as a whole. Here the results may be compared with evaluations from other places using the same practice language concerning children, care and treatment environments, and programmes. Frequently the central question involves asking, 'What kinds of children are participating in the group care service, under what circumstances, and what does that imply for management and treatment?' (Warren 1973).

Section I: Social policy mandate and philosophy of the centre

(a) The definition of centre mandate

So many are the variables concerning children, staff, programmes, strategies, and even length of time in care, the arguments so recurring about what approaches work best, that optimally many decisions about programme design, general philosophy, and methods of working may need to be taken outside the group care unit. The leaders and those already working in a setting, if they have already been hired, make representations to managers or administrators about their views on child assessment, prescribed actions, and broad outlines of intervention. It is clearly advocated that decisions such as these about mandate should not rest with the team leader and his immediate staff group alone. Frequently such important decisions are left to team leaders because an agency has no coherent way of describing children or staff programmes in an integrated whole. Care and treatment goals are frequently written in vague, 'fuzzy' terms (Kushlik 1975; Mager 1972) such as 'realising a child's potential', 'broadening experience and skills', 'increasing self-confidence and ability to make relationships', or 'to aid insight into self-defeating processes'.

What is unhelpful is the realization that most group care centres adopt such statements as basic beliefs or as an accepted part of their service claims. The British Association of Social Workers (1977) in the opening pages of its document defining 'The Social Work Task' offers an example of how 'fuzzy' language (Mager 1972) is adopted by a professional body. A mandate written in such global terms, with words likened to a belief system, is not helpful for a team of workers who require clarity of expectations about the fundamental direction and ethos of their programme. A mandate written in global terms can lull an agency into the false impression that it actually has detailed direction for its various programmes. However, when many programme descriptions are examined closely, frequently one finds that no integrating formula holds the scheme together: neither the care and treatment strategies for particular children, the characteristics and traits of staff needed, nor methods for systematically monitoring and evaluating change.

To summarize: chaos and disillusionment are more likely to exist and be in evidence unless there is a statement of policy expectations or mandate about what kind of children the programme will serve and general ideas about the treatment strategies expected. Those working in group care programmes might well ask themselves: (1) What is the policy mandate for our present work setting? (2) Who decided these expectations? and (3) What are the concepts which underpin the policy mandate and what assumptions are used to integrate children, staff, and programme? Asking staff to write down their individual answers to these three questions and then asking the staff group to examine their replies during a team meeting provides its own revelation of similarity, difference, and confusion.

When setting up a new service, a team leader may well have the luxury of working out key areas of the programme prior to hiring staff. If the staff group are already in post, as happens in most establishments, an effective tactic which can assist staff to develop their work occurs naturally through the developmental process which an action plan uses. It evolves from within the staff group, under the clear leadership of the team manager, and seeks to use the aspirations of each staff member. Minimum requirements are that the team leader needs a knowledge of group dynamics and the workers should not be totally inexperienced at working in staff groups where, at different times, the members may be challenging, confronting, intimate, and revealing. If the majority of a team have little knowledge of group dynamics and the steps through which groups develop and regress, then the action plan exercise may get bogged down with interpersonal problems that get in the way of its primary task. Menzies (1977) referred to this as anti-task activity. If it happens, then the team leader needs to acquire (or needs to be instructed about) guidance in group dynamics, sensitivity training, or something similar.

(b) Philosophy of the unit
To be realistic, it must be remembered that an action plan provides detailed statements on the whole variety of aspects of group care practice, a centre's rules, resident group culture, staff, and so on. It is not a solution and decision-making print-out of every variable likely to confront a worker in the course of a shift. The action plan is used to clarify issues about the establishment's philosophy and beliefs, the principles underlying child management practices, communication approaches, and aspirations. When these issues

are clearly articulated and written so as to be understood and endorsed by all who work in the centre (or in association with a centre), so there develops the basis for a shared approach to practice. Real differences and individual preferences amongst staff members will be highlighted during what can become a long-drawn-out process of coming to a negotiated agreement about a shared language of practice. Conflicts emerging in relation to different orientations, backgrounds, experiences, beliefs, and life-styles are essential steps in the development of an Action Plan, and also the level of commitment to the plan which is likely to result thereafter.

At least three questions need to be asked of staff as they engage in this step of the Action Plan process. It is comparatively easy for all workers to give initial responses to these questions separately and in writing, in a task involving about 5–10 minutes. Staff members are asked:

1 What are the guiding principles which underlie the work of this centre, its work with children, staff, neighbours, and other professionals?
2 What ideas or concepts are used to explain the unit's work with children?
3 Describe in a few words the communication or interpersonal approach used in interactions between staff and children, between children, and between staff.

This kind of written exercise is frequently a stimulus for people to take such a 'fuzzy' or ideological question seriously. Responses from staff in different units are given as examples:

- No responses at all were given, with workers unable to formulate a written statement of philosophy for themselves, let alone a philosophy that might incorporate principles for the whole unit. In such a case, specific instruction, experiential work, and clarity of thinking were necessary in order to get the workers to think in terms of philosophy.
- Clearly articulated statements which were in conflict with the statements of other workers. Such statements were products of the different backgrounds from which the workers had come as compared with a common definition about the resident group.

– At different times in a very short period, the same workers answered the three questions very differently, revealing the temporary nature of the centre's philosophy. Statements that are based on the past few shifts of work are often presented in subjective terms.
– A coherent, systematic response was obtained from a fourth team, indicating the successful completion of important ground-work which was necessary in order for workers to perform with a shared approach to practice.

Section II: Child development and orientations to group living

(a) Child development
This section outlines the particular features involved and events that take place in the centre which give the setting a uniqueness. This involves such items as:

(1) influencing children's group culture;
(2) transmitting values to children;
(3) children's rules and procedures;
(4) children's meetings.

The team leaders are encouraged to make certain that in thinking of child development, the subheadings of an Action Plan will reveal important norms that may be distinctive features of the centre. Not everything taking place with children needs to be mentioned, otherwise the Action Plan document will be so large that it cannot be used as a staff guide or handbook.

In a way similar to that which was detailed above concerning philosophy, benefit can come from asking individual workers to spell out in writing what they consider to be the ideal culture initiated and enacted by staff with children in the centre. Writing this up on large paper and posting it around the wall (wallpapering) offers an insight to everyone about the common and divergent attitudes held by staff members towards the children. If the unit is already functioning with children, each worker can also be invited to write how they assess the present children's group culture. Comparisons between the ideal and present group cultures are important and frequently result in productive discussion.

Different strategies for influencing and having an impact on children's group culture are readily available. Jones (1968) advocated a participative approach, Vorrath and Brendtro (1974) outlined a peer responsibility approach, while Brown and Christie (1981) or Pizzat (1973) have offered social learning approaches to practice. The basic philosophy of the centre – already completed – must be compatible with and reinforce the key interventions planned with a group of residents. Feedback from workers who have struggled with these two sections in an Action Plan has revealed that these sections are frequently the least tangible of the lot. They are the most difficult to sort out and yet the most important, because all other aspects of the Action Plan build from a coherent statement about the centre's philosophy and its orientation to the children's population it serves.

(b) Values and attitudes to child behaviour

Once the basic orientation to work with children is clear, and the workers have clarified major expectations which they have for the children, then a series of more specific questions need to be asked. A highly relevant, but seldom asked, question for all workers is: 'What are the specific values that we want the children to learn?'

In practice this question can be considered with staff, using an exercise similar to that already described. At a staff meeting, workers can be asked to 'Write down six basic values you want children to learn.' Such an exercise can demonstrate, in reasonably relaxed way, the important differences in social background which exist between workers, and therefore different priorities given to teaching children. The individual value preferences can be wallpapered around the wall, giving staff an opportunity to note whether their recommended values are acknowledged. Various patterns have been highlighted as group care workers have engaged in such an exercise:

– Some staff have similar values.
– Some values may be wrapped up in a personal language which disguises the basic value, and to which several other values can be imputed. Many workers hold the value, for example, that 'residents should attend a dentist every six months'. Here the value is not seeing the dentist but perhaps ensuring that a child keeps his/her teeth for a lifetime or maintains his/her

good looks. Alternatively the worker may be saying, 'I don't want you to have to suffer a lot of dental work, therefore it is better to do something each day than it is to wait until your teeth rot,' in other words a stitch in time saves nine.

- Some values held by workers are total absolutes, such as 'always tell the truth', or 'telling the truth in certain circumstances'. Does telling the truth mean truthful replies only when asked a question, and does it include voicing opinions when someone expresses dislike or revulsion – as when seeing a dirty, intoxicated man asleep in a chair? Such absolute values, and how they should be applied in a given setting, are opened for debate amongst workers.
- Workers tend to find absolutes and procedures easier to recall than to identify values which they might find helpful to reinforce with children in day-to-day practice.

Group care teams are encouraged to refine a half dozen social values which the workers' group can reinforce over and over again, during any shift, whether events go well or badly. In so doing, a group care team helps to promote consistency and enable children to assimilate learning through repetition time and time again. This is especially relevant for egocentric, impulsive children whose interests are solely in the present. It is also helpful for those who have surges of emotion which dominate mind and body.

When value orientation has been considered, on both sides of the Atlantic, some workers have objected to the notion of filling children's minds with a particular set of ideals. Such an approach has been thought contradictory to the notion of individual freedom. These workers want to emphasize values where children are allowed to pick and choose for themselves and change their own values.

To counter these arguments, proponents of the Conceptual Level Matching Model have shown that a large proportion of residents in some centres have not become dependent on any clearly defined norms or values. For this reason, until personal values become part of a child's pattern of functioning, it is neither appropriate nor possible for that child to start being independent or commence working out his own beliefs. Brill (1979) highlighted the importance of flexibility in negotiation and expressiveness in work with children who *had* internalized personal values. However, approaches such as these have often been misused with children who are physically mature, but whose egocentricity is extreme and whose interpersonal maturity is low. Brill and Reitsma (1978) demonstrated that significant behaviour problems come about as the result of staff wanting young people to work out their own value systems. Such findings serve to reinforce the argument that group care workers all too frequently use idiosyncratic approaches in their practices with children.

Relevant values for egocentric children might include the following:

- Stop and think (before acting or responding).
- Listen to what others say.
- Do unto others as you want them to do to you.
- Face up to others.
- Face up to problems.
- Your views and ideas are important.

Group care workers seem to have little difficulty considering what these values might involve in practice. They also tend to support decisions about using all happenings, whether positive or negative, to emphasize these value prescriptions with *direct suggestions* about their importance. After frequent use and practice, the workers may start to use *indirect suggestion* by telling stories or using metaphors which contain these values (Grinder and Bandler 1979; Lankton 1979).

(c) Rules and expectations

Workers will have to decide what to include in this section and more important what to miss out. A statement of all rules and expectations will be so huge and overpowering that it will alienate most children, staff, and others. Procedures and rules can include the daily routine or timetable with specific indications as to when events occur. Important expectations and rules can also be included, especially those that are fundamental to the smooth functioning of the establishment along certain lines. Some rules come to the forefront of the mind because of contravention on a regular basis, and others because, when broken, these rules cause difficulties for staff. Basic expectations can be spelled out around daily living routines, including:

- Chores, details, or daily jobs.
- Leaving the centre, weekend or holiday absences, absconding, and so forth.
- Formal or informal counselling sessions.
- Pocket money and other.

Rules might include statements such as:

- No violence against any person.
- No drugs or alcohol.
- No visiting each other's bedroom after 9 p.m.
- No sex on the premises.

However much effort workers put into spelling out rules, most of them are likely to be written in negative terms. Some centres have stated the penalties which will be imposed for non-compliance with expectations or violation of the rules. Other centres have tended to reinforce daily compliance. Still other centres have been known to bring violations to a regular group meeting.

Putting only basic rules and expectations down on paper often results in the claim made by some outsiders that more rules and expectations should be written into the Action Plan. Ultimately the decision about what to include will necessitate each group care worker listing all the rules and expectations as they see them in the centre, and then everyone rank ordering their importance. The revelation that comes from workers through such an exercise is that different staff see norms, rules, and expectations differently. Some rules and expectations might apply with some members of staff, while others might operate quite differently. For example, it may be discovered that some workers have a rigid approach to ensuring the children go to bed at the stated time. Others, however, may allow television to be watched until the end of a programme, or until activities have been completed. The smaller the unit with fewer staff working alongside each other, the more likely it is that very different procedures will evolve for different shifts. Again using the evidence supplied by Brill and Reitsma (1978), and that of Hunt (1972), the more egocentric and lower the interpersonal maturity of a child, the more learning approaches should emphasize systematic and consistent interactions throughout his waking day.

The very fact of consolidating rules and expectations in workers' minds will force them to clarify particular demands or prohibitions used in their centre. The end result for an Action Plan is that while numerous agreements will be made concerning basic prompting and general compliance from residents during certain events, only a few rules will actually need to be written down. Otherwise, the list becomes never ending and forever changing. A crucial function at staff meetings is to review and update rules and expectations at regular intervals for everyone's benefit!

Section III: Links with family, peers, and significant others

(a) Family development

Questions posed in this section involve the centre's approach to working with families. Here, workers are invited to consider the attitudes that are held towards involving parents in the life of the programme. For instance a particular group home had a clear objective about intensive work with parents. This objective was written into their social policy mandate by the agency which funded them. Basic expectations concerning work with families were stated, involving at least two contacts with the family by each worker each week, with at least one of these meetings being at the group home. A specific contract was to be negotiated with the parents at the time of referral. Any home visits would be followed up by detailed discussion so as to examine how the visit had gone. Parents were actively encouraged to use the same techniques with their child at home as the group care workers were using, most frequently a Behaviour Modification approach.

In other establishments, contact with families may be less intensive. Whatever the level of contact, it is important that practices carried out with families are clearly stated and workers know what actions are expected of them in this respect. If the philosophy and attitudes underpinning practice are to ensure that parents become partners in helping (Whittaker 1979), then the methods which are used to engage parents as partners will need to be stated. Conte explores this practice issue further at a later stage in this volume. It is worth remembering the evidence supplied by Taylor and Alpert (1973) who found that, more than anything else, the determining factor about future adjustment following an institutional care placement is the frequency of contact between parents and child.

(b) Involvement of peers and others
The friends and associates of children will inevitably have contact
with a group care centre. Whether school friends or work mates
are concerned, the Action Plan should make a basic statement
about how these involvements should be managed. Parties in the
early morning hours, under-age drinking, or sexual involvements
give some indication of issues that might develop. Involvements
with other 'outsiders' should also be noted whether these include
health and social service workers, police, neighbours, shop
deliverymen, volunteers, or others. This subsection of an Action
Plan is rarely complete. Rather, workers are required constantly
to upgrade their involvements with others in practice.

(c) After-care
Centre workers are asked to consider their relations with children
who have left the centre and gone elsewhere. Any contact which
is planned or engineered to provide continuing encouragement
and support for ex-residents should be stated. Sinclair (1971) and
Moos (1975) have argued that basically adjustment to living
outside a group care centre is correlated with the after-care
environment that a person will be living in. The implication is
that a child is more likely to succeed with any social skills taught
in a group care centre if those prompting these skills in an after-
care environment include the people who have struggled with
him/her in close proximity during previous weeks and months.
Of course, if this is to happen, it may only be possible when
those using a centre live in close proximity and have few problems
concerning transportation. This step in the Action Plan process
enables numerous changes and adjustments to be made, and
identifies practical ideas about after-care which could become part
of the service.

Section IV: staffing and staff development

A summary statement about how the staff function together as
a team, including reference to the consultation and supervision
available, is very different from the statements made in the child
development areas. In itself, this section can be brief. There is
opportunity for a team leader and team members to expand or
contract the Action Plan headings to suit the particular orientation

of the centre. The issues referred to here give an illustration of what could be expected in some settings. It is interesting to note how people identify subjectively with the notion that what happens within the staff group is often reflected back in what happens with the children. Thus, the level of energy available in a team, its commitment to interpersonal and intra-personal development, the workers' orientation to staff meetings, availability of consultation and supervision: all contribute to the morale, satisfaction, and effectiveness of group care workers.

In writing on this matter and his use of the Group Environment Scale (Moos, Meel, and Humphrey 1974) to assess team climates, Brill indicated that a moderate level of Leader Control appeared to be a necessary, but not all-sufficient condition for efficient team functioning. It would seem that Leader Control should be combined with (1) a high level of organization and clarity around daily norms, expectations, and routines, and (2) teamwork to minimize workers' loss of energy through frustration and anger, and to maintain a high task focus. Under such conditions, it is expected that staff morale would be higher and rates of turnover considerably reduced (Brill 1979: 120–23).

The corollary to this is that an inefficient series of staff meetings, no predictability around consultation and supervision, or a lack of clarity about who does what, when, and how, are likely to be reflected in low morale amongst residents, more behaviour which is out-of-control and more complaints about the handling of different situations. Thus it is that a brief section about care for the care-givers is an important feature of any Action Plan. As Maier argued, 'It is inherent that the caretakers be nurtured themselves and experience sustained, *caring* support in order to transmit this quality of care to others' (1977: 17).

(a) Staff meetings

Some statement should be made about the frequency of staff meetings and who is obliged to attend. This would influence the rostering of staff. If different people attend for different sessions this is likely to alter the way in which meetings can be conducted. Action plans can spell out expectations about staff meetings using short statements concerning the organization of each meeting and how this reinforces the philosophy of the unit. Increased efficiency and positive feedback about how time spent in meetings has become more productive is the consistent response from workers using this approach. Workers seem to be especially pleased with the increased cohesion which is reported in relation to work with residents and in planning for the future.

(b) Staff consultation and supervision
The Action Plan should note how an establishment stands with regard to the team leader providing a formal consultation and supervision service. If a unit is committed to such a service, the Action Plan needs to spell out how it will be conducted. This contrasts dramatically with a team leader and staff meeting simply because of a perceived obligation and without clarity of purpose and organization. Such *ad hoc*, unplanned meetings are so frequently time wasting. The system of staff consultation and supervision, spelled out in an Action Plan, might involve:

(1) a review of previous decisions;
(2) a review of key worker activity;
(3) the health, job satisfaction, and morale of workers;
(4) fulfilling the tasks of the job;
(5) any other business;
(6) a summary of decisions taken; and
(7) an evaluation of the meeting.

The Action Plan might make formal note of the importance of consultation by specifying a minimum number of meetings per month and obligations associated with taking notes at meetings. An alternative route is to ensure that a meeting is never adjourned without setting a date for the next session.

Section V: Key worker responsibilities

An aspect of group care practice which is becoming increasingly common involves a direct care worker co-ordinating all aspects of care and treatment for a particular child. Such a worker also disseminates information about that child to all other staff. In some places this person is termed the 'primary worker', in other places this person is called the 'key worker'. If such a system operates, then the basic responsibilities of a key worker need to be spelled out in the Action Plan, describing how the key worker will carry out these tasks. This might include planning care and treatment activities, report writing, liaison concerning job finding or school attendance, formal counselling sessions, working with family, and so on. An Action Plan seeks formally to incorporate this feature into the overall service.

Section VI: Evaluation of staff performance

Another important area in the Action Plan involves specification of how performance and actions of each worker will be monitored and evaluated. An Action Plan with clear philosophy and procedures will be a waste of paper unless there is clarity around evaluation of staff performance. It is important for a team leader to be involved in setting up a recording system which can monitor how each worker is performing. Thus, a clear record of performance can be used to focus discussion on actual practices at staff meetings, individual consultations, and during in-service training sessions. Without this section being clearly articulated, there is no definite reason for workers to conform to the Action Plan. A useful exercise involves staff being asked to identify in writing those practices which they believe are going well, those which are unproductive, and those which are likely to need oversight in order to guarantee consistent performance. It is a frequent cause for surprise that many workers request an inspectorial approach so as to improve their own individual performance and to enforce changes in the performance of others.

Section VII: Programme development and evaluation

This final section is oriented towards examining what happens over the course of time with children, the group care workers, and the setting. Whatever the major interests of the team, these will be reflected in the information collected.

(a) Resident change

Some centre teams are oriented towards looking at criminal activity, violence, and problem incidents while the child is in residence. If this is so, then the Action Plan should state how the required information is collected. Such information might also include the rate with which children are unfavourably discharged or removed from the centre. Others might be interested in overall changes experienced by a child during his time in receipt of services, so diagnostic testing at the beginning of his stay would be replicated at pre-determined intervals. The increased demands for care and treatment accountability make this issue of service evaluation a very important consideration in any Action Plan for practice.

(b) Unit environment
Only a few programmes look at evaluation measures concerning a centre's environment. The environment scales developed by Moos (1974, 1975) can be used to assess the environment of group care along nine comparative dimensions, including the *Relationship dimensions* of involvement, support and expressiveness; the *Personal Development dimensions* of autonomy, orientation, and achievement; and *System Change dimensions* of order and organization, clarity of expectations, and control. This is done by using a questionnaire completed separately by each worker and resident. The information obtained from such environmental analysis enables future development of the service. For instance, with low Conceptual Level adolescents in an institutional setting certain environmental profiles would seem to enable the establishment to run most smoothly (Brill 1979). If more mature people are in residence, then other profiles are necessary. Chase (1973) correlated certain environmental patterns that went with a reduction in absconding, where less absconding was found in environments with reasonably high staff control and a high emphasis on expressiveness by both staff and residents. Such findings further emphasize the importance of systematic evaluation in group care practice. It is on this basis that the Action Plan and future development of the service can proceed.

(c) Information about staff
Finally, it is important to consider the information about staff which might interest a centre. The rate of staff sickness in a centre is an important consideration. In recent years there has been a growing interest in job satisfaction and staff morale, and changes or trends in satisfaction and sickness which take place over time. If these issues are important to workers, then a monitoring of basic information about staff attendance and performance may help to reduce the amount of sick leave in a centre. High levels

of sick leave frequently put heavy demands on other workers who can have their hours increased with little warning. This, in itself, can influence job satisfaction amongst team members, as demonstrated in a study of group home staff (Johnson *et al.* 1978) where those working in excess of fifty hours per week were more likely to report symptoms of 'burn-out' and feelings of despondency. The opposite results may be found in teams where workers concentrate on staying 'well' and dealing with practice issues as they emerge.

Conclusions

A shared language for practice in group care has been suggested through the development of a centre Action Plan. It is not intended that all the features suggested here should be dogmatically adhered to by those seeking to develop an Action Plan for the first time. Rather, they are offered as examples which illustrate the Action Plan framework. A range of exercises have also been suggested which can enable workers to produce a coherent statement about how their service will operate.

Certain assumptions have been made throughout this chapter about the importance of a common theme that draws together the disparate characteristics of children, treatment environment, and intervention strategies. The Action Plan is intended to be a negotiated statement of common themes which tie people and programmes together. In so doing, an Action Plan can help workers to reduce the level of conflict, competition, or despair which can all too easily develop in daily practice. Since the development of an Action Plan involves a team process, it is likely to increase the clarity of focus expected for each worker. The completed document is also useful in public relations with other professionals and referral agencies.

Notes

1 Stephen Casson is Residential Child Care Advisor for the City of Newcastle Social Services Department in England.

References

Brill, R. (1977) Implications of the Conceptual Level Matching Model for the Treatment of Delinquents. Paper presented at Conference of the International Differential Treatment Association, Rensselaerville, New York.

—— (1979) *Development of Milieux Facilitating Treatment* (Final Report No. 4). Montreal: Université de Montreal, Groupe de Recherche sur L'Inadaptation Juvenile.

Brill, R. and Reitsma, M. (1978) *Action Research in a Treatment Agency for Delinquent Youth* (Final Report No. 1). Montreal: Université de Montreal: Groupe de Recherche sur L'Inadaptation Juvenile.

British Association of Social Workers (1977) Report of Working Party on 'The Social Work Task'. London: BASW Publications.

Brown, B. J. and Christie, M. (1981) *Social Learning Practice in Residential Child Care*. Oxford: Pergamon Press.

Chase, M. M. (1973) *A Profile of Absconders*. New York: New York State Division for Youth, Research Department; World Trade Center.

Grant, J. D., Grant, M. Q., and Sullivan, E. D. (1957) The Development of Interpersonal Maturity: Applications to Delinquency. *Psychiatry* 20: 272–83.

Grinder, J. and Bandler, R. (1979) *Frogs into Princes*. Utah: Real People Press.

Harvey, O. J., Hunt, D. E., and Schroder H. M. (1961) *Conceptual Systems and Personality Organization*. New York: John Wiley.

Hoghughi, M. (1980) *Assessing Problem Children – Issues and Practice*. London: Burnett Books.

Hunt, D. E. (1966) A Conceptual Systems Change Model and Its Application to Education. In O. J. Harvey (ed.) *Experience Structure and Adaptability*. New York: Springer.

—— (1972) *Matching Models in Education*. Toronto: OISE.

Johnson, K. W., Rusinko, W. T., Girard, C. M., and Tossey, M. (1978) Job Satisfaction and Burn-out: A Double-edged Threat to Human Service Workers. Washington, DC: Academy of Criminal Justice Science Meeting, March.

Jones, M. (1968) *Social Psychiatry in Practice*. Harmondsworth, England: Penguin.

Kushlik, A. (1975) Some Ways of Setting, Monitoring and Attaining Objectives for Services for Disabled People. *British Journal of Mental Subnormality* 21 (41) (December).

Lankton, S. R. (1979) *Practical Magic: The Clinical Application of Neuro-linguistic Programming*. Cupertino, California: Meta Publications.

Mager, R. F. (1972) *Goal Analysis*. Belmont, California: Fearon Publishers.

Maier, H. (1977) *The Core of Care*. Stirling, Scotland: Aberlour Child Care Trust, The First Aberlour Trust Lecture.

—— (1981) Essential Components in Care and Treatment Environments for Children. In F. Ainsworth and L. C. Fulcher (eds) *Group Care for Children, Concept and Issues*. London: Tavistock.

Menzies, I. E. P. (1977) *Staff Support Systems: Task and Anti-Task in Adolescent Institutions*. London: Tavistock Institute of Human Relations.

Moos, R. H. (1974) *Evaluating Treatment Environments – A Social, Ecological Approach*. New York: John Wiley.

—— (1975) *Evaluating Correctional and Community Settings*. New York: John Wiley.

Moos, R. H., Meel, P. M., and Humphrey, B. (1974) *Combined Preliminary Manual: Family, Work and Group Environment Scales*. Palo Alto, California: Consulting Psychologists Press.

Palmer, T. (1967) Personality Characteristics and Professional Orientations of Five Groups of Community Treatment Project Workers: A Preliminary Report of Differences among Treaters. Sacramento, California: Community Treatment Project.

—— (1968) Revisions by G. Howard (1972) Rating Inventory for the Selection and Matching of Treatment Personnel. Sacramento, California: Community Treatment Project 1968b.

—— (1972) *Differential Placement of Delinquents in Group Homes, Final Report*. Sacramento: California Youth Authority and the National Institute of Mental Health.

Pizzat, F. (1973) *Behavior Modification in Residential Treatment for Children*. New York: Behavioral Publications.

Report of Care and Children Committee (The Curtis Report) (1946) Cmnd 6922. London: HMSO.

Sinclair, I. (1971) *Hostels for Probationers*. London: HMSO.

Taylor, D. A. and Alpert, S. W. (1973) *Continuity and Support Following Residential Treatment*. New York: Child Welfare League of America.

Vorrath, H. H. and Brendtro, L. K. (1974) *Positive Peer Culture*. Chicago: Aldine.

Warren, M. Q. (1973) Community Corrections: For Whom, When and Under What Circumstances? What the Research Tells Us. Sacramento, California: Community Treatment Project.

Whittaker, J. K. (1979) *Caring for Troubled Children*. San Francisco: Jossey-Bass.

5 Personal care and treatment planning

Gale E. Burford[1]

Introduction

Over the past decade or more, changes have occurred with respect to criminal justice and social welfare institutions which have had a profound impact on group care practice with children on both sides of the Atlantic. These changes have been brought about in part by economic conditions, by advances in technology, and by alterations in the legal codes of most parts of the United States, Canada, and Great Britain. The evidence of change can be found in the diverse language contained in the group care literature, such as: protection, remediation, rehabilitation, life skill development, care, control, punishment, education, re-education, special education, retraining, treatment, and therapy. Any attempt to understand the needs, wants, and problems of young people in receipt of group care services is a complex undertaking. This is particularly true with respect to young people who are referred because of identified or predicted threat, delinquency, acting-out, disturbance, or maladjustment.

In this chapter, consideration is given to a number of contemporary trends in behavioural management, the provision of education and social opportunities, and the offer of treatment to troubled and troublesome young people. It is argued that personal care and treatment can only be understood if assessment and evaluation methods are sufficiently precise as to account for important differences between: the variety of care and treatment programmes, the setting in which these services are offered, the differential characteristics of young people admitted, and the varying levels of involvement with respect to families and local communities. To meet this challenge, any approach to personal care and treatment planning is dependent upon the use of a differential assessment typology. In what follows, research findings based on the results of one such typology are summarized, and implications for group care practice are discussed.

Background and assumptions

Behavioural management
The impact of economic recession and the increased emphasis on individual rights and responsibilities for children have supported the social policy notion of accounting for minimum standards of care. Generally speaking, such standards involve guarantees of personal safety and security in both physical and emotional terms. In practice, physical safety and security have been translated to mean: freedom from attack or access to protection when threat is perceived; food, clothing, and shelter; and rest or stimulation based on physiological needs (e.g. large muscle exercise). Emotional safety and security have been taken to include: the need for physical space in which items of personal symbolic worth can be stored, where feelings of worth can be nurtured or tension internally governed; and the need for sufficient social stimulation as to prevent psychological withdrawal.

While such minimum requirements may be administered in stark terms by group care practitioners, research (Moos 1975) supports the notion that lower rates of absconding and other rule-breaking behaviours are associated with the level of satisfaction reported by residents about their living unit environment. Moos's cogent statement summarizing research in residential group care bears repeating:

'There is no reason for not converting the large proportion of control oriented programs in correctional and psychiatric settings into treatment oriented programs of the appropriate types. This would at the very least, enhance the satisfaction and morale of the residents and staff who live and function in these programs.'   (Moos 1975: 129)

While trends in the rights and responsibilities of young people have sought to follow the principle of least interference, economic conditions have required that the methods used be cost-effective. At the same time, influences from learning theory (Bandura 1969), field theory (Lewin 1951), and the theory of symbolic interaction (Cressey 1965; Mead 1974) have found enhanced expression in group care practice. This has resulted in an expectation that behaviour to be managed will be specified more clearly, that important variables in the person—environment context will be isolated, and that more insightful use will be made of peer group influences in behavioural management.

Research shows that positive behavioural changes can be effected with many residents in a range of different types of programmes (Gendreau and Ross 1979; Lipton, Martinson, and Wilks 1975; Ross and Gendreau 1980; Taylor and Alpert 1973). However, one is left with the impression that most youngsters do not maintain acquired changes following release from group care services. This is particularly so when all residents and all programmes are aggregated together for evaluation purposes, regardless of the important differences between them. In spite of widespread acceptance of the notion that behaviour is a function of a particular person in a particular environment, most research has grouped all residents in all programmes together using the same measures of progress. Jones's (1977) summary of research on the social, psychological, and physiological effects of expectancies, Bronfenbrenner's (1979) review of ecological variables and Moos's (1975) work on social climates all reveal the complexity which must be taken into account in any study of reciprocal relations between people and environments.

The provision of education and social opportunities
If nothing else, children and young people continue to age during their period of placement in a group care centre and continue to share the same requirements as other young people living in the community. In addition, many young people in receipt of group care services also have problems with learning, and some have a

variety of physical and emotional problems, such as allergies, nutritional deficiencies, enuresis, and motor disturbances. While these problems do not appear to be valid predictors of behavioural problems, clear associations are evident (Hippchen 1978; Sapir and Nitzberg 1973). Arguments have been put forward for a decade or more that educational, social, and health-oriented services could solve the problems which bring children into care, or at a minimum such services should be provided to prevent children and young people progressing further into anti-social behaviour. Structuring time through the use of pro-social activities and pursuits has become virtually synonymous with the term programme, especially in the North American context. That such activities represent forms of social control or behaviour management must be recognized, even though it is important to recognize that the same services are used to enforce social control for young people not in care.

Research has shown that considerable gains in skill development, academic achievement, and improvements in attitude may be made during periods of group care and treatment. However, these gains cannot be associated globally with measurable success in subsequent school performance, job stability, or reduced recidivism (Gendreau and Ross 1979; Lipton, Martinson, and Wilks 1975; Ross and Gendreau 1980; Warren 1983). Once again, as in the case of behavioural management, such findings may simply reflect problems in measurement as much as anything else, especially in those studies which group all residents in all programmes together for evaluation purposes. Thus, there is no rationale for failing to provide the usual social, health, educational, and legal opportunities and services, unless it can be shown that these tend to introduce other types of difficulty for children. Even if such services caused harm, it is still difficult to know with whom the services are harmful and under what conditions this would occur when different types of youngsters and programmes are evaluated merely in global terms.

Treatment
The term treatment is used here in a manner which is synonymous with the execution of a plan of intervention, the purpose of which is to influence the youngster to make pro-social decisions in the future. In this sense, for a service to qualify as a treatment *per se*,

expected outcomes must be stated beforehand, noting what the service intends to do and what outcomes are anticipated. Regardless of whether the results are beneficial, credit cannot be given to treatment unless the preceding conditions are met. The need for rigour on this issue cannot be overstated. Without an explicit statement of intent or plan, it is impossible to distinguish between actions which are initiated primarily in the service of social control, those which are initiated in the well-intentioned belief that something 'ought' to be good for a youngster, and actions which are based on a testable hypothesis.

This definition can be said to apply in settings where the desired outcomes may focus on symptom reduction and other specific behaviour changes, as in the case of criminal justice settings where social policy has emphasized recidivism as the measure of success. Perhaps this stringent demand is related to a social perception that juvenile delinquents are 'less deserving' than other groups of children and young people. Such a definition of treatment does not exclude any effort – therapeutic, educational, environmental, ecological, etc. – so long as that effort yielded an explicit and testable plan beforehand. While some research indicates that many individuals make positive changes during treatment, it is also clear that recidivism rates and the future expression of behavioural symptoms remain. Once again, a general conclusion is that the majority of young people do not maintain positive changes once they leave treatment.

Differential treatment
One of the most widely publicized reviews of treatment effectiveness with delinquents in the United States carried out before 1967 (Lipton, Martinson and Wilks 1975) stands as a rich source of information supporting many treatment efforts, even though conclusions reached by these authors had the opposite effect. The 'nothing works' argument (Martinson 1974) portrayed the failure of treatment when all the subjects and all programmes of care and treatment under all conditions were taken together. Others (Jesness 1975; Moos 1975; Palmer 1978; Ross and Gendreau 1980) have argued that programmes of care and treatment are not all the same and that when certain differences are taken into account, some treatments do bring about success with some subjects, under certain conditions. There is, therefore,

adequate justification for continued practice, careful evaluation, and research.

Neither the 'nothing works' arguments nor the judicial moves to ensure 'fair practices' impede treatment necessarily, so long as 'fairness' allows for public and private purchasers of service to choose a particular treatment that is known to decrease the likelihood of recidivism or future recurrence of a problem. Eventually such practices might encourage families and others to become more involved in choosing which services are best for them and the possibility of moving to an alternative service if a better option is discovered (Moos 1975). Masked in statistics and data on outcome are findings which can only be understood if one takes account of certain differences among the young people who come into care, their families and perhaps communities, programmes of care and custody, treatment methods, techniques of evaluation and research, and the characteristics of counsellors, educators, and care staff.

Researchers have noted the masking effect that occurs when programmes (or courses of action) are evaluated with all the human subjects grouped together (Gendreau and Ross 1979; Grant and Grant 1959; Hunt 1971; Jesness 1965, 1971a; Palmer 1978; Quay 1977). At the same time, attempts to control for these variables across settings, while continuing to account for the unique experience of individual subjects presents one with all the same problems as confronts other research on human behaviour in a social context. What constitutes individual counselling, group or family therapy, life skill development, and even behaviour therapy varies between settings and practitioners. Elsewhere in this volume consideration is given to the organization, provision, and evaluation of group care services for children, whether involving the education, health care, criminal justice, or social welfare resource networks. The subsequent focus of this chapter is on care and treatment planning for individual children and young people who are prone to be admitted or readmitted to group care in the criminal justice or social welfare systems.

One last word, however, is required by way of introduction. This is, that while an understanding of the interplay between people, settings, and conditions is still in its embryonic stage of development, group care centres cannot back down from the requirement that each will operate from carefully written descriptions of the services they offer, preferably written for each individual living-unit.[2] Some programmes so lack a sufficiently detailed explanation of what they offer that they fail to inform managers and practitioners about whether the mandated service is actually being provided. Other programmes may have clear descriptions of intention but lack the resources and capability as to maintain outcomes over time (Quay 1977) or to monitor 'program drift' (Johnson 1981).

Differential assessment and research

In an ideal world, group care practice might include provision for a unique care and treatment plan which would fit the special requirements of every individual in receipt of services, with any problem in every situation. However, approaches which are individualized to this extent contribute little to our understanding about effective ways of allocating resources to youngsters whose problems, situations, and perceptions are similar. At the same time, individualistic approaches serve merely to complicate the task of conceptualizing programmes of personal care and treatment. Even though some writers support the idea that important differences are to be noted between children and their families, and between programmes (Apter 1982; Maier 1979, 1981; Whittaker 1979), there is less agreement about which differences are important for planning group care and treatment. There is also little agreement about which characteristics are the most significant influences for individual children and families. Still, there is probably more support for a differential approach to group care practice than for approaches which operate on the assumption that a single or simple solution can be found to service the needs of broad categories of children and young people.

Differential assessment and research inevitably involve the use of a conceptual typology which is used to classify information about a person with a problem in an environment. Such classifications with human subjects must never lose sight of the fact that a typology is merely a starting point against which a decreasing application of a label is measured (Toch 1970). If a typology is used, the rationale for its use must be stated beforehand to avoid any confusion about what the various activities associated with classification actually mean (Levinson 1982). For example, assignment to a group care programme can easily be for control purposes rather than treatment, or such a placement might be to take advantage of or avoid some other service, such as prison. It is assumed in this chapter that assessment typologies are used with the aim of matching people with appropriate resources. In so doing, assessment typologies can only be used to develop optimal resources if they withstand the demands of scientific rigour. In reality, it is probably more accurate to suggest that one seeks to find a 'good enough' fit. The 'good enough' or minimum requirements approach should not impede the development of treatment approaches so long as consideration is given to the satisfactions of life in each resident's daily routine. Minimum standards may be applied to ensure that the overall quality of life for residents is maintained, and to ensure the quality of specific goal-directed activities, such as recreation or counselling.

Rather than to single out any one assessment typology as being the best, suffice it to say that the choice is a complex one depending, of course, on the specific purpose and the cost, balanced against the demands made on the setting, including demands associated with the social policy mandate imposed externally (Fulcher 1983). In selecting an assessment typology the following considerations should be made at the very least (Megargee 1977):

- A typology should be reliable so that two independent workers will agree on the same assessment.
- An assessment typology should be valid, to ensure that the individuals actually have the characteristics which the typology hypothesizes that they possess.
- An assessment typology should include almost all the members of a particular class (e.g. delinquents).
- An assessment typology should have theoretical and practical relevance to planning, decision-making, and the development of appropriate service responses.
- An assessment typology should seek to reduce or eliminate potential dangers from labelling, the unnecessary use of social control and ill-conceived or harmful practices. For example, a typology based on 'normal' human behaviour in social

environments would be preferable to one which is biased towards individual abnormality or pathology.
– Assessment typologies which have been used extensively in practice and research should be thought to have particular relevance.

While many assessment typologies have been tested, ranging from head shape to psychiatric disorder, fewer have evolved in conjunction with rigorous evaluation as to their reliability, validity, and social desirability. Others, such as the Moral Development Scheme (Kohlberg 1964, 1969), the Minnesota Multiphasic Personality Inventory (Megargee *et al.* 1979; Meyer and Megargee 1972), and the Conceptual Level Matching Model (Brill 1978; Hunt and Hardt 1965) show promise in their capacity to guide care and treatment efforts with rigour. However, each of these typologies has not been used extensively enough as to guide practice in a variety of settings. While it is tempting to infer differences which two systems might describe, verification of such differences must be left to rigorous cross-classification studies. There are some behavioural systems (Jesness 1971a; Quay and Parsons 1970; Quay 1977) which have demonstrated relevance in developing care and treatment programmes and measuring outcome, but these seem to be less revealing when used independently of other measures. Alone, each typology does not account for which person made what changes, in what circumstances. It would seem that typologies based on personality still offer the most reliable and valid methods of highlighting personal variables in this equation.

One of the most extensively used assessment typologies based on personality characteristics is the Interpersonal Maturity Classification System: Juvenile (Warren 1966). Research with this typology has yielded a unique compilation of behavioural, demographic, and psychological data about juvenile delinquents in general and those in group care and treatment in particular. This typology has been used to support personal care and treatment planning, programme development and research in residential and community settings involving families, family group homes, boarding homes, institutional facilities of various size for all levels of security, day centres, classrooms, and other short-term reception and detention centres. The practice research findings associated with these efforts will be summarized below as they relate to the role of group care centres and to the development of personal care and treatment plans. Before doing this, however, it should be noted that the Interpersonal Maturity (I-Level) typology was developed in the main for delinquent adolescents and young adults. Certain implications are evident for the education and treatment of other troubled young people and these will be noted where appropriate.

The Interpersonal Maturity Classification System: Juvenile

What is comparatively unique to this typology is that while the maturity levels represent theoretical descriptions of normal development, the behavioural descriptions are associated with empirical differences identified between different young people assessed to be at the same level of interpersonal maturity. Nine different sub-types of delinquent young people (Warren 1966) and three sub-types of non-delinquent young people (Harris 1978) have been described using this assessment typology. While some of these descriptions are based on larger numbers of subjects than others, each has relevance for practice in a number of settings. For example, it would seem that lower maturity young people are likely to be referred to health care, special education, or other social welfare services rather than to criminal justice or correctional settings. The primitive and unsocialized manner of presentation which is characteristic of lower maturity young people is comparatively obvious and is probably more understood by practitioners who deal with severe child neglect. Care and treatment strategies have been developed for lower maturity young people in both residential and community settings with positive results (Warren 1983). The majority of young people assessed with this typology can be summarized within three subgroupings: passive-conforming, power-oriented, and internally conflicted young people (Palmer 1974).

Passive-conforming young people
Described as middle maturity,

> This type of young person usually fears, and responds with strong compliance to, peers and adults who [they] think have

the "upper hand" at the moment, or who seem more adequate and assertive than [themselves]. [They] consider [themselves] to be lacking in social "know-how", and usually expect to be rejected ... in spite of [their] efforts to please [others].'

(Palmer 1974: 12)

An example may be found in the case of a sixteen-year-old boy who came from a home where he was treated one minute as though he were much younger than his actual age and the next minute with physical terror. The youth was brought before a juvenile court having been found with burglary tools in the security area of a large office complex at night. When apprehended, he acted as though he had been a 'bad boy' and co-operated with the arresting officers by showing them where his friends were hiding on the fire escape waiting to be let into the building. The nature of his interpersonal maturity was revealed further at the police station when he discovered that his friends were angry with him. At this point the boy began talking under his breath and acting belligerently about being arrested. When challenged by one of his friends and when given a knowing glance by the arresting officer, this boy made a daring escape from the police station while the other boys were waiting. A crisis was precipitated for this youth in the form of a conflicted set of allegiances, leaving him – in his view – with no way of conforming to both.

Although important differences have been found between youngsters in this assessment subgrouping (Palmer 1971), the general pattern of acquiescence to power, coupled with what has been described as a 'soft' exterior or affect is usually evident. As for goals of intervention with this group of young people, both behavioural management and the provision of a number of other services are feasible under a variety of conditions. Care and treatment efforts aimed at reducing recidivism have ranged from moderate success to outright failure (Jesness *et al.* 1972; Palmer 1974; Warren 1983).

Behavioural management goals in group care practice are comparatively easy to accomplish with these youngsters because of their adaptability in a variety of settings with different types of young people (Jesness 1971a; Palmer 1972, 1976). These young people also offer apparent satisfactions for staff who work with them as reported elsewhere in this volume with Fulcher.

Behavioural management tasks may be carried out as part of a general yet supervised programme of activities emphasizing consistency, attachment, firmness, and caring. More important than any single method or technique of behavioural management is the pressing need for any care and treatment plan to reduce the sources of fear, threat, and anti-social influences in these young people's environment. For example, passive-conforming young people would seem to respond to group activities, team sports, clubs, and other pursuits involving physical activity. When levels of structure and certainty are reasonably high, these young people are willing to co-operate. This factor, plus their being likeable and amenable to supervision in groups, can present risks if passive-conforming young people remain too long in institutional care or are not challenged sufficiently as to overcome their vulnerability to delinquent and anti-social influences. For this reason, it is especially important that the goals of institutional placement are specified and evaluated carefully to avoid complacency in the care and treatment of passive-conforming young people.

This same pattern appears to hold true with regard to educational goals where measurable improvements in attitude, academic achievement and skill development have been demonstrated as possible and feasible practice attainments with this group of young people (Jesness et al. 1972). In one experimental study using carefully matched lesson plans, classroom environments, and teaching styles, passive-conforming youngsters outperformed all other types of students (Andre and Mahan 1972). Yet gains in behaviour and educational developments do not appear to be predictive of non-recidivism for this group of young people as a whole (Jesness et al. 1972; Palmer 1976; Warren 1983).

The outcome of efforts to treat the problem of delinquency for this group is mixed. Many passive-conforming young people commit more offences after certain patterns of care and treatment than they did beforehand, and more than other passive-conforming young people who had received no treatment at all (Warren 1983). While according to Palmer (1978) variations in treatment outcomes are almost certainly related to differences within this group of young people, Lukin (1981) found that passive-conformists with high post-test scores on enthusiasm, measured by the Jesness Behavior Checklist (1971b), performed better after institutional release than those who remained depressed or unenthusiastic. This gives credence to a long-standing clinical impression that passive-conforming young people can overcome their basic pessimism about themselves and, as such, self-assertion is a worthwhile goal to pursue in practice with such young people.

The selection of care and treatment methods for this group of young people in institutional programmes appears to be of secondary importance, presumably once again related to their adaptability in the setting (Jesness 1971a, 1975; Palmer 1972). In community settings where group care placements have been used as an adjunct to other therapeutic methods, the use of psychodrama (e.g. role play or 'rehearsing' for job interviews) and family education approaches would seem to be preferable to family group therapy which emphasizes familial ownership of problems. Family therapy and Guided Group Interaction approaches (similar to practices found in a therapeutic community) seem to produce higher drop-out rates with the passive-conforming young people, presumably because of the heavy reliance in both approaches on the use of confrontation (Warren 1983). The use of an intensive, treatment-oriented approach with sound unit management and continuous feedback to both staff and young people would seem to be preferable to placement in a traditional, custodially oriented training school, youth treatment centre, or young offenders institution (Jesness 1980).

Even under favourable conditions, treatment successes with these youngsters would seem to be low. More disturbing is the realization that these youngsters seem to have low rates of recidivism *while* being supervised in certain community-based programmes. As long as they are closely supervised, it appears that these young people stay out of trouble (Warren 1983). Research findings such as these pose certain social policy questions about the care and treatment of passive-conforming young people. While placement in a residential setting which rigorously adheres to a treatment approach can make a difference, long-term supervision in the community would appear to have other benefits. Patterns of supervision using differential treatment methods can beneficially form networks around this type of youngster which can provide non-delinquent associations and create obstacles for criminal and delinquent influences. The problem associated with this option is that such methods of intervention do not seem reliably to achieve the goal of preparing passive-conforming young people for situations where they will need to resist criminal influences after supervision is withdrawn.

It may be that programmes involving volunteers and networks of community neighbours, teachers, and other resources in the 'ecological' environment will find more success with this type of young person. Successes with this approach should be easy to determine, since flight or rearrest is imminent for these young people when delinquent influences or fear prevail. For group care teams, these youngsters present a special challenge. Treatment success almost certainly involves helping them to overcome their pessimism about growing up and standing up for themselves. Care and treatment which seeks to increase these youngsters' interpersonal complexity and helps them internalize a set of personal values would seem to be realistic and worthwhile goals to pursue. Whatever the method, intervention should seek to involve the youngster as an enthusiastic ally in a carefully considered process of developmental learning.

Power-oriented young people
Subgrouping of young people described as middle maturity,

> 'This group is actually made up of two somewhat different kinds of individuals, who nevertheless, share several important features with one another. The first [cultural conformist] like to think of [themselves] as delinquent and tough. [They are] more than willing to "go along" with others, or with a gang, in order to earn a certain degree of status and acceptance, and to later maintain [their] "reputation(s)". The second type [anti-social manipulator or counteractive young person] ... often attempts to undermine or circumvent the efforts and directions of authority figures. Typically this second type of youngster will attempt to assume a leading "power role" for [themselves].'
> (Palmer 1974: 12)

The first type of power-oriented young person can be illustrated in the example of a boy who during an admissions interview stared 'daggers' at the interviewer and answered questions in monosyllables, volunteering very little information. The young person's social and delinquency history, plus descriptions extracted from conversations where the lad was more willing to talk,

revealed a picture of someone who had few experiences of a
social world beyond his involvements with a very distinctive peer
group. During a period of observation the lad was seen to 'melt'
into the institutional routine. As far as staff were concerned the
youngster subtly took on roles of power and loyalty to peers.
Clearly not a leader, the youth fell into the role of protector,
extortionist, and 'muscle man' with a subgroup of residents who
were physically stronger and more street-wise than others in the
centre. When staff moved in to reduce the influence this subgroup
had in the living-unit, the boy in question assaulted a staff member
from behind, using a weapon he had concealed in a unique and
creative place, making it both handy and lethal. Research has
shown that young people of this type commit significantly higher
rates of violent offences as compared with any of the other
delinquent sub-types (Warren 1983).

The second type of power-oriented youngster, the anti-social
manipulator, has been described as being closest to the description
of 'psychopathic', 'sociopathic', or even 'character disordered'
personality as found in other assessment typologies. The term
'anti-social manipulator' has come under disfavour by many
practitioners using this typology, thereby prompting a move from
group care workers and others to change the term to refer to
'the counter-active youngster'. This move is aimed at removing
what is perceived as stigmatization associated with the label. This
apart, there is no disagreement about the way these youngsters
present themselves in practice.

One youth of this type described a situation leading up to his
arrest with a friend, after the two 'just happened' to go to the
home of an acquaintance for a visit. During the visit, the friend
pulled a knife on the host and this youth thought it had something
to do with money owed to his friend. During the financial
transaction, the counter-active youth decided he would listen to
the stereo, turned it up to full volume and entertained himself by
dancing in the room while the other two boys discussed the
method and timing of repayment. Not long after he and his friend
left the house, the two boys were arrested in front of the same
house when the host pointed them out to the police. When asked
why he and his friend had stayed in front of the house, the boy
replied that they had not really stayed in front of the house. Since
it was a nice evening, they had decided to walk around the block

two or three times. The boys just happened to be passing the friend's house when they were arrested.

Research findings support the view that placement in residential group care using specific care and treatment approaches is the best option for some 'power-oriented' young people (Jesness 1975; Warren 1983). Even placement in a traditional, custodially oriented training school appears to be a better choice than community-based treatment, including the use of different types of group homes (Palmer 1976; Warren 1983). While it would seem that substantial gains may be achieved in educational objectives, psychological growth, and behavioural management, such gains do not appear to be predictive of future job and school successes or non-recidivism (Andre and Mahan 1972; Jesness 1971a, 1972; Palmer 1976). Findings on treatment outcome with power-oriented young people would suggest that the selection of an appropriate care and treatment approach is a critical variable. Jesness (1975) found that counter-active young people responded better to treatment if they were in a programme which used transactional analysis as compared with those who were treated in a programme which used behaviour modification.

In sum, while it would appear that these youngsters respond better in circumstances where structures and controls are known and expected, and where sanctions are both timely and warranted in the eyes of the peer group, some of the power-oriented young people seem to benefit from alternative methods of treatment. A major problem in recommending care or treatment plans for this group, beyond the 'minimum requirement' of justice, is that present measures of progress have not been shown to distinguish between young people who will be rearrested, reconvicted, and reincarcerated, and those who will not. In other words, no measures of progress are readily apparent upon which to base continuation or discontinuation of care and treatment approaches. Palmer (1974) found that all the middle-maturity groups, including the power-oriented type, tended to respond better to care and treatment efforts if the youngsters were admitted before the age of sixteen.

The implications arising from findings such as these are complex. It could be that positive results are to be attained through the use of time-limited periods of residential supervision in treatment-oriented group care centres. Such uses of residential supervision and control may, however, seem severe if sentencing guidelines do not take account of differential assessment and research findings. In short, two people committing similar crimes could receive different responses. This problem is reduced, in part, because cultural-conformists may self-select institutional placement with their assaultive offence histories. Obviously, assessment typologies cannot be used in isolation from other facts, or as the sole basis for institutional placement. However, the implication remains that when anti-social or delinquent behaviours begin, they tend to persist with all young people (Loeber 1982), but such persistence is particularly significant with the power-oriented young people (Warren 1983). Changes can be fostered with some of them but high structure appears to be necessary, if only to forestall patterns of re-offending or to provide a basis from which a care and treatment programme can operate.

Internally conflicted young people
In this group of higher maturity young people,

> 'We find two separate personality types which share certain important characteristics with one another. The first type [acting-out] often attempts to deny — to [themselves] and others — conscious feelings of inadequacy, rejection, or self-condemnation. Not infrequently, [they] do this by verbally attacking *others* and/or by the use of boisterous distractions plus a variety of "games". The second type [anxious] often shows various symptoms of emotional disturbance — e.g. chronic or intense depression, or psychosomatic complaints. [Their] tensions and conscious fears usually result from conflicts produced by feelings of failure, inadequacy, or underlying guilt.'
> (Palmer 1974: 12)

The internally conflicted group accounts for the largest number of adolescents found in settings for delinquent young people (Warren 1983). This is also the group for which qualified treatment success can be reported. One girl, assessed as acting out, sat patiently through a meeting with her father who had come to visit her in a residential centre. After the father repeatedly told her 'how hurt your mother is over this whole affair' and how 'they still loved her', the girl shrugged her shoulders and returned to her bedroom. Hours later she exploded. Within the space of a few minutes she wrecked her room, cut herself and smashed her best friend's Christmas gift. All the while she made obscene curses and shrieks of pain. Afterwards the girl said 'Everything is OK now, I just want everyone to get off my back.' For this girl, acting out was a familiar way of achieving a measure of relief from her pain.

The anxious group of internally conflicted young people typically use introspection as a temporary, and ultimately self-defeating, relief from inner turbulence. One boy, who had just met a new staff member in a group home, sat up all night talking about the problems he had with his own parents. Encouraged by the boy saying he 'felt better' after their talks, the counsellor repeated this activity for two more days. At the weekend, the boy became depressed for no apparent reason. Subsequently, it was discovered that the boy had interpreted this worker's actions to mean that he thought the boy 'needed' extra help. The boy had become immobilized through his personal style of 'mind-reading'.

Research has shown that internally conflicted young people can be successfully treated in carefully planned and evaluated programmes of care and treatment (Jesness 1975; Palmer 1974, 1976). Some important features of successful treatment approaches would seem to be:

- Initial placement in a residential centre is recommended for those who exhibit high levels of emotional disturbance, commitment to self-destructive relationships, behaviours which emphasize denial or avoidance, or commitment to a life-style of self-destructive substance abuse (Palmer 1974). In applying such criteria, Palmer (1976) found that erring in the direction of choosing a setting with too much structure (e.g. a 'closed' setting) was preferable to erring in the direction of too little structure (e.g. a community group home). Specific treatment-oriented settings can be expected to impact favourably on outcome (Jesness 1980; Moos 1975; Palmer 1976).
- Careful 'matching' of these youngsters with a community or field worker who can follow them both in and out of residential care is apparently crucial (Barkwell 1976; Jesness 1980; Palmer 1976).
- Personal care and treatment plans based on differential

assessment, supported by sound case management and ongoing evaluation would seem to be important (Jesness 1980; Palmer 1976).

A range of residential group care resources would seem to have played important roles in the successful treatment of internally conflicted young people. Different types of group home, shelters, and other short-term, back-up units and day resources have been used to achieve a variety of goals (Jesness *et al.* 1972, 1980; Palmer 1972, 1976). Summarizing the characteristics of different settings and types of group care resources which have contributed to success with internally conflicted young people is an extremely complex and perhaps dangerous task. For example, judging a treatment approach in one setting with one type of young person as successful may have little bearing on the same type of young person in a different type of setting. For this reason, only general clinical impressions will be given.

The use of personal contracts is generally supported. This seems to hold true for behavioural management (Jesness *et al.* 1972; Moos 1975), education (Andre and Mahan 1972); and type of treatment (Jesness 1980; Palmer 1976). The findings support the clinical view that internally conflicted young people can and should be involved as knowing partners in any care and treatment efforts. In short, staff must work to elicit the perspective and meaning which each of these young people places on the daily events in their lives. It is not possible to 'merely supervise' internally conflicted young people. These young people must be engaged as individuals, consciously to support them in their use of psychological controls and their enactment of purposeful behaviour. This requirement for personal involvement may help to explain the unique patterns of frustration reported elsewhere in this volume for group care personnel working with internally conflicted young people.

So far, it would seem that success in the residential phase of care and treatment is more closely related to differences between the acting out and the anxious types of internally conflicted young people than to the selection of treatment methods. Jesness and his associates (1972) found similar success rates for all internally conflicted young people when comparing a programme which used transactional analysis with another one which used behaviour modification. Furthermore, both of these treatment-oriented options were found to offer better results than placement in a traditional, custodially oriented institutional setting (Jesness 1980). When Lukin (1981) accounted for pre- and post-test differences on the Jesness Behavior Checklist (1971b), she found that acting out youngsters were less prone to recidivism if they had improved on certain measures (e.g. friendliness and responsibility). For the anxious-conflicted group, Lukin found that success meant change in the *opposite* direction, that young people who performed better after release had shown a decrease in anger control and social control during their period of residence. Such findings could pose problems for any service which viewed a reduction in anger control or an increase in anti-social behaviour as evidence of failure. Other measures on the California Psychological Inventory support the idea that treatment progress can be documented amongst internally conflicted young people (Warren 1983).

Although specific academic and life skill achievements may be attained in residential and day care programmes, particularly in specialized classrooms, such achievements cannot be associated necessarily with future job and school successes, or reduced recidivism (Andre and Mahan 1972; Jesness *et al.* 1972; Palmer 1976; Warren 1983). While such findings do not come close to the definitive statement on care and treatment for internally conflicted young people, the findings do establish some key assumptions which are of importance to social planners, group care practitioners and others involved in work with youngsters such as these. First, some residential programmes committed to planned care and treatment may have an impact on the psychological conflicts which these young people have and thereby reduce their chances of recidivism at some time in the future. Second, such programmes need to be flexible enough to take into account the important differences between residents when administering and evaluating care and treatment activities. Third, group care programmes working with internally conflicted young people must be skilfully managed so that they work closely and co-operatively with other community services, as a part of a larger effort with these youngsters and their families.

While statements such as these may seem obvious to many practitioners, they have been challenged repeatedly in North

America and Great Britain (Cornish and Clarke 1975; Lerman 1975; Lipton, Martinson, and Wilks 1975; Romig 1978). No summary of research findings from the California Youth Authority programmes has failed to comment on the accusation that the data generated by these programmes was 'managed' (Robinson and Smith 1971). Others have more cautiously pointed to possible flaws in the research related to the ways in which many repeat offences may have gone unreported by treatment workers during the period of community supervision (Becker and Herman 1972; Lerman 1975). Such criticisms continue to cloud the findings that four years after all formal contact had ceased, follow-up data favoured by large margins the internally conflicted young people who had received particular types of treatment (Warren 1983). In spite of the criticisms associated with the cost of treatment and the amount of social control involved (Lerman 1975) group care practice can ill afford to ignore the successful outcomes achieved through the use of differential care and treatment efforts with internally conflicted young people.

Presentation of the assessment

Of course, no assessment typology can provide more than a reference point from which to study and evaluate other assessment data. A differential assessment typology can be used to develop an interactional perspective in situations involving person–problem relationships. At the very least, assessments of this type should include:

1 A summary description of the young person, home and family, community, and cultural ties, which incorporates information associated with social, legal, medical, educational, and psychological assessments.
2 A summary statement of problems, needs, and wants, with elaboration as required to pinpoint their specific nature. In most cases there is no reason why such statements cannot be verified, or at least examined and evaluated by the young person's family throughout the early stages of treatment.
3 A statement of goals and long-range issues which will be taken into account in working with the youngster.
4 Identification and discussion of immediate issues or recommendations.

5 Statement of risks, limitations and minimum expectations which
will be maintained for the young person for a given period of
,time.

Assessments may involve a variety of personnel but the actual
integration of the material into a set of working statements should
be prepared by someone who has an overview, as well as a
practical understanding of the care and treatment options available.
Such a person(s) should understand differential assessment concepts
and research issues sufficiently well as to be able to write
behavioural objectives. This latter skill is vitally important since
the assessment will need to be written and interpreted across a
wide variety of group care practitioners. In instances where the
assessment worker is enlisted to help define objectives, or to give
specific consultation and advice for staff, the Offender Intervention
Scales (Palmer 1978) may be of particular relevance. For example,
a goal for one young person might be to increase his or her
perception of the world and of themselves. However, workers
may be presented with problems of apathy and indifference. The
Offender Intervention Scales offer some possibilities for direction:

– get the resident to be more evaluative and responsive to his
  social world;
– encourage resident to more actively care about what happens
  to him;
– insist that the resident be more reactive to the events in his/her
  life and take a more active stance in what happens to them.

Still it remains for group care workers to translate such advice
into their pattern of practice in a residential or day care centre.
Maier's (1979) summary of research and comments about the
rhythmicity between children and care-givers in nurturing, caring,
and purposeful interaction are of particular relevance. The
introduction of differential diagnostic and assessment information
into group care centres can create tensions for teams of workers
who want assessments to give prescriptions about what to do,
rather than provide a framework, from which to consider a young
person's behaviour within a total plan. It must be remembered
that the onus of responsibility, for developing successful group
care and treatment programmes, rests with the agency which
provides the service. As such, the goals for an individual young

person must be sufficiently broad as to embrace both residential and non-residential resources but practical enough to be meaningful for those working directly with a youngster. Much of the expertise needed to translate these goals into achievable objectives must come from the group care workers who manage and provide direct services in a chosen resource.

This is no small matter, as is evidenced in the following example of a sixteen-year-old boy whose behaviour in a residential centre led to heated discussion amongst staff about what each should be doing with the lad. Some felt that immediate behavioural sanctions should be imposed. Others said they had forestalled the need to do this by not reacting directly to the boy's behaviour and by redirecting or diverting the boy's attention. One staff member claimed that the boy was 'challenging our authority' and another said that the boy was 'just trying to be one of the group'. The assessment process revealed a boy who was so internally conflicted that he took all interactions very personally. Staff agreed to view his behaviour as an anxious request for personal attention. The boy subsequently told his counsellor that he was 'not sure who he was at times' and that he felt silly for acting the way he had when he was admitted. While any number of responses might be appropriate for some young people, this boy's 'make-up' would indicate that a carefully formulated care and treatment plan had special relevance for him.

Conclusions

Personal care and treatment plans are rendered uniquely difficult in group care settings by the powerful emotional involvement engendered by residential living. Feelings are known to touch on the beliefs and attitudes of all involved, and not just the group care workers, who have varying conceptions of 'what youngsters need' and how these needs should be met. Research evidence obtained through the use of 'matching' in education and other treatment settings (Hunt 1971; Palmer 1967, 1976) presents a powerful argument for differential assessment in group care and treatment settings. Brill (1978) demonstrated the utility of the Conceptual Level Matching Model in residential centres which assign a 'primary worker' to do a variety of tasks with and for residents. This method (Reitsma-Street 1982) of matching worker and resident according to perceived need for structure in their social environment is comparatively easy to use and has found support from direct practitioners, managers, and researchers.

Others have found that even simple assessment distinctions between young people can provide valuable assistance to those engaged in group care practice: Agee (1979) 'instrumental vs. expressive'; Dockar-Drysdale (1975) 'integrated vs. non-integrated'; Maier (1981) 'go-go vs. living radars'. Teams will only integrate and use as many assessment distinctions as there are sound options available when it is felt their resource is not 'best' or 'good enough' for a particular resident. If teams operate on the assumption that their programme is best for all or even most youngsters, then such an attitude will cloud the development of particular areas of strength. While tensions can arise, it is also the case that differential assessment can be of immediate benefit to the selection of workers, a particular regime of activities, or even more specialized routines of care, education, and treatment. Group care teams require assessment information which is sufficiently complex as to enable them to achieve personal involvement with each youngster over time, but not information that is so complex that frustration will be generated about issues which are insoluble or not fully understood.

Finally, practitioners are left with the question of whether an assessment should attempt to provide information which is specific to a particular treatment method. For example, if a programme uses behaviour modification, transactional analysis, or perhaps even Goal Attainment Scaling (Bartelt and Colon 1982), should the assessment provide information on base-line behaviours, life script, and so forth? The answer is probably no, in most cases. Once again, it is important to remember that assessments cannot take the place of a clearly formulated personal care and treatment plan. The inclusion of behavioural objectives is recommended in most instances, and practitioners who aspire to do particular treatments must learn to write intervention objectives as an integral part of their care and treatment approach.

Notes

1 Gale Burford is Assistant Professor of Social Work at the Memorial University of Newfoundland, St Johns, Newfoundland, Canada.

2 See Palmer 1978; Moos 1975; Fulcher and Ainsworth 1981 for guidelines on the preparation of programme descriptions.

References

Adams, S. (1977) Evaluating Correctional Treatments: Toward a New Perspective. *Criminal Justice and Behavior* 4: 323–29.

Agee, V. (1979) *Treatment of the Violent Incorrigible Adolescent*. Toronto: Lexington Books.

Andre, C. R. and Mahan, J. A. (1972) *Final Report on the Differential Education Project*. Educational Research Series, No. 11. Sacramento: California Youth Authority.

Apter, S. J. (1982) *Troubled Children/Troubled Systems*. New York: Pergamon Press.

Bandura, A. V. (1969) *Principles of Behavior Modification*. New York: Holt, Rinehart & Winston.

Barkwell, L. J. (1976) Differential Treatment of Juveniles on Probation: An Evaluative Study. *Canadian Journal of Criminology and Corrections* 18 (4) (October): 363–78.

Bartelt, R. and Colon, I. (1982) Implementation of Goal Attainment Scaling in Residential Treatment: An Administrative Model. *Child Welfare League of America* 0009–4021/82/070424–11. Reprint.

Becker, J. and Herman, D. S. (1972) A Critical Appraisal of the California Differential Typology of Adolescent Offenders. *Criminology* May.

Brill, R. W. (1978) Implications of the Conceptual Level Matching Model for Treatment of Delinquents. *Journal of Research in Crime and Delinquency*: 229–45.

Bronfenbrenner, U. (1979) *The Ecology of Human Development*. Cambridge, Mass.: Harvard University Press.

Cornish, D. B. and Clarke, R. V. G. (1975) *Residential Treatment and Its Effects on Delinquency*. Home Office Research Study 32. London: HMSO.

Cressey, D. R. (1965) Theoretical Foundations for Using Criminals in the Rehabilitation of Criminals. *Key Issues* 2 January: 87–101.

Dockar-Drysdale, B. (1975) Staff Consultation in an Evolving Care System. In J. Hunter and F. Ainsworth (eds) *Residential Establishments: The Evolving of Caring Systems*. Dundee, Scotland: Dundee University, Department of Social Administration.

Fulcher, L. C. (1983) Who Cares for the Caregivers – A Comparative Study of Residential and Day Care Teams Working with Children. PhD Thesis. Stirling, Scotland: University of Stirling.

Fulcher, L. C. and Ainsworth, F. (1981) Planned Care and Treatment: The Notion of Programme. In F. Ainsworth and L. C. Fulcher (eds) *Group Care for Children: Concept and Issues*. London: Tavistock.

Gendreau, P. and Ross, R. (1979) Effective Correctional Treatment: Bibliotherapy for Cynics. *Crime and Delinquency* October: 463–89.

Grant, J. D. and Grant, M. Q. (1959) A Group Dynamics Approach to the

Treatment of Non-Conformists in the Navy. *The Annals of the American Academy of Political and Social Science* 3 (22): 126-35.

Grant, J. D., Grant, M. Q., and Sullivan, E. D. (1957) The Development of Interpersonal Maturity: Applications to Delinquency. *Psychiatry* 20: 272–83.

Harris, P. (1978) The Interpersonal Maturity of Delinquents and Non-delinquents. PhD Thesis, State University of New York at Albany.

Hippchen, L. J. (ed.) (1978) *Ecologic-Biochemical Approaches to Treatment of Delinquents and Criminals*. New York: Van Nostrand Reinhold.

Hunt, D. (1971) *Maturity Models in Education: The Coordination of Teaching Methods with Student Characteristics*. Toronto: Ontario Institute for Studies in Education.

Hunt, D. and Hardt, R. (1965) Developmental Stage, Delinquency and Differential Treatment. *Journal of Research in Crime and Delinquency* 2: 20–31.

Jesness, C. (1965) *The Fricto Ranch Study: Outcomes with Small vs. Large Living Groups in the Rehabilitation of Delinquents*. Sacramento: California Youth Authority, Research Report No. 47.

—— (1971a) The Preston Typology Study: An Experiment with Differential Treatment in an Institution. *Journal of Research in Crime and Delinquency* 8: 38–52.

—— (1971b) *Jesness Behavior Checklist Manual*. Palo Alto, California: Consulting Psychological Press.

—— (1975) Comparative Effectiveness of Behavior Modification and Transactional Analysis Programs for Delinquents. *Journal of Consulting and Clinical Psychology* 43 (6): 758–79.

—— (1980) Was the Close-Holton Project a 'Bummer'? In R. Ross and P. Gendreau (eds) *Effective Correctional Treatment*. Toronto: Butterworth.

Jesness, C., Derisi, W., McCormick, P., and Wedge, R. (1972) *The Youth Center Research Project: Final Report*. Sacramento: California Youth Authority and American Justice Institute.

Johnson, V. S. (1981) Staff Drift: A Problem in Program Integrity. *Criminal Justice and Behavior* 8 (2) (June): 223–32.

Jones, R. A. (1977) *Self-Fulfilling Prophecies: Social, Psychological and Physiological Effects of Expectancies*. Hillsdale, NJ: Lawrence Erlbaum Associates. Distributed by Halsted Press, Division of John Wiley.

Kohlberg, L. (1964) *Stages in the Development of Moral Thought and Action*. New York: Holt, Rinehart & Winston.

—— (1969) Stage and Sequence: The Cognitive-Developmental Approach to Socialization. In D. Goslin (ed.) *Handbook of Socialization, Theory and Research*. Chicago: Rand McNally.

Lerman, P. (1975) *Community Treatment and Social Control: A Critical Analysis of Juvenile Correctional Policy*. Chicago, Ill.: University of Chicago Press.

Levinson, R. (1982) A Clarification of Classification. *Criminal Justice and Behavior* 9 (2) (June): 133–42.

Lewin, K. (1951) Psychological Ecology. In D. Cartwright (ed.) *Field Theory in Social Science: Selected Theoretical Papers by Kurt Lewin*. New York: Harper & Row.

Lipton, D., Martinson, R., and Wilks, J. (1975) *The Effectiveness of Correctional Treatment: A Survey of Treatment Evaluation Studies*. New York: Praeger.

Loeber, R. (1982) The Stability of Anti-social and Delinquent Child Behavior. *Child Development* 53: 1431–446.

Lukin, R. (1981) Recidivism and Changes Made by Delinquents During Residential Treatment. *Journal of Research in Crime and Delinquency* January: 101–12.

Maier, H. W. (1979) The Core of Care. *Child Care Quarterly* 8 (3): 161–73.

—— (1981) Essential Components in Care and Treatment Environments for Children. In F. Ainsworth and L. C. Fulcher (eds) *Group Care for Children: Concept and Issues*. London: Tavistock.

Martinson, R. (1974) What Works? Questions and Answers About Prison Reform. *The Public Interest* 35: 22–54.

Mead, G. (1974) *Mind, Self and Society*. Chicago: University of Chicago Press.

Megargee, E. I. (1977) The Need for a New Classification System. *Criminal Justice and Behavior* 4: 107–14.

Megargee, E. I. and Bohn, M. J. Jr., with Meyer, J. Jr. and Sink, F. (1979) *Classifying Criminal Offenders: A New System Based on the MMPI*. Beverly Hills, California: Sage Publications.

Meyer, J. Jr. and Megargee, E. I. (1972) Development of an MMPI-Based Typology of Youthful Offenders. *FCI Research Reports* 4 (2): 1–21.

Moos, R. (1975) *Evaluating Community and Correctional Settings*. New York: John Wiley.

Palmer, T. (1967) *Personality Characteristics and Professional Orientation of Five Groups of Community Treatment Workers*. Sacramento: California Youth Authority. Mimeographed paper.

—— (1971) *Patterns of Adjustment Among Delinquent Adolescent Conformists*. Sacramento: California Youth Authority, Community Treatment Project Report Series, No. 1, Spring.

—— (1972) *Final Report: The Group Home Project. Differential Treatment Environments for Delinquents*. United States Public Health Service, Research Grant No. MH14?79 (Center for Studies of Crime and Delinquency).

—— (1974) The Youth Authority's Community Treatment Project. *Federal Probation* March: 3–14.

—— (1976) *Final Report of the Community Treatment Project, Phases 1, 2 and 3*. Sacramento: California Youth Authority and National Institute of Mental Health.

—— (1978) *Correctional Intervention and Research: Current Issues and Future Prospects*. Lexington, Mass.: D. C. Heath.

Quay, H. (1977) The Three Faces of Evaluation: What Can Be Expected to Work. *Criminal Justice and Behavior* 4: 341–54.

Quay, H. and Parsons, L. (1970) *The Differential Behavior Classification of the Juvenile Offender (Technical Report)*. Morgantown, West Virginia: Robert F. Kennedy Youth Center.

Reitsma-Street, M. (1982) A Critical Review of the Conceptual Level Matching Model and Its Relevance for the Treatment of Maladjusted Youth. *The Differential View: A Publication of the International Differential Treatment Association – Sixth Annual Conference Proceedings*. Issue 12, September.

Robinson, J. and Smith, G. (1971) The Effectiveness of Correctional Programs. *Crime and Delinquency* 17 (1) (January): 67–80.

Romig, D. (1978) *Justice for Our Children*. Lexington, Mass.: Lexington Books.

Ross, R. and Gendreau, P. (1980) *Effective Correctional Treatment*. Toronto: Butterworth.

Sapir, S. and Nitzberg, A. (1973) *Children with Learning Problems*. New York: Brunner/Mazel.

Taylor, D. and Alpert, S. (1973) *Continuity and Support Following Residential Treatment*. New York: Child Welfare League of America.

Toch, H. (1970) The Care and Feeding of Typologies and Labels. *Federal Probation* 34 (3): 15–19.

Warren, M. Q. (1966) *Interpersonal Maturity Level Classification: Juvenile, Diagnosis of Low, Middle and High Maturity Delinquents*. Sacramento: California Youth Authority.

—— (1983) Application of Interpersonal Maturity to Offender Populations. In W. S. Laufer and J. M. Day (eds) *Personality Theory, Moral Development and Criminal Behavior*. Toronto: Lexington Books.

Whittaker, J. (1979) *Caring for Troubled Children*. San Francisco: Jossey-Bass.

6 Teaching competence in group care practice[1]

Richard W. Small[2] and
Leon C. Fulcher

Introduction

Any discussion about specialized helping environments for children would be incomplete without reference to the relationships which can be found between practice in group care centres and in schools. After all, a large proportion of each child's day is spent in some type of formal classroom experience. Moreover, many of the important advances in the education of children with special needs (Mann and Sabatino 1974) are of relevance to group care practice with children. Piaget (1970) and Montessori (1964, 1973), amongst others, have influenced the development of teaching methods based on children's interactions with their physical environment in all learning situations. Some of the approaches derived from their work are of direct relevance to activity programming outside the classroom (Silberman 1973; Weihs 1971), a practice theme which VanderVen considers elsewhere in this volume. Other educators have contributed directly to our knowledge about practice with children who have learning disabilities (Bangs 1968; Cruickshank 1971; Cruickshank and Johnson 1975; Frostig and Maslow 1973; Frostig 1976; Kirk 1966).

The development of behaviour modification techniques in the

special education classroom has paralleled advances in the wider
field of child care, especially in the United States. The literature
provides a rich source of practical advice for those working with
children in the group care field (amongst others cf. Bijou 1971;
Bradfield 1971; Brown and Christie 1981; Hewett 1969; Homme
1969; Meisels 1974; and Pizzat 1973). Special education has given
considerable attention to the management of surface behaviour
in the classroom. Swift and Spivak (1974) offered a detailed review
of the contributions made by teachers in this area of practice.
However, in spite of the potential for common ground between
teachers and group care workers, such common ground is not all
that frequently recognized in practice. Some have attempted to
illuminate the common themes between special education and
group care practice, most notably Apter (1982), Brendtro and
Ness (1983), Brown and Christie (1981), Hobbs (1966), Kashti
(1979), and Nash (1976) amongst others. From an ecological
perspective, the school classroom must be considered as a
significant influence on child and family life. More importantly
the classroom should be considered as an integral part of group
care and treatment for children. Both the school and the group
care centre offer a sophisticated technology and legitimate goals
which can be used for teaching competence skills to children with
special learning needs.

Individual learning style and the teaching of competence

When attempting to think of a child's total environment as a
curriculum for teaching competence, one is faced with the problem
of relating the goals and techniques used by a group care worker
to those used by the classroom teacher and others. In many
respects, shared practice involves finding a language which all
staff can share, as suggested by Casson elsewhere in this volume.
In other respects the task involves making a conscious effort to
deal with a child's functioning in the present, thereby avoiding
the temptation to make diagnostic conclusions which over-
emphasize difficulty in one area as the cause of learning problems.
The initial strategy for effective competence teaching should be
to set aside — at least temporarily — the labels and stereotypes
which children bring with them, so that observable behaviour can
be analysed, and some conclusions reached about what is likely

to work best with each child. In this way, it is possible to build a common vocabulary for teaching, by looking at a child's *personal learning style*.

Learning style is something far more comprehensive than the rate at which a child acquires learning or his overall temperament. Here, learning style can be said to refer to the level of competence that each child brings to learning. Competence is shaped by a particular balance of developmental strengths and weaknesses which can be observed, recorded, and supplemented by specific teaching strategies. Implicit in this notion is a view of the learning process which considers each child as a *whole*: as a unique being who receives, associates, and expresses him/herself through the interactions of five developmental modes – perception, cognitive functioning, affect, language, and motor functioning. Assessment of competence skills in each of these modes of functioning should assist workers more directly to meet the special needs of children in group care practice.

Perception
The manner by which the brain interprets stimuli received by the sense organs – or perception – depends on the integration of previous sensory experience and individual neurological patterns. Perception skills are critical for learning and can vary greatly from child to child. Children who are referred to group care services are frequently misperceivers, in relation to both human interactions and perception of basic sensory data. Both visual and auditory perception require consideration. Competence in the area of visual perception influences the extent to which a child can 'tune in' to learning situations. Some children are especially oriented to visual experience and would seem to learn most effectively through this channel. However, a child who is seriously lacking in these skills may consistently lose his place when reading, be unable to find things when they are right in front of him, or become disoriented in familiar surroundings. If a child is unable to judge distances and spatial relationships with confidence, then he may exaggerate his footsteps when moving up or down stairs, or move awkwardly across open ground. Many of the symptoms associated with the condition labelled 'dyslexia' seem related to visual-perceptual confusion.

A social and educational learning environment which emphasizes structure, repetition, and consistency can help a child to organize his day around specific tasks, and is therefore strongly indicated for children with visual-perceptual difficulties. Some of the elements which may be expected to influence practice relationships include:

- *Laterality:* Social competence is affected by a child's ability to see him or herself as the central figure in a space, distinguish right side from left side, top from bottom, and front from back. Competence in this area is necessary for such tasks as moving through crowded spaces (a busy train, a shopping centre, rugged terrain) or distinguishing right and left body parts (getting dressed, personal hygiene).
- *Directional tendency:* A child's social competence is influenced by his ability to orient his/her body towards a space outside him/herself. Competence in this area is necessary for such tasks as map reading, following directions to school or the shops, or helping with the laundry.
- *Figure–ground relations:* Social competence is limited by a child's ability to perceive objects in the foreground while at the same time blocking out background distractions. Competence in this area is necessary for such tasks as focusing attention on one word on a page while reading, or finding a cooking utensil in a drawer while helping prepare a meal.
- *Discrimination:* Social competence in this area involves the ability to pick fine visual detail in distinguishing one form or object from another. Competence in this area is necessary for learning tasks such as discriminating between the letters *f* and *t*, and recognizing a smile or frown in social relations.
- *Closure:* A child's social competence in this area involves his ability to fill in the missing parts of an object when only some parts are shown. Competence in this area is necessary for such tasks as spelling in written form, reading road signs from the bus, or playing video games.
- *Position in space:* Social competence in this area involves a child's ability to discriminate between objects which have the same general form, but vary in their spatial position. Competence in this area is necessary for such tasks as seeing that the letters *b* and *d* are different while reading, drawing pictures or geometric patterns on sheets of paper, or finding a room in a high-rise office block for an interview.

While some children are 'all eyes' as they make sense out of their environment, others are 'all ears', learning most efficiently through the auditory channel. The child with weak auditory perception is likely to say 'Huh?' as a first response to questions or instructions, although he may have had little difficulty hearing what was said. Such a child may forget instructions or follow them in the wrong sequence. During a lesson when the teacher is speaking, such a child may be paying attention to workmen, birds, or motor sounds outside the classroom window. When asked to bring something to class the next day, she/he may forget or bring the wrong object. As with children who have problems of visual perception, children with limited social competence in the audio perception sphere may encounter, as well as create, a great deal of frustration in their social relations. Such children may become withdrawn or stubbornly 'deaf' in situations where they are unsure or frightened.

Auditory perception is the interpretation of stimuli sent from the ear to the brain. When working with children who lack competence in the audio perception area, practitioners need to resist quick interpretations of emotional conflict or resistance (even though these may be apparent symptoms). Until simple accommodations are made by children to their immediate environment, they will be unable to engage in learning. Practice tasks may include: providing a quiet place for the child to work or play: presenting tasks one at a time; using pictures of words for items and activities in the environment; emphasizing hand movements; and insisting on eye contact so that a child can 'hear' what is said through watching the speaker's lips. Some of the elements workers can expect to encounter in their practice relationships include:

- *Foreground–background:* Social competence in this area involves a child's ability to focus on foreground sounds and block out background sounds. Competence in this area is necessary for such tasks as hearing the teacher give assignments in a noisy classroom or paying attention to the instructions given by an adult at the dining room table.
- *Discrimination:* Social competence is limited for a child if she/he is unable to discriminate between different sounds or auditory stimuli. Competence in this area is necessary in order to hear

the difference between *sat* and *sad* during a spelling test, or the difference between *no* and *now*, when an adult is giving instructions.

– *Sequence:* A child's social competence in this area involves his/her ability to interpret what she/he hears in correct order of presentation. Competence in this area is necessary for such tasks as hearing the difference between *bets* and *best,* or hearing which is done first when making breakfast: put the egg into a pan of boiling water, or put the egg into a pan of water and bring it to the boil.

– *Closure:* Social competence is affected by a child's ability to fill in missing parts of a whole word or meaningful sequence of sounds. Competence is important in this area for such tasks as learning new words, discerning accents or speaking with someone over the telephone.

Cognitive functioning
It is tempting for the teacher and some group care workers to dwell on *cognitive* functioning as the most important determinant of individual learning style. It is certainly the case that cognitive ability plays an important part in all areas of physical and social development. In practice, however, one can become very unclear about the precise nature of a child's social competence in this area, as distinct from others. In what follows, an arbitrary distinction is made between language, on the one hand, and specific, measurable skills associated with cognitive functioning on the other. It is hoped that such a distinction will assist practitioners to make clearer distinctions between several aspects of a child's social competence in the cognitive area.

The ability to think clearly, to move beyond concrete events to abstract ideas, to form complex concepts and to assign objects or ideas to categories are but a few of the cognitive skills necessary in learning social competence. As with language, the precise manner in which the brain develops and carries out these operations is not entirely understood. On the evidence available, it would seem that cognitive skills are partly constitutional and partly based on the relative variety and intensity of sensory experience in early childhood (Piaget 1963; Piaget and Inhelder 1969). Actual opportunities to manipulate, touch, smell, or otherwise experience concrete objects and people can be said to aid concept formation throughout life. Some of the essential cognitive operations associated with learning social competence include:

- *Abstraction:* Social competence in this area involves a child's being able to discern between numerous concrete events, elements, characteristics, and relationships. Competence in this area is necessary for a child to find his/her home in a row of similar terraced houses. This requires dealing with the idea of home as different from the other houses that look the same as the one in which the child lives.
- *Categorization:* A child's social competence in this area involves his/her ability to group experiences and objects into classes, based on similarity of type or function. Competence in this area is necessary for a child to understand basic geometry, handle tools, or simply separate the laundry.
- *Generalization:* Social competence will be restricted in this area if a child lacks the ability to infer causal relationships from specific events and particular consequences. Competence in this area is necessary for a child to use the Highway Code while riding his/her bicycle across town, as compared with simply knowing how to ride a bicycle. Understanding the rules associated with advanced arithmetic, or figuring out that hitting the baby will always make mother angry are other cognitive skills in this area.
- *Time sense:* Social competence in this area involves the ability to be oriented to time and changes measured in time. Competence in this area is necessary for planning ahead or for matching energy available to the duration of a given task.
- *Number concepts:* In this area, a child's social competence is influenced by his/her ability to count and use simple numbers to represent quantity. Competence is required in relation to number concepts if a child is to engage actively in the vast range of social encounters in a technological age.
- *Arithmetic reasoning:* Social competence in this area involves the ability to manage such concepts as equality, inequality, computation, and distribution in daily life. Competence in this area is necessary for such tasks as shopping, making change, and estimating costs.

A child with noticeable confusion in his pattern of cognitive functioning may seem far more of a puzzle than other youngsters in a group. Such a child might have persistent trouble with 'simple' tasks such as grouping, counting, or sorting objects by category. She/he may become confused when asked to list everything she/he can think of that is used in a workshop, or may be unable to predict adult responses following repeated episodes of interaction. Children like these may count on their fingers, and be unable to give change or tell time. In many ways, a group care placement is ideally suited to the task of managing cognitive difficulty, given the potential for restructuring and reinterpreting the social environment for each child. The primary tasks for teachers and group care workers in this context can be seen as promoting a child's *inner* organization by shaping learning environments which 'make sense' for each child. The classroom or group home provides a venue in which social competence can be rehearsed for use in future environments.

Affect

Social competence in relation to affect, or emotional functioning, can be said to involve a broad category of skills, each of which is expected to influence a child's overall pattern of functioning. Mastery in this area includes the skills required to manage emotional turmoil, personal thoughts, and feelings. Competence in this area also involves a range of skills associated with presentation of self in interpersonal relations. Such skills might be considered with respect to the following areas:

- *Self-image:* Social competence in this area involves a child having accurate and positive thoughts and feelings about himself/herself. Competence in this area is necessary for meaningful social interactions and for such tasks as tolerating one's own mistakes or learning to be more assertive in social relationships.
- *Impulse control:* A child's social competence in this area involves his/her ability to monitor and control personal thoughts and actions. Competence in this area is necessary for a child to sustain attention in a given task or to learn that she/he must 'Wait their turn'.
- *Social perception:* Social competence in this area involves a child's being able to 'read' the emotional communications of

others and to 'hear' what is expected of him/her in a given social setting. Competence in this area is necessary for learning to make friends, for becoming part of a group or avoiding expulsion from the library.

– *Social judgement:* In this area, a child's social competence is influenced by his/her ability to weigh the alternatives, probabilities, and potential consequences of his actions in different social situations. Competence in this area is necessary for such situations as knowing when to be aggressive and when to walk away from a fight.

– *Delayed reward:* Social competence will be restricted for a child in this area if she/he is unable to postpone gratification for future gain. Competence in this area is necessary for such tasks as saving one's pocket money to buy an expensive toy or budgeting for cigarettes between one pay packet and another.

– *Foresight:* Social competence in this area involves the ability to consider future events in the midst of current activities. Competence in this area is necessary for planning ahead and for conscious self-control of behaviour.

– *Motivation:* A child's social competence in this area involves his/her ability to take pleasure in and derive satisfaction from semi-autonomous achievement. Competence in this area is necessary for learning to read for pleasure, pursue hobbies, ride a bicycle, or any other type of self-learning activity.

– *Adaptability:* Social competence in this area involves a child's ability to remain calm, oriented, and persevering in the face of change. Competence in this area is necessary for mastering the anxiety involved with transitions, such as moving to another town, changing schools, starting work, and so forth.

– *Body image:* Social competence for a child in this area involves an internal awareness of feelings in his/her body and body parts, as well as a conscious awareness of his/her body feelings in space and time. Competence in this area is necessary to help a young person prepare for a first date, to modify impulses to behave dangerously, or to maintain involvement with selected peers.

Learning is clearly hampered in a child who is handicapped by anxiety, rage, or distorted self-image. Learning is also impaired in a child who is unable to give affection. In more subtle ways, learning is hampered in a child who cannot deal with sadness, joy, or excitement, or who constantly falters in social situations because she/he misreads the emotional responses of others and her/his effect on others. A child lacking in emotional competence may be unable to heed danger or may be paralysed by anxiety. She/he may be unable to think ahead, to know when the teacher or foster parents are angry, or to understand why other children in the playground avoid playing with him/her. Finally, she/he may be unable to risk making mistakes which are a part of social learning.

Language
Most children learn to manipulate language from a very early age in life. Word games and the nuances of meaning are a continual delight to them. For some children, however, language may be slow or problematic. For these children, words and the use of words may be less a tool of social interaction than a perplexing barrier to entering into the life of things. Several of the processes involved in language functioning are outlined below:

— *Simple vowel and consonant sounds:* Social competence in this area involves an ability to discriminate among language sounds and to produce particular sounds correctly. Competence in this area is necessary for pronouncing words correctly or for learning a foreign language.
— *Vocabulary:* In this area, social competence involves a child's ability to understand the meaning of words, including the comprehension of different meanings in different contexts. Competence in this area is necessary for the correct interpretation of written and spoken communication, and for fluency of speech.
— *Grammar:* A child requires a degree of social competence in this area in order to understand both surface and depth structures of sentences. Competence in this area is necessary for determining when a collection of words is a sentence, when sentences have meaning, when sentences with different word order can mean the same thing, and how the arrangement of words in a sentence indicates their relationship to each other.
— *Auditory and visual reception:*[3] Social competence in this area involves a child's ability to derive meaning from verbally

presented or visually presented bits of information. Competence in this area is necessary for grasping the complex differences involved in the question, 'Did you hit Jimmy or did he hit you?' following a fight in the bedroom. Competence in this area is also necessary in order to understand the action in a comic strip or to read non-verbal expressions on the face of an adult.

– *Auditory and visual association:* In this area, social competence involves a child's ability to understand the relationships between words or concepts when presented orally and visually. Competence in this area is necessary for such tasks as filling the salt cellar and sugar bowl with a white, granular substance, selecting categories of picture on a video screen, or for anticipating danger when seeing a young child run into the street.

– *Verbal and manual expression:* Social competence in this area involves the ability to express simple and complex meanings in both verbal and non-verbal means. Competence in this area is necessary for a child to tell a friend or adult about a school outing, or when a child needs to explain which hand tool he needs if he has forgotten its name. In short, competence in this area is necessary for complete communication in almost all social situations.

Emotionally closed-up youngsters who also have distinct language difficulties may refuse to speak or may use mostly single words and simple sentences in their speech. Sentences they do use may seem confusing. In dealing with these children, both the teacher and group care workers need to be aware of a child's difficulty with language and what this means for that child. A child may easily distort the meaning of words in communications with others because of this difficulty. In order to be certain that a meaningful exchange is taking place, an adult needs to determine whether the child cannot understand what is expected of him, or whether he understands but is unable to express himself in response. If the child cannot understand what she/he hears, she/he can be helped to attain greater competence by allowing him/her more time to respond, by simplifying the sentence, or by using pictures or gestures to aid meaning. If the child has trouble with expression, she/he can be assisted by adults asking questions that elicit more precise responses. For example, if the question 'What would you like to do this afternoon?' elicits no response, 'Would you like to go shopping?' may be more productive.

Motor functioning
An accurate evaluation of a child's motor abilities is of critical importance for teachers as well as group care workers. Many children function best when they are actively involved physically in any number of learning tasks. Movement and activity are likely to be distinctive features of their learning style in most situations. For the child who is reasonably competent in terms of motor functioning, workers need to provide positive means for such skills to be exercised, as well as maintaining a focus on the control of excess energy. The child with weak motor skills may be able to read or watch television, but be unable to write legibly. For such children, the classroom teacher may need to provide a tape recorder in order to avoid struggles which are related more to the physical problem of shaping words on paper than to emotional blocks to expression. Similarly, a group care worker may need to arrange personal practice sessions before exposing a child such as this to competitive play situations, where he may experience failure and humiliation.

The general area of motor functioning may be examined as the integration of large and small muscle activity. Functioning in the motor skills area is likely to include the following elements of performance:

– *Gross motor skills:* Social competence in this area involves the ability to use and co-ordinate the large muscles of the body, including legs, arms, and back. Competence in this area is necessary for such activities as running, jumping, or climbing.
– *Fine motor skills:* In this area, social competence involves the ability to use and co-ordinate the small muscles of the body, including fingers and wrist, and so on. Competence in this area is necessary for such activities as drawing, writing, or cutting with scissors.
– *Eye–hand co-ordination:* A child's social competence in this area involves his/her ability to control both eye and hand at the same time to perform a task. Competence in this area is necessary for gross motor activities such as catching or kicking

a ball. It is necessary for such fine motor activities as drawing a picture or operating a self-powered wheelchair.

- *Balance:* Social competence in this area involves the ability to co-ordinate large and small muscles to maintain balance equilibrium. Competence in this area is necessary for such activities as riding a bicycle or hopping on one foot.
- *Posture:* In this area, social competence involves a child's ability to hold his body erect. Competence in this area is necessary for sustained activities such as sitting, standing, walking, or bicycle riding.

Motor skills are important for adaptation to every part of the environment. Motor functioning is an excellent area for highlighting ways in which curriculum goals in the life space of group care and curriculum goals in the classroom overlap. With the provision of motor skill training, such as football or dance practice during recreation periods, a child will increase proficiency as well as develop skills for interacting with a peer group. Furthermore, motor skill training also helps improve body awareness, self-confidence, and even specific skills, such as handwriting in the classroom. There would seem to be a great deal of potential in this area, for positive collaboration between teachers and group care workers – collaboration which would enhance their practice with children.

To summarize, consideration has been given to five developmental modes of functioning which influence individual learning styles and social competence amongst children. The five developmental modes involved perception, cognitive functioning, affect, language, and motor functioning. It must be emphasized again, however, that learning is very much a dynamic process in which interaction takes place between all five of the developmental modes referred to above. In short, some level of integration is achieved across all five modes of functioning, and this integration is likely to shape learning style and patterns of social competence for a child.

Other abilities, such as attention and memory, are also influenced by the integration of developmental skills within the individual child. In many ways, a child's ability to 'pay attention' – when involved in a particular task – is the most delicate of all developmental competence skills. Memory is also a highly variable capacity in each person. Some children may have trouble with specific recall of words and names, while others are at ease reciting the alphabet backward. Some children may have the uncanny ability to remember details in physical space, while others need to keep asking directions to the bus station. Social competence for children in receipt of group care services requires the support and encouragement of teachers and group care workers whose practices are complementary.

Learning style and the learning environment

The value of looking at the whole child and emphasizing social competence with observable skills is that workers can be eclectic in their approach to learning tasks with children. More to the point, the emphasis on individual differences in learning style, rather than individual pathology, may assist workers to make more practical sense out of assessments and to formulate more clearly practical goals in learning environments committed to teaching competence skills. Most important, since the focus of attention is the child as a whole person with a consistent learning style, then the *methodological emphasis* of an educational or group care programme changes as interventions are redefined.

By turning attention to each child being helped to acquire competence skills in any or all areas of functioning, workers can emphasize personal strengths and only secondarily focus attention on individual weaknesses. This represents an important technical and clinical shift in thinking for those engaged in group care practice. Although a child's weak or problem areas are acknowledged, primary attention is given to existing competence skills which can be exploited (and which a child can learn to use on his own) in any new learning situation. The whole group care programme thus becomes a comprehensive *learning environment* which is responsive to learning style as well as special learning needs. Several programme features require consideration if workers are to use their group care centre as a learning environment for children, where social competence skills receive primary attention.

Assessment of competence
In setting up an effective learning environment, group care workers must compile a record of information about the personal learning style of each child. Such a record may be informally held

amongst a team of workers, or more helpfully written in summary form in a quickly referenced file, as in the Kardex or Problem-Oriented Record systems. Compiling a record of information about a child's functioning must be understood as involving a process of continuous assessment, rather than a diagnosis of the 'problem'. All too frequently, workers are tempted to use assessment typologies to 'diagnose' a child's problems and, just as frequently, such an approach has resulted in constant struggles around a child's incompetence in social situations. With the focus on deficiency, everyone working with a child − and more importantly the child himself − may be blind to areas of strength in his overall pattern of functioning. Even the most seriously handicapped child has some capacity to learn, and more importantly, she/he approaches learning with his/her own special combination of strengths as well as weaknesses.

The daily curriculum
In daily programme terms, an emphasis on social competence requires that the learning opportunities available for children should possess three basic attributes. First, the daily curriculum and expectations for every participant in the programme should be easily *comprehended by each child*. A child should be able to understand where she/he is headed with particular learning tasks, what skills she/he is using or struggling to master in a given task, and how she/he can use the skills she/he does have to engage in problem solving. Second, the daily curriculum should be directed at *specific goals*, both in academic terms and in relation to daily living. Non-specific or esoteric objectives may result in basic survival skills − reading, writing, and arithmetic − being unlearned, thus undermining the social competence of a child when she/he reaches school-leaving age. Basic cookery, laundry, and self-care skills should probably become concrete goals in any group care centre for adolescents. Finally, the daily curriculum should be *continuous*, in that formal academic learning parallels learning in other areas of a child's life. Ideally, a child should experience learning to read as part of the process of growing up and changing, which includes learning how to make friends, purchase an item of clothing at a shopping centre, or deal with angry feelings after an argument.

Selection of curriculum materials
The books, games, papers, puzzles, and other objects a teacher brings into the classroom as aids to learning are part of the concrete reality of curriculum design. Such materials are important factors in defining the physical impact of the classroom as a learning environment. The group care centre, in the same way, makes use of curriculum materials which can be used in the teaching of social competence, where a range of materials can be adapted to the learning style of each child. Two things are implied by such an approach. To begin with, curriculum materials should include *variety*, to take account of different learning styles, different learning content, and changes in the weather. Both indoor and outdoor curriculum materials are required so that children can attain social competence skills which can be used in a wide range of situations. The second point implied by this approach is that curriculum materials need to be chosen with *maximum flexibility* in mind. Here, the idea is that materials need to be used with more than one child, in different situations, and in combination with other materials. In the group care centre, this issue is encountered with respect to recreation and leisure-time materials, including games equipment or craft supplies.

Use of physical space
Teachers can use the shape of their classroom as a physical instrument which can enable implementation of curriculum objectives. In a similar way, group care workers can use their centre as a 'classroom' for teaching social competence. To begin with, teachers and group care workers need to consider how *responsive* the physical environment (classroom or centre) is to individual learning style and the varying demands that are made by children and staff. As Maier suggests, 'The Space We Create Controls Us' in many subtle and not so subtle ways (1982). A second consideration involves the question of whether the physical environment is *instructive*, communicating the message that this is a learning environment where social skills are used and competence is possible. The physical environment can invite or intimidate those who inhabit that environment. To use a theatrical metaphor, the physical environment does not provide the 'script' used in the learning drama which unfolds. The 'script' is provided by the 'actors and actresses', each with their own personal learning

style. The physical environment provides the 'staging and props' which give 'context' to the drama, and thereby influences the 'intensity' of a given sequence of activities. The significance of purposeful activity with children is considered further by VanderVen elsewhere in this volume.

Social climate in the learning environment
At least five important features will need consideration if the climate of group care and treatment is to facilitate social competence learning. One of the most obvious features involves a climate of *respect for individual differences*. Since few behaviour management techniques are both effective and meaningful for every child in a group, so workers should be willing and able to adjust certain rules or regulations accordingly. A second feature which influences the climate of a centre can be said to involve *clarity of expectations* in all areas. There should be no unnecessary mysteries in the classroom or group care centre. Each developmental step of the living and learning curriculum should be as clear and unambiguous as possible. A third feature which requires consideration is the *attitude of support* that is present within the climate of a centre. Low morale, disinterest, boredom, or an interest in different priorities elsewhere can have a significant impact on the learning potential available in a centre. This feature is frequently influenced by a fourth feature, the presence of sufficient and instantly available *back-up support* to help manage disruptive behaviour. No one person should be expected to engage extremely disruptive behaviour on his own. Management of disruptive behaviour needs to arouse as little attention as possible – to avoid either active or covert positive reinforcement – until both child and worker(s) can agree to resume their learning tasks. Such an approach requires considerable staff teamwork and an acceptance of back-up as another of the learning resources available, not a sign of staff weakness. Finally, careful *attention to group composition* may help to minimize extreme variability in the behaviour patterns of a group of children. This feature is given further attention by Burford and Fulcher elsewhere in this volume.

Collaboration with and support from others
When seeking to establish learning environments which teach social competence skills, it is necessary to consider all those in

direct contact with children as teachers in the broadest sense. The classroom teacher orients his or her learning objectives towards one set of goals and the group care workers are oriented to another set of goals. To the extent that learning goals are complementary in both the school classroom and group care centre, then social competence learning will be facilitated. The same argument holds for the service goals pursued by an attached social worker, a social worker based elsewhere, or social service managers. Each staff member working with individual children, or a group of children, will benefit from knowing which learning approaches seem to work best for the other workers. It may be helpful if time can be scheduled for different workers to spend some time working in the others' domains, such as a teacher being involved in after-school activities, a group care worker helping in the classroom, or a social worker helping with recreation activities. Such overlaps may help to generate a fuller appreciation of the importance of co-ordinating all aspects of the learning environment. The administrative supports available in any group care centre should include mechanisms for bringing workers together to share their daily experiences with children. Rigid scheduling patterns and territorial boundary disputes can, and frequently do, undermine collaborative efforts in group care practice. In this way, important sources of support can be removed from workers and children in their shared task of promoting social competence.

Conclusions

An overall commitment to promoting competence skills rather than curing illness is perhaps one of the most important goals of practice in the group care field. Such a goal is more readily achieved if all those working with a child – teachers, group care workers, and others – take account of his overall pattern of functioning and his personal learning style. Functioning in the areas of perception, cognitive functioning, affect, language, and motor skills are all important considerations in teaching children skills which will enhance their social competence in different situations. Assessment of competence, as compared with 'diagnosing the problem', will help to inform the daily curriculum of practice and the curriculum materials needed to promote learning. Planned uses of the physical environment can help to facilitate a social climate in the centre which encourages learning. Finally, collaboration with others involved in a child's life can offer valuable support to both children and care-givers alike. In short, the whole centre programme can be conceived as a learning environment in which the goals of formal education in the classroom and goals in the life space of group care are closely co-ordinated. Elsewhere in this volume, Hopkinson and Conte explore some of these issues further when considering practice in inter-disciplinary teams and working with parents.

Notes

1 This chapter draws heavily on an earlier work published with Clarke (1979). The concepts outlined in this earlier paper have been re-examined and extended, so as to make them more applicable to a wider readership.

2 Richard Small is Assistant Professor of Social Work at the State University of New York at Albany, New York, USA.

3 The Reception, Association, and Expressive categories used in this section on language functioning are based on the comprehensive work by Kirk (1966).

References

Apter, S. J. (1982) *Troubled Children/Troubled Systems*. Oxford: Pergamon Press.

Bangs, T. (1968) *Language and Learning Disorders of the Pre-Academic Child*. New York: Appleton-Century-Crofts.

Bijou, S. (1971) *The Exceptional Child: Conditional Learning and Teaching Ideas*. New York: M.S.S. Information Corp.

Bradfield, R. (1971) *Behavior Modification of Learning Disabilities*. San Rafael, California: Academic Therapy Press.

Brendtro, L. K. and Ness, A. E. (1983) *Re-educating Troubled Youth: Environments for Teaching and Treatments*. New York: Aldine.

Brown, B. J. and Christie, M. (1981) *Social Learning Practice in Residential Child Care*. Oxford: Pergamon Press.

Clarke, R. B. and Small, R. W. (1979) Schools as Partners in Helping. In J. K. Whitaker, *Caring for Troubled Children*. San Francisco: Jossey-Bass.

Cruickshank, W. M. (1971) *Learning Disabilities in Home, School and Community*. Syracuse, NY: Syracuse University Press.

Cruickshank, W. M. and Johnson, G. (1975) *Education of Exceptional Children and Youth*. Englewood Cliffs, NJ: Prentice-Hall.

Frostig, M. (1976) *Education for Dignity*. New York: Grune & Stratton.

Frostig, M. and Maslow, P. (1973) *Learning Problems in the Classroom*. New York: Grune & Stratton.

Hewett, F. (1969) *The Emotionally Disturbed Child in the Classroom.* Boston: Allyn & Bacon.

Hobbs, N. (1966) Helping Disturbed Children: Psychological and Ecological Strategies. *American Psychologist* 21 (12): 1105–151.

Homme, L. (1969) *How to Use Contingency Contracting in the Classroom.* Champaign, Ill.: Research Press.

Kashti, Y. (1979) *The Socializing Community: Disadvantaged Adolescents in Israeli Youth Villages.* Tel Aviv: University of Tel Aviv, Studies in Educational Evaluation, Monograph No. 1.

Kirk, S. A. (1966) *The Diagnosis and Remediation of Psycholinguistic Abilities.* Urbana: University of Illinois Press.

Maier, H. W. (1982) The Space we Create Controls Us. *Residential Group Care and Treatment* 1 (1): 51–9.

Mann, L. and Sabatino, D. (1974) *The Second Review of Special Education.* New York: Grune & Stratton.

Meisels, L. (1974) The Student's Social Contract: Learning Social Competence in the Classroom. *Teaching Exceptional Children* 7 (1): 34–6.

Montessori, M. (1964) *The Montessori Method [1912].* New York: Schocken Books.

—— (1973) *From Child to Adolescence [1939].* New York: Schocken Books.

Nash, C. (1976) *The Learning Environment: A Practical Approach to the Education of the Three-, Four- and Five-Year-Old.* Toronto: Methuen.

Piaget, J. (1963) *The Language and Thought of the Child.* New York: Basic Books.

—— (1970) *Science of Education and the Psychology of the Child.* New York: Grossman, Orion Press.

Piaget, J. and Inhelder, B. (1969) *The Psychology of the Child .* New York: Basic Books.

Pizzat, F. (1973) *Behavior Modification in Residential Treatment for Children: Model of a Program.* New York: Behavioral Publications.

Silberman, C. (1973) *The Open Classroom Reader.* New York: Random House.

Swift, M. and Spivak, G. (1974) Therapeutic Teaching: A Review of Teaching Methods for Behaviorally Troubled Children. *Journal of Special Education* 8 (3): 259–89.

Weihs, T. J. (1971) *Children in Need of Special Care.* London: Souvenir Press.

7 Activity programming: its developmental and therapeutic role in group care

Karen D. VanderVen[1]

Introduction

While there has been growing evidence that activities play an important role in human development, health, and personal well-being (Erikson 1950; Erikson 1976; Redl and Wineman 1957), practice in the field of group care has traditionally placed secondary emphasis on activity programming whether as the *modus operandi* for delivering care and treatment services, or as an essential skill required by group care workers. The primary focus in group care practice has emphasized interpersonal skills, especially in North America, though less so in Europe. Educationally oriented writers, such as Brendtro and Ness (1983), Guindon (1970), Hobbs (1974), in the North American context, or Rasmussen (1984) and Tugginer (1984) in Europe, have long emphasized the importance of purposeful activity in group care practice. Nevertheless, it remains the case that in practice, a legitimate focus on inter-personal relations can frequently ignore the importance of purposeful activity and its meaning for children and adults.

The significance of activities in promoting growth and well-being from infancy to adulthood is emphasized throughout what follows. The term 'activity programming' is used in this chapter to mean any planned involvements with children where a variety of methods and materials are used to influence their behaviour towards particular goals or enhanced well-being. Activities with children have been viewed traditionally as being at worst time-fillers and at best a means of preventing unmanageable behaviour by keeping children busy.

Recent advances in the field of group care have shown activity programming to be a central component of the care and treatment process with children (Davids 1975; VanderVen 1972; Whittaker 1969). This chapter begins with a brief examination of activities as a means of intervention. Attention then turns to a consideration of guidelines for activity programming. Finally, consideration is given to the task of involving children and encouraging workers to use purposeful activity in group care practice.

Activities as intervention

Activities have no rival in the wide range of group care methods for contributing to an individuals's sense of *mastery* and *self-esteem*. Through involvement in one sort of activity or another, a child comes to better understand his world and his own abilities in that world, as well as gaining a sense of relative competence as a contributor in activities whenever he is invited to perform. Erikson (1976) provides a strong rationale for the implementation of activity programs which counter dependency and passivity in group care environments. The emotional significance of purposeful activity is articulated for each of the psychology stages articulated by Erik Erikson (1950). At each stage, a child's successful negotiation of life tasks requires engagement in the world with support from others to foster social competence and personal well-being.

A review of the group care literature since the Second World War will highlight the wide swings of the pendulum concerning practice trends and fashions. The psychoanalytic tradition was heavily challenged by the social learning advocates; individual methods have been challenged by group methods; short, sharp shock treatments have been advocated over self-actualization or therapeutic community approaches. When there is a strong response in one direction, there is a shift eventually in the opposite direction (VanderVen 1984). One example amongst many might involve the attitudes held in society towards children working.

The child labour laws sought to ensure that children would not be deprived of the opportunity for health, play, and education by having to work long hours, under poor conditions, at menial and exhausting jobs. Over the years, the pendulum has swung in the direction of assuming that no demands should be placed on children to participate in the 'work of the world'. This so-called 'freedom' helps to ensure that adults and machines will be able to do these jobs, and do them more quickly as well. Many adults who experienced the Great Depression and social conditions of the 1920s and 1930s, and who are now policy makers and community leaders, have sought to provide for children what they themselves never received.

Several examples of this orientation to work can be found in group care practice. In many day nurseries or playgroups, children are not expected to help pick up their playthings at the end of a session. In homes, parents have frequently 'done the work themselves' rather than insist that children will carry out chores which give them participation and responsibilities in the 'routine' activities of family life. Older youths might show their lack of involvement in a social environment – be this a school or project centre – by doing sloppy work, writing graffiti on walls, hooting during meetings, or throwing food during lunch breaks.

In recent years, more reasoned arguments have been put forward which seek to span the extremes between captive labour and total passivity in group care practice with children. Maier (1981) has shown how play and work are not mutually exclusive in children's development. It does not follow that, by encouraging children to 'work', they are therefore deprived of important experiences provided by play. Those who advocated so-called 'free' play for children have gone so far as to argue that little or no guidance, support, or direction should be introduced by adults. 'Free' play is the practice. Smilansky (1968) challenged this notion by calling attention to the significance of theme-oriented dramatic play for children in group situations. This type of play was found to encourage *cognitive development* and enhance school readiness amongst pre-school children. The point was also made that, for many children, play required the attentive interventions of teacher or care-giver in a variety of ways.

It is now acknowledged that encouragement of 'work' skills as early as pre-school age can play a significant part in helping children acquire personal habits such as attention, persistence, and tolerance of frustration, all of which are essential for successes at school. Adult responses which facilitate the development of these skills include: being supportive, supporting independent activity, encouragement and reinforcement without being overly directive, and not giving *too much* reinforcement, allowing achievement to become its own reward (Stipek 1983). Traditional therapeutic approaches with children have focused attention 'inside-out'. That is, practice has tended to assume that by addressing the internal psyche of children, their feelings and behaviours could be modified in ways that would remove barriers to reality testing and actual achievement. Much less attention goes into providing the external circumstances and straightforward guidance which could lead to better achievement. Activity programming, in this sense, consists of an 'outside-in' approach in which knowledge and skills are acquired through participation in competence-building activities. Emotional states are influenced accordingly.

Guidelines and techniques for activity programming

The contemporary practitioner should be familiar with a range of activities which take place in, or might be introduced at, a group care centre. With the development of group care for infants and toddlers, activity programming is being used to ensure that services provide more than physical care and offer a truly developmental service to vulnerable and rapidly growing children. For pre-school children, the emphasis in activity programming centres on play. The importance of play at this stage stems from its educative, developmental, and therapeutic aspects that have been documented elsewhere (Curry 1971; Smilansky 1968; VanderVen 1976). Attention has now turned to matching environmental conditions and personal learning styles to achieve specific developmental outcomes (Duke 1975; Hunt 1966; Olds 1977). Of course play is a major feature of activity in social environments for both normal and exceptional children. Powers (1980) found in this respect that exceptional children require more support and encouragement from adults to sustain play behaviour.

After-school care, for children of working parents, is another arena where activity programming offers rich potential. Parents frequently report a wish for their children to be involved in 'games' and in opportunities to 'make things' (Common Focus 1983: 4). In group care settings, activities are used in daily living situations and are also used to foster social competence in situations outside the centre. Whittaker (1976) has considered the use of activities in group treatment for emotionally disturbed children. Activity group therapy has been used by VanScoy (1972) as a means of helping children make the transition between play and work. Ross and Bernstein (1976) advocated the use of planned activities in helping emotionally disturbed children with behaviour problems, while Alwon (1979) and Wilson (1977) have stressed the therapeutic uses of activity programming in small centres. Meanwhile, Krueger (1977) has urged care workers and teachers to view a total 'program day' for activity planning in group care. Elsewhere in this volume, Small and Fulcher consider activity programming as a means of teaching social competence in group care practice with children.

Important advances have been made in the use of planned activity for adolescents of school leaving age or younger. Volunteer service projects (Allen and Mitchell 1982) have been used with emotionally disturbed children, while volunteer placements have been used successfully for children leaving care (Brewis 1984). Such findings serve to reinforce the importance of purposeful activity in group care practice with children. Activity programming also extends to work with parents (VanderVen and Griff 1978). Elsewhere in this volume, Conte explores how group care workers can engage parents, so as to help them become more effective parents with their children.

Because group care services are provided for such a diverse population of children, workers are frequently required to accommodate and adapt generic skills to the different children they encounter (VanderVen and Mattingly 1980). To assist workers in this transfer process, some guidelines are offered for activity programming with different groups of children at various times of the living and learning week.

Guideline 1: The principle of universal adaptation
This principle suggests that there is no activity that cannot be adapted so that at least some of its components can be performed by a child of any age, normal and exceptional, with the possible exclusion of young infants and the profoundly handicapped. This

principle is analogous to the educational premise put forward by Bruner, who stated, 'Any idea, problem or body of knowledge can be presented in a form simple enough so that any particular learner can understand it' (1968: 44). An example of this principle is given for the sceptical reader:

> 'For years a child care worker conducted arts, crafts and other activities with profoundly disturbed children who functioned as if they were mentally handicapped and whose overt behaviour could be quite bizarre. Other staff were astonished when they saw that these children could glue tiles, lay ice lollipop sticks in rows, paint completed projects, saw wood, hammer nails, pour moulds. In "cooking", they could stir and cut dough, sprinkle decorations, form patties, and slice. (For safety, they did not handle sharp knives or hot pots.) These children could also arrange chairs, sweep with brooms, tidy up the floor and throw waste paper in the basket.'

How can such performance be explained? Careful scrutiny of many activities will show that there are underlying components which relate to skills required in the very earliest stages of development. For this reason, almost any children – even those with fairly severe developmental handicaps – can perform such skills. For example, *basic physical motions* are fundamental to many activities such as crafts, food preparation, games, housekeeping chores, and others: in–out, grasp–release, up–down, back–forth, over–under, push–pull, squeeze–release, stirring, and so on. Such physical movements emerge as capabilities early on in life, in all but the most profoundly handicapped children. Thus, apparently complex activity is actually composed of basic physical motions that are learned and performed by infants in the earliest months of life. This makes performance of certain activities accessible to any child who has developed functionally through infancy, so long as the *cognitive organization and thematic content* is supplied as needed by a supportive person and where initial guidance may be given to help children make the appropriate motions.

The principle of universal adaptation can be used to involve difficult or poorly developed children who may on the surface seem incapable. In so doing, it offers a further advantage in that it expects participants to engage in socially appropriate interaction. Universal adaptation also addresses the problem in the selection of activities. Practitioners often make the mistake of selecting materials which are far below the interest level of children. The result is that an activity is often rejected by the children. Using the principle of universal adaptation, a thoughtful practitioner can pick an activity with a level of meaning closer to a child's individual learning style, even though the operations necessary to perform the activity are simple.

Guideline 2: Activity transforms passivity
Popular writers insist that children are forced too soon into taking on adult activities and should be 'kept children' longer. Emotionally, children may be exposed to too much, too soon. However, this does not seem to be the case for involvement in activities offered by children's centres. The opposite, in fact, seems closer to the truth. Much programming, particularly that for exceptional children, seems to 'do' more for children than it does in helping them learn to 'do' for themselves. The premise that organized services keep clients, be they children or adults, passive and dependent has been well documented (Cumming and Cumming 1962; Maier 1981). Yet, activities provide essential 'rehearsal practice' (Maier 1981) for children, helping them to develop skills for living in the community. As such, specific effort is made to prevent institutionalization – in which the longer children remain in a restricted setting, the less able they become to function outside of it.

Well-planned activity programming has the potential to transform passivity into activity. Sophisticated pre-schools for years have encouraged children to do things for themselves: button their coats, serve their own food. Institutional settings, particularly those serving mentally and physically impaired children, have been much less oriented towards encouraging activity and independence. There seem to be two main reasons for this. One is the institutional structure itself, which, with an eye to efficiency, functions like a small community to generate the services it needs without involving clients in this effort. To illustrate this, a large institution might do all laundry collectively, or prepare all meals in a central kitchen. The second reason is that children, particularly those who are small or handicapped, readily call forth a feeling in adults that little can be expected of them. Feeling more competent themselves if they perform tasks for the children, adults contribute to children's passivity and dependency. Those who supervise new volunteers frequently report how one of their major tasks is to discourage the volunteers from 'babying' the children whom they find 'adorable'.

Thus, the implication for workers who use activity programming is to ensure maximum involvement by the children. *Figure 7.1* offers some examples of ways in which workers can either activate children or reinforce passivity. Naturally the ages and capability of children must be given consideration. Older, more capable children are likely to assume more initiative and responsibility. Still, even toddlers can be provided with opportunities for appropriate participation at their developmental level. These examples are not meant to imply that children should never attend a planned party or take part in an organized sport, nor that children should prepare all their meals and do all the maintenance work in their settings. However, some participation in such activities offers valuable opportunities for children to learn to behave appropriately in public situations.

Guideline 3: Process and product
Process (the means to the end in an activity) and product (its end product) have often failed to receive a balanced emphasis in children's activities, although both are essential in developing self-esteem and encouraging learning. Little League or Junior football, for example, has often been criticized for its emphasis on winning (the product) rather than providing children with the experience of playing (the process). Conversely, a student teacher who was a competent guitarist and folk singer offered to lead a group of pre-schoolers in singing children's folk songs. The person in charge refused her offer saying that this would 'over-define' the children's musical experiences. Here, perhaps, the notion of process was over-emphasized: music is fine as long as children do not learn any songs.

Attitudes towards process and product seem to reflect the tendency of many in group care practice to think dichotomously: either one approach or the other must be emphasized, rather than considering the possibility of both being employed simultaneously (VanderVen 1984). Thus, the traditional approach for pre-schoolers has been to value activity for its own sake. The experience itself

Figure 7.1 Examples of passive and active approaches to activities

Activity area	Passive approach	Active approach
Daily living and self-care	Meals and snacks planned, prepared, served, and cleaned up after, completely by adults	Children participate in planning, preparing, serving, and cleaning up
	Children's rooms and play area completely cleaned for them	Adults encourage children to take responsibility for keeping their areas orderly
	Adults choose clothing	Adults state general standards for appropriate clothing and help children choose their own within these guidelines
	All decorating done 'professionally' or little decorating at all	Children make appropriate decorations
	'Grounds' care and maintenance done by paid staff	Children participate in grounds care and maintenance, perhaps as 'apprentices' to paid staff
Recreation and entertainment	Television constantly turned on with children randomly sprawled in front of it	Care-givers and children together select appropriate programs and watch them together
	Children taken to watch ball game, swimming event, etc.	Children taught to play ball and are taught to organize their own games; children are taught to swim and develop skill
	Children taken to watch play, concerts, etc.	Children guided in putting on their own performances, to learn to play musical instruments
Ceremonies and marker events	Commercial decorations for holidays are bought and put up by adults	Children make decorations and put them up themselves
	Adults plan and conduct parties or hire outside group to do it	Adults help children plan and conduct parties themselves

has primary social and learning value and the final outcome does not really matter. As children proceed up the developmental scale, tangible, meaningful results become increasingly important. Recalling what Erikson (1950) expected at each developmental stage, it can be argued that a sense of industry is crucial for school age children. By this time they are cognitively aware of their competence in sports, games, crafts, and other activities, and have established judgements about what constitutes good performance.

With reasonable adult support and an orderly environment, children are able to achieve reasonably positive outcomes in their activities. Children who are deprived of adult support and perform in a disorganized fashion may never see their efforts yield anything other than disappointing results. In such instances, a child's already low self-esteem is lowered further, making it all the less likely that his next experience in that activity will be a positive one. Observers of many children's treatment centres have observed how these facilities may have the most sophisticated therapists and consultants, and yet a walk into the 'day' room yields the vision of chaotic, inappropriate, and unfocused activity. The reasons are readily apparent: materials and equipment are poorly stored and poorly cared for; there are old, torn magazines and games or jigsaw puzzles with pieces missing; broken crayons, felt-tipped pens without lids, and used colouring books, etc. Even if the workers were interested in children's activities, they would have very few suitable resources with which to work.

Guideline 4: Structure precedes creativity and freedom
A similar guideline to that of emphasizing both process and product in activities is that involving structure. *Structure* refers to the provision of a prescriptive or directive framework in the organization of activities. The notion of structure implies that more emphasis may be given to the provision of guidance and instruction than on the options for unmodified expressiveness. The following examples show the contrast in behaviour when there is structure and when it is lacking:

A group care worker, feeling that the 'acting out' adolescents to whom he was assigned needed to 'express their angry feelings', randomly laid some fingerpaints out on a table. Soon, the adolescents were laughing at the obscene forms one of them had made with the paint, as well as the antics of several others who, having painted themselves, were beginning to chase another worker with paint-covered hands outstretched in front of them.

Discounting what she had 'heard' about painting by numbers 'stifling creativity', a different worker had several waiting when her adolescent group came home from school. Attracted by the pictures of sports figures, the boys gravitated to the paintings and each selected the one he wanted. The worker remained on hand, giving suggestions about the amount of paint to put on brushes, completing all of one number before starting on another, and similar guidelines as needed. While the boys made 'noises' about receiving suggestions, they followed them and were pleased with their paintings, when finished.

Structure is particularly necessary for exceptional children with limited experience, or for impulse-ridden children with low frustration tolerance. These children simply do not have the concepts and skills necessary for true creativity and expressiveness. Somehow, misguided values about 'repressing children' and 'stifling creativity' have been applied to these children who need *to learn the concepts and practise the skills associated with an activity before using it* in a freer and more undefined area. Structure is important for normal children too, as shown by the following example:

An intending child care worker, along with several classmates, was sent to an art class in an elementary school for observation. The teacher distributed construction paper to the children and gave very specific instructions about how it was to be cut and assembled to make a picture of a sailboat. When a child faltered, the teacher very carefully repeated her instructions. The student worker watched carefully for resistance and for children giving up, but she saw none of this. Instead there was intense concentration and when the children were finished, pride and pleasure as they held up their results. With the exception of colour, the results were identical and well executed. Several of the child care students were appalled that the teacher 'did not let the children be original'.

What the students missed, however, was that this art lesson was indeed *a lesson*. This experience was providing children with fundamental skills – cutting, pasting, arranging, and so on – which are prerequisites to doing meaningful creative work. Basic techniques and operations must be known before they can be applied to make unique constructions and combinations.

The group of children who probably need the least amount of formal structure in their activities are normal infants and pre-school children who are able to use an environment with potential for random explorations. Even this group, however, require a supportive structure in the form of a safe and inviting setting, easy access to materials, and availability of care-givers for guidance if necessary. These features tend to encourage purposeful activity even though there is little emphasis on a finished product.

Without an appropriate degree of structure, even the most well-organized children can be lured into undirected behaviour which ultimately leads to anxiety or boredom. Veteran school teachers often tell novices to 'start strict, then you can ease up later'. This also applies to the use of activities with children in group care where it is easier to set limits or impose limitations at the beginning. Then, as children are ready, begin to allow them more freedom. This avoids the unproductive situation where inadequate limit setting results in behaviour which 'gets out of hand'. The sudden imposition of controls merely builds up resentment and resistance. Some examples of unstructured and structured approaches to activities with children are shown in *Figure 7.2.*

Guideline 5: Creating a climate of involvement
Current organizational theory, as applied to group care practice, emphasizes the relationship between the general climate or implicit 'message' given by a setting and the degree to which that environment is successful in achieving its goals. In the group care field, of course, provision of a setting which encourages constructive interaction between children and adults is a basic feature of practice. Activity programming not only promotes ego development and learning in children but it also provides a much more facilitating climate for effective group interaction (Ross and Bernstein 1976). When children are lacking in social skills, activities provide a framework around which interaction occurs. For example:

Figure 7.2 Some examples of unstructured and structured approaches to activities

Activity	Unstructured	Structured
Play	Undifferentiated space, random assortment of toys available from a pile in the toy box. Adults sit and talk to each other or watch children	Planfully set up physical setting with 'activity areas' and materials in good repair, carefully arranged to invite involvement and constructive behaviour. Adults may make suggestions to help children get started; then observe but are available to make suggestions or interventions
Arts and crafts	Clay randomly placed on table	Each participant receives piece of moulding material; demonstration and practice with moulding techniques provided
	Crayons, paint, and paper laid out; children randomly approach and use them as they see fit	Sponge painting, small object printing, spatter painting or crayon resists
Sports	'Free' swim	Swimming instruction
	Mats inviting informal wrestling and tumbling on the floor	Gymnastic instruction and practice

A worker suggested to a group of adolescent boys slumped around the television set, not really watching, that they listen to records. 'Oh, that's just as boring as TV,' groaned one, but another said, 'Let's get out Jim's guitar and see if we can make some noise.' Soon the boys had 'found' some other instruments and were actively involved in making music. The worker's suggestion of an activity provided the impetus for constructive, positive interaction amongst the teenagers.

Jerry was a non-verbal autistic child who preferred to sit spinning objects for hours on end. He ardently refused efforts to get him involved in 'conversation'. He would simply continue his spinning when someone spoke to him. However, workers continued to approach him when an activity was at hand. Even though he tried to 'shake them off', the fact that the workers had something specific around which to initiate interaction made the communication between them more purposeful and productive. In short, they had 'something to talk about'.

The strategic use of activity programming to facilitate group processes in a centre can help prevent the all-too-frequent occurrence of children and staff developing *adversary* relationships with one another. This is most likely to occur in settings where lack of activity initiates a cycle of: boredom/acting out/staff counter-response (often in the form of punishment)/children's anger at the staff/acting out behaviour designed to provoke and test the staff/and a repeat of the cycle. Once this counter-productive cycle has become established, the centre may become 'crisis-oriented' which means that workers are unable to make an 'instrumental' approach to their work, being engaged alternatively in 'putting out fires' fuelled by continued 'acting out' (VanderVen 1975). This, of course, restricts the developmental and therapeutic potential in a centre. Activity programming can become a significant force for achieving group cohesion and successful group efforts. Sherif's notion of the *superordinate goal* as described by Bronfenbrenner (1977) is of particular interest to workers seeking to create a positive group climate. A superordinate goal is an embracing purpose, extending beyond the more routine experiences of daily activity, which by its very nature draws out the most energetic of those engaged in a particular situation. Attention to a mutually important goal helps to bypass the usual blockages caused by negative inter-personal relations, while at the same time encouraging problem-solving behaviour.

Another major benefit of the superordinate goal in group care practice is that it provides a means of bringing the dignity of ceremony and 'marker events' back into the lives of children. The loss of 'special' occasions has been lamented by some writers (Elkind 1983; Mand 1983), while others have emphasized the use of ceremony in a re-education process (Hobbs 1974). Ceremonies include concerts, open houses, recitals, graduations, events at the completion of an activity (school, camp, etc.), club inductions, parties, etc. Inclusion of ceremonies such as these in a total activity program reduces the degree of monotony that can creep into group care programs (Mand 1983) and also provides a common goal for all to work towards.

Guideline 6: Goal setting

The notion of goal setting, as used in education and business, has found increasing use in human service agencies, to define agency mandate, to design services, and to develop individual care and treatment plans. All three uses of goal setting are of relevance to practice with children in group care settings. The presence or absence of purposeful activities in a setting can be said to reflect the particular goals of that setting. For example, agencies which claim to offer a therapeutic milieu must consider programme activities as a major feature of their service. Such agencies must also provide both the resources and administrative support necessary to ensure that the activities take place. Agencies need to be sure that goal statements on paper find actual implementation in service delivery. For example:

> The Green Trees Agency stated that it was preparing children for return to their communities. However, such activity programming as the agency offered was limited to activities which took place within the walls of the institution.
>
> Another agency, the Cross Corners Centre, stated in brochures for parents that it developed problem-solving skills in pre-schoolers. Observation studies, however, showed that children were given patterns to copy and pre-academic work based on rote learning.

It is the responsibility of senior managers in an agency to provide workers with the logistical support necessary for translating agency goals about activity programming into actual program elements. Similarly, activities for specific groups of children in a setting need to be goal-directed, achieving aims consistent with the purpose of the centre, while at the same time being careful that no members of the group are harmed. Thus, activities can be used to help individual children achieve goals established in personal care and treatment plans, as noted by Burford elsewhere in this volume.

A goal–objectives–evaluation approach, as summarized in *Figure 7.3*, offers a simple but useful method for stating goals that can be attained, designing activities that support their achievement, and assessing the degree to which they have been successful. This standard approach uses goals as *broad statements of purpose*, and objectives as specific *outcomes* of an intervention, outcomes which

Figure 7.3 Standard goals–objectives–evaluation planning approach

Goals	Statements about the general purpose of a project or activity
Objectives	Specific outcomes to be achieved by the project or activity that are observable or measurable
Program	Actual activities or interventions provided in order to achieve the objectives
Resources	Personnel, supplies, and resources needed to provide the program
Evaluation	Assessment of the degree to which a program achieves its objectives and the degree to which a goal was met

can be observed and measured. If the objectives have been achieved, then one can assume that the goal from which they were derived has been attained. The advantage offered by goals and objectives is that, when appropriately stated, they literally 'spell out' the type of activities needed to achieve an objective. The less vague and 'fuzzy' the objectives (Mager 1972), the more likely it is that supportive activities will accomplish their intended purpose, and their success can be evaluated. The following examples illustrate this approach:

Goal: Children will learn to function in the community.

Objective: To select a mode of transportation, take it to the town centre and return safely to the agency.

Program: Activities designed to instruct children in the use of transportation services, and supervised practice in actually making the journey.

Evaluation: Given money for fare, the child will go to the bus or train stop, board, go to the town centre, telephone a worker from the town centre and return by 12 o'clock.

Goal: Children will develop concern for their physical surroundings.

Objective: To put all clothes away in a drawer or closet at night.

Program: Activities and supervision designed to orient children towards picking up and putting their clothes away at the end of the day.

Evaluation: By bedtime, all clothing shall be in children's drawers or closets.

The emphasis on accountability (demonstration of results) in the human services, and the recognition that practitioners need feedback about the success of their efforts (VanderVen 1975) lends further support for the use of this approach in practice. However, since many practitioners are not accustomed to thinking in a goal-oriented way, technical assistance may be necessary to help them use the approach with comfort and skill. There are a number of useful manuals on writing goals and objectives. Mager (1972) offers a particularly clear and easy guide to follow. The use of 'action' verbs is a frequently recommended strategy for preparing effective objectives. Focusing on 'outcome or results', rather than on the 'means to an end', is also encouraged.

The alert practitioner will be aware of several pitfalls associated with using goals and objectives. One criticism has been that they are too mechanistic and do not allow the opportunity for changes that may be required as an activity develops. Another criticism is that objectives often fail to come close to achieving lofty goals. For example, a service may state that its purpose is to 'prepare children for school entrance', with stated objectives such as: 'a child will name the primary colours'; 'a child will count to 100'; and 'a child will recite the alphabet'. Such limited objectives barely take into account the array of social and cognitive skills children must have for successful school performance.

Guideline 7: Activity analysis in time and space
Once the objectives of an activity programme have been set, the next task involves selecting the appropriate activity and integrating it within a supportive time–space structure. Effective strategies for doing this have been outlined in a number of relevant works over the past two decades or so (Krueger 1978; Mand 1983; Redl and Wineman 1957; VanderVen 1972; Whittaker 1969, amongst others). Several ideas suggested by these writers are summarized below.

The first step in selecting a specific activity is to perform a task analysis, which breaks down an activity to determine its basic components. In this way, the activity's relationship to given needs or goals can be more clearly discerned, and a decision made as to whether the activity is appropriate to use with a specific group or individual. Task analysis is a powerful way of ensuring that activities can be expected to achieve desired goals, or whether the activities might actually harm the participants. A more detailed consideration of activity analysis can be found in VanderVen (1972) and Gorres (1977).

Different activities in time and space are important considerations when encouraging orientations to reality (Cumming and Cumming 1962). Activities reduce confusion, boredom, and feelings of detachment, as well as unmanageable behaviour. Activities break up time and space, and thereby contribute to the therapeutic or developmental potential of a group care centre. Effective time–space planning can be highly supportive of activity programming as follows:

Space design
  – Physical activities require a comparatively large space, without breakable or dangerous objects in the way. Similarly, messy activities should be conducted in areas where maintenance or cleanliness is not a first priority. For example, finger painting would not be conducted on a carpeted floor.
  – The activity should be compatible with the message of the space, ensuring what Savicki and Brown (1981) refer to as 'cue congruence'. For example, finger painting would not be conducted over a carpeted floor; or dodge ball in a parlour.
  – 'Small muscle' activities should be carried out in such a way that there is sufficient space for a complete range of motion for each participant.
  – The degree to which materials should be openly accessible depends on the nature of the group, and the safety and attractiveness of the materials. For example, impulse-ridden children may concentrate better if the materials needed for sequential steps of a project are visible and available only as needed. If workers want pre-school children to explore the materials at hand, then these need to be placed at the children's eye level so they can see and reach for them easily.
  – Group activities such as crafts and games are often facilitated by spatial arrangements encouraging face-to-face interaction. Tables will want to allow seating at which participants can see each other.
  – Assignment of individual workers to subgroups, rather than several workers overseeing a larger group together, can be an

effective way of encouraging interaction amongst all participants and providing support for children who need special guidance.

Time structure
- In line with Wolfensberger's (1972) principle of normalization, the time allocated for an activity should be appropriate for the time of day and the interests of the participants. For example, a game of football is probably not a suitable 'wake up' activity.
- There should be sufficient time allotted to an activity so that children experience a reasonable sense of closure or completion. For example, to have only ten minutes in which to set up and begin work on a model aeroplane would result in frustration and difficulty when ending the activity.
- Clear beginning and ending points for activities are necessary. For example, a formal schedule can help ego-deficient children to orient themselves to the social environment.
- The time allocated for an activity should be sufficient to allow for setting up, orienting the participants, terminating the activity, and, if necessary, cleaning up.
- Orientation to the activity and the time allocated to it should be given to the children. For example, 'We will be working on your model projects for the next hour or so.'
- Warning should be given prior to the formal ending of an activity: such as, 'Try to finish in about ten minutes as it will be time to get ready for dinner.' This point cannot be overstressed as a means of preventing anger and acting out. Even adults have difficulty when leaving activities they are interested in. Time is needed to prepare for a change.
- Activities should end before participants lose interest and/or behaviour deteriorates (Whittaker 1969). An activity will always look more attractive next time, if participants have a memory of interest being even slightly unfulfilled.
- Transition activities are useful in setting up and successfully maintaining attention as children move from one type of involvement to another. Bringing the group together after one activity and before starting another is one of several 'transitioning' techniques suggested by Krueger (1983). Transitions are also appropriate times for a worker to 'break the ice' with a special childhood trick or demonstration. She/he might, for example, pull a button on a string out of a back

pocket saying, 'Have you ever seen one of these?' and then show some children how to spin it.

Involving children in activities

Once activities are planned, selected, and set up, the challenge still remains of catching and sustaining the children's interest and participation. Many children with normal curiosity need little incentive to become eagerly invested in an activity. This is not always true of children with special needs. Several pointers are offered which may assist group care workers to involve children in activities.

– *Positive expectation:* Positive expectation (VanderVen 1972) means that the total demeanour of the person offering an activity assumes that the children will follow his/her bidding to participate. The unspoken message (at least to begin with) given by the worker is, 'Everyone is going to join in; I fully expect you to.' Strength of conviction often gives recalcitrant children very little chance to resist, they are simply swept up in the worker's enthusiasm. Positive expectation is actually a method of communication reflected in the worker's tone of voice and stance; Savicki and Brown (1981) and Trieschman, Whittaker and Brendtro (1969) have shown these variables are important influences on the outcome of a worker's approach to a child.
– *Using the 'Hawthorne effect':* The 'Hawthorne' or novelty effect (Parsons 1974) has little recognized, but important, implications for activity programming. These implications are that sudden exposure to something new in an environment is likely to provoke an intense response. In children's environments, the introduction of a *new* activity or plaything can have amazing results, drawing positive attention and involvement from all children. Ultimately, and since repetition of the same stimulus leads to a diminished response, a new activity should be introduced every so often, or re-introduced at periodic intervals.
– *Standards of performance:* It is paradoxical perhaps that activities which have a standard of performance (either enforced by staff or inherent in the quality of the outcomes) actually *attract* children, even impulse-laden children with low frustration

tolerance. Somehow, children rise to the expectation that they can and should deliver a good-quality performance. Contrary to popular belief, many children's services fail to make expectations for each child's performance. Knowledge of child development has often been used, and appropriately so, to ensure that expectations and performance standards for children have not been too high. However, perhaps because workers lack awareness of a child's *upper* limits of capability, such children have not been called upon to meet challenges or try to 'rise to an occasion'. Thus, workers need to be alert to assess the degree to which children can meet a particular performance standard, and then help them do so. This seems to provide children with the special feeling of mastery which is so important. Perhaps this is another reason why children do not shun activities which may have taxed them.

— *Praise and reinforcement:* 'Common sense' would suggest that a generous dose of praise now and again will motivate and sustain children's positive behaviour. However, not only does praise need to be given judiciously, but praise can also even act as a discouragement (Krueger 1978; Stipek 1983; VanderVen 1972). Activities may indeed nudge children along towards enhanced performance, encouraging praise from workers. However, care needs to be taken to ensure that praise will not imply to the child that he must always perform at this level. From fear of failing to reach his/her previous high standard, a child may, on the next occasion the activity is presented, refuse to try it, although she/he has previously been successful. Stipek (1983) recommends encouraging children to let the successful completion of an activity serve as its own reward. This does not mean that children are not praised at all. Rather, well-timed praise, carefully related to the accomplishment, is more likely to be successful. For example, 'I like the way you painted those colours on the paper,' instead of, 'Son, you're very clever,' or, 'I like the way you did that work for me.' As compared with praise, simple reinforcement techniques are often helpful in both encouraging children to complete the various steps of an activity, and in completing tasks they may perceive as unpleasant. For example, a worker may say, 'As soon as you finish sandpapering your birdhouse' — many children do not like sanding — 'you can put this bright new paint on it.' The

Premack Principle (cited by Krueger 1978) implies that a more pleasant activity can be used as a reinforcer or motivator to aid completion of a less pleasant activity that must be completed first. Following this principle, a worker may say, 'If you get your homework done, we will go out for a game of football,' or, 'When your rooms are tidied up, we can start making the snacks.'

– *Staff investment:* The *investment* of staff in helping children sustain their interest and involvement in an activity has been cited as an important variable by a number of writers (VanderVen 1972; Whittaker 1969). Such investment takes the form of workers using themselves as specific supporters and guides to help children get started in the activity. From time to time they may lose concentration and need to be helped to 'refocus' or be helped over 'snags'. The degree to which children will need staff intervention depends upon the general competence and social level they possess. At times, staff support and investment is appropriate, even for pre-school children, who frequently need intervention from adults in order to organize, focus, and sustain constructive play behaviour (Smilansky 1968).

– *Monitoring stimulation levels:* The amount and quality of environmental stimulation is a powerful influence on children's behaviour in any setting. Light, sound, texture, colour, and even smells are all worthy of consideration. The very fact of an activity taking place automatically provides some organization of sensory input. Obviously, a large gymnasium in which there is a game of dodge ball or a living room in which a group is playing table games are going to present different stimulation messages. Such messages will contrast graphically with a large room in which children are sprawling on chairs while the television drones on with its programme re-runs. There is a need, therefore, for workers who use activity programming to 'stage' stimulation so as to facilitate smooth conduct of a particular activity. Major aspects for concern are under- and over-stimulation.

Often under-stimulation in an environment is a cause for hyperactive, unfocused, irritable behaviour. Because there is not enough stimulation, children 'supply their own' by increasing their activity level. Interestingly, this viewpoint contradicts an earlier one in which children's hyperactivity was thought to be related to over-stimulation or more information coming in than they could process. Under-stimulation can also lead to withdrawn behaviour when, if there is nothing to draw the child's attention, she/he does not attend to much.

Over-stimulation can have similar effects: it can either elicit over-active behaviour or encourage withdrawal. For example, interest in infant stimulation led those unfamiliar with the needs of infants to bombard them with noise mobiles, bright toys, and incessant bouncing or chatter. For many infants the result was withdrawal and evidence of stress. With older children too, over-stimulation can have both an over-activating and a repressing effect. Birthday parties which last too long are a prime example: as the noise level rises and the amount of movement increases, children become increasingly restless and hard to manage.

Jimmy's fourth birthday party at pre-school was beginning to turn into a disaster. A contagious round of giggling had been precipitated by one of the group games and soon children were screaming and running around in circles. As the birthday child, Jimmy himself was particularly excited. A worker caught him as he sailed by, holding him until he calmed down and whispering an alternative activity for him. By this time, the others, with the help of staff, had also settled and it was possible to start a new, quieter activity.

As this illustration shows, practitioners can *actively* control the amount of sound, light, and movement in their settings, and one of the major tools for doing this is themselves. They 'mediate' the stimulation very much in the tradition of a parent who comforts an infant frightened during a storm, by picking him up and cuddling him. For children with ego deficits, mediation of stimulation by the worker is essential (Bergman and Escalona 1949).

Conclusions

This chapter has emphasized the meaning of activities in group care practice with children. Because activities also have meaning to the adults who provide them, it seems appropriate to conclude this chapter with a summary statement about how activities can be of help to the worker. There are persons in the group care field whose repertoire of activity skills is limited. For some, this may be due to an absence of knowledge. For most, the reason is probably related to a limited awareness of their own personal resources and the relevance these resources have for the children with whom they work. Some might suggest that 'being good at art' is the major prerequisite for working with children. Perhaps recalling a difficult experience with an art teacher (it is amazing how frequently this experience has been repeated) such workers resist initiating activities with children.

Because of the strong influence group care workers have as role models for the children in their care (Bertscher 1973) it is important that workers overcome their reticence and be able to show enthusiasm and a degree of competence in selected activities. This in itself serves as a strong force to involve children in purposeful activities. There are several ways of encouraging workers to be more comfortable with activities. Some suggestions might include:

- Experiential activities which provide direct exposure to different materials and then encourage practitioners to recall similar experiences in childhood. This usually yields a sudden rush of productive memory as illustrated by the following example.

   Group care workers were shown the old trick of placing a coin under a piece of paper and then rubbing it sideways with a pencil to make an outline of the coin on the paper. Many recalled having done this themselves as children, and then went on to further recall similar activities: stringing paper clips, cutting paper snowflakes, making 'cat's cradles'.

- Art experiences (in particular) where materials of varying degrees of structure are used (perhaps different shapes of pasta) to demonstrate how one does not have to be 'artistic' in order to produce many aesthetically pleasant art objects.
- Permission to be playful can be very helpful. Most child care workers have a strong identification with childhood (VanderVen 1978). This makes it all the more easy for them to be 'put in touch with' their own childhood pleasures experienced in

play and playfulness, and to recognize the acceptability of encouraging playfulness as an adult.

When the social climate of a centre is productive and interesting, it is much more likely to be so for staff as well. Recent studies of stress in group care suggest that aspects of the milieu which are not helpful for children are similarly demeaning and debilitating for the adults who 'live there too'. This contributes to diminished investment amongst workers, burn-out, and increased turnover amongst staff (Reed 1977). For this reason, staff have a lot to gain from making activity programming successful. They become more sympathetic and engaged workers who benefit from their involvement in activities in many of the same ways that children do.

This point could not be illustrated better than in the account of 'The Acorn People' (Jones 1977) which was written by a counsellor in a summer camp for severely handicapped children. The dignity of the children engaged the investment of an initially indifferent counsellor. The children were supported and their participation was encouraged in a range of 'normal' activities that they should not have been able to do. These activities included climbing a mountain in wheelchairs with the resultant experience of exhilaration and accomplishment. These children wielded a complete transformation on the attitudes of their workers as a result of their quest for programming which could bring them into the mainstream: another demonstration of the power of activity programming.

Notes

1. Karen VanderVen is Professor of Child Development and Child Care, School of Health Related Professions at the University of Pittsburgh, Pennsylvania, USA

References

Adler, J. (1976) *The Child Care Worker: Concepts, Tasks and Relationships*. New York: Brunner/Mazel.
Allen, A. J. and Mitchell, M. L. (1982) Helping the Community: An Untapped Resource for Troubled Children. *Residential Group Care* Fall: 1–4.
Alwon, F. J. (1979) An After School Activity Club Programme. *Child Care Quarterly* 8 (4): 266–78.

Argyris, C. and Schon, D. (1981) *Theory Into Practice*. San Francisco: Jossey-Bass.

Berger, J. H. (1979) The Multifaceted Levels of Play for Preschool Children. *Child Welfare* 58 (5): 327–32.

Bergman, P. and Escalona, S. (1949) Usual Sensitivities in Very Young Children. *Psychoanalytic Study of the Child*. New York: International Universities Press.

Bertscher, H. (1973) The Child Care Worker as Role Model. *Child Care Quarterly* 2 (Fall): 178–91.

Brendtro, L. K. and Ness, A. E. (1983) *Re-educating Troubled Youth: Environments for Teaching and Treatments*. New York: Aldine.

Brewis, R. (1984) *Young People in Care: A Study of the Community Service Volunteer's Children in Care Schemes, Scotland*. Stirling: University of Stirling Social Work Services Group.

Bronfenbrenner, U. (1977) Toward an Experimental Ecology of Human Development. *American Psychologist* 32: 513–30.

Bruner, J. (1968) *Toward a Theory of Instruction*. New York: W. W. Norton.

Buckholdt, D. R. and Gubrium, J. F. (1979) *Caretakers: Treating Emotionally Disturbed Children*. Beverly Hills, California: Sage Publications.

Center for Early Adolescence (1983) 3:00 to 6:00 p.m.: An Issue for the 80's. *Common Focus* 5 (2): 1–8.

Committee on Child Psychiatry (1973) *From Diagnosis to Treatment: An Approach to Treatment Planning for the Emotionally Disturbed Child*. New York: Group for Advancement of Psychiatry.

Cumming, T. and Cumming, E. (1962) *Ego and Milieu*. New York: Atherton Press.

Curry, N. (1971) Consideration of Current Basis Issues on Play. In G. Engstrom (ed.) *Play: The Child Strives Toward Self-Realization*. Washington, DC: National Association for the Education of Young Children.

Davids, A. (1975) Therapeutic Approaches to Children in Residential Treatment. *American Psychologist* 32: 809–14.

Duke, L. A. (1975) The Organization of Day Care Environments: Formal Versus Informal Activities. *Child Care Quarterly* 4 (3): 216–22.

Elkind, D. (1983) Speech delivered at the annual meeting of Pittsburgh Association for the Education of Young Children, March. Pittsburgh, Pennsylvania.

Erikson, E. (1950) *Childhood and Society*. New York: W. W. Norton.

Erikson, J. M. (with David and Joan Loveless) (1976) *Activity, Recovery, Growth: The Communal Role of Planned Activities*. New York: W. W. Norton.

Foster, G. W., VanderVen, K., Kroner, E. R., Carbonara, N. T., and Cohen, G. M. (1972) *Child Care Work with Emotionally Disturbed Children*. Pittsburgh, Pennsylvania: University of Pittsburgh Press.

Freud, A. (1966) *The Ego and the Mechanisms of Defense*, revised edition. New York: International Universities Press.

Gorres, C. (1977) Activity Programming for Disturbed Adolescents. Unpublished Master's Thesis. Pittsburgh, Pennsylvania: University of Pittsburgh.

Griff, M. (1983) Family Play Therapy. In C. Schaefer (ed.) *Handbook of Play Therapy*. New York: John Wiley.

Guindon, J. (1970) *Les étapes de la ré-éducation*. Paris: Editions Fleurus.

Herron, R. T. and Sutton-Smith, B. (1971) *Child's Play*. New York: John Wiley.

Hobbs, N. (1974) Helping Disturbed Children: Psychological and Ecological Strategies. In M. Wolins (ed.) *Successful Group Care: Explorations in the Powerful Environment*. Chicago: Aldine.

Holmes, D. J. (1964) *The Adolescent in Psychotherapy*. Boston: Little, Brown.

Hunt, D. E. (1966) A Conceptual Systems Change Model and Its Application to Education. In O. J. Harvey (ed.) *Experience, Structure and Adaptability*. New York: Springer.

Jones, R. (1977) The Acorn People: What I Learned at Summer Camp. *Psychology Today* June: 70–81.

Klein, A. (1975) *The Professional Child Care Worker*. New York: Association Press.

Krueger, M. A. (1977) The 'Program Day' as School Day in Residential Treatment. *Child Welfare* 56 (4): 271–78.

—— (1978) *Intervention Techniques for Child Care Workers*. Milwaukee, W.I.: Franklin.

—— (1983) *Careless to Caring for Troubled Youth*. Wauwatosa, Wisconsin: Tall Publishing.

Mager, R. (1972) *Goal Analysis*. Belmont, California: Fearon Publishers.

Maier, H. W. (1981) Care and Treatment Environments. In F. Ainsworth and L. C. Fulcher (eds) *Group Care for Children: Concept and Issues*. London: Tavistock.

Mand, C. (1983) Re-education Through Recreation. In L. Brendtro and A. Ness *Re-educating Troubled Youth*. New York: Aldine.

Olds, A. R. (1977) Why Is Environmental Design Important to Young Children? *Children in Contemporary Society* 11 (1): 5–7, 33.

Parsons, H. (1974) What Happened at Hawthorne? *Science* 183 (8 March): 922–32.

Peterson, R. and Brown, R. (1982) The Child Care Worker as Treatment Coordinator and Parent Trainer. *Child Care Quarterly* 11 (3): 188–203.

Powers, D. (1980) *Creating Environments for Troubled Children*. Chapel Hill, North Carolina: University of North Carolina Press.

Rasmussen, H. C. (1984) Group Care: Towards a Definition. Unpublished conference paper presented at Group Care Practice: The Challenge of the Next Decade. London: Community Care.

Redl, F. and Wineman, D. (1957) *The Aggressive Child*, 3rd edition. Glencoe, Ill.: Free Press of Glencoe.

Reed, M. J. (1977) Stress in Live-in Child Care. *Child Care Quarterly* 6 (2): 114–20.

Ross, A. L. and Bernstein, N. D. (1976) A Framework for the Therapeutic Use of Group Activities. *Child Welfare* 55 (9): 627–40.

Rubin, J. A. (1978) *Child Art Therapy: Understanding and Helping Children Grow Through Art*. New York: Van Nostrand Reinhold.

Savicki, V. and Brown, R. (1981) *Working with Troubled Children*. New York: Human Sciences Press.

Smilansky, S. (1968) *The Effects of Sociodramatic Play on Disadvantaged Pre-school Children*. New York: John Wiley.

Spivak, G. and Shure, M. (1978) *Problem-solving Techniques in Childrearing*. San Francisco: Jossey-Bass.

Stipek, D. (1983) Work Habits Begin in Pre-school. *Young Children:* 38: 25–32.

Trieschman, A. E., Whittaker, J. K., and Brendtro, L. K. (1969) *The Other 23 Hours.* Chicago: Aldine.

Tugginer, H. (1984) Staff Training and Development in Group Care Practice. Unpublished conference paper at Group Care Practice: The Challenge of the Next Decade. London: Community Care.

Vaillant, G. E. and Vaillant, C. O. (1982) Natural History of Male Psychological Health: Work as a Predictor of Positive Mental Health. In S. Chess and A. Thomas (eds) *Annual Progress in Child Psychiatry and Child Development 1968.* New York: Brunner/Mazel: 602–19.

VanderVen, K. (1965) Activity Programming for Ego Development of Severely Disturbed Children. Unpublished Master's Thesis. Pittsburgh: University of Pittsburgh.

—— (1972) Activity Programming. In G. Foster, K. VanderVen, N. Carbonana, E. Kroner, and Q. Cohen *Child Care Work with Emotionally Disturbed Children.* Pittsburgh: University of Pittsburgh Press.

—— (1975) Agency Administration, Effective Child Treatment and Professionalization of Child Care Workers: Some Relationships and Suggestions. Unpublished paper delivered at Child Care sessions, American Orthopsychiatric Association, Atlanta, Georgia.

—— (1976) The Impact of Play: How Play Facilitates Optimal Growth and Development. *Children in Contemporary Society* 9 (March): 50–2.

—— (1977) Art in the Therapeutic Milieu. In *Perspectives on Art Therapy: The Proceedings of the Second Pittsburgh Conference on Art Therapy.* Pittsburgh, Pennsylvania.

—— (1978) A Paradigm Describing Stages of Personal and Professional Development of Child Care Practitioners with Characteristics Associated with Each Stage. *Proceedings of Ninth International Congress of the International Association of Workers with Maladjusted Children.* Montreal, Canada.

—— (1984) How Adults Think About Children; A Significant Variable in Their Development and Potential Well Being. To be published in *Pittsburgh Association for the Education of Young Children, Anniversary Publication.*

VanderVen K. and Griff, M. (1978) Expanded Roles for Child Care Workers: Work with Families. Unpublished paper.

VanderVen, K. and Mattingly, M. (1980) Action Agenda for Child Care Education in the 80's: From Setting to Systems. *Child Care Quarterly* 10 (3): 279–88.

VanScoy, H. (1972) Activity Group Therapy: A Bridge Between Play and Work. *Child Welfare* 51 (8): 528–34.

—— (1976) The Child Care Worker as an Activity Group Co-therapist. *Child Care Quarterly* 5 (3): 221–28.

Whittaker, J. K. (1969) Program Activities. In A. E. Trieschman, J. K. Whittaker and L. K. Brendtro *The Other 23 Hours.* Chicago, Ill.: Aldine.

—— (1976) Differential Use of Program Activities in Child Treatment Groups. *Child Welfare* 55 (7): 459–67.

—— (1979) *Caring for Troubled Children.* San Francisco: Jossey-Bass.

Wilson, T. (1977) Creating a Diversified Activity Program in a Small Psychiatric Institution for Children. *Child Care Quarterly* 6 (4): 248–58.
Wolfensberger, W. (1972) *The Principle of Normalization in Human Services.* Toronto: National Institute on Mental Retardation.

Section III

Indirect work on behalf
of children

8 Resident group influences on team functioning

Gale E. Burford and
Leon C. Fulcher

Introduction

This study was carried out as part of an overall staff development and training effort begun in 1977 at Shawbridge Youth Centres in Montreal, Canada. Prior to that time, changes in the social policy environment at provincial, regional, and community levels had so impacted care and treatment programs in the agency, that rapid change and expansion were commonplace.[1] An increase in the number of secure unit beds and the addition of detention services, along with the sudden admission of girls into a service established for boys, forestalled most efforts aimed at treatment in the agency. In some instances, rapid change threatened to compromise the agency's own expectations concerning quality of care and education for the children and young people it served. Staff development and training activity was established around two major objectives: (1) to support staff in fulfilling the expectations of their job and living-unit programme descriptions; and (2) to introduce a set of practice standards for child care in the agency as a whole.

The action research project which accompanied staff training and development sought to develop further understanding about the nature of staff team functioning as a central component of residential group care and treatment. Since 1968 Shawbridge Youth Centres have used differential classification as a diagnostic basis for planning the control and treatment of delinquents admitted into its residential, day, and fieldwork programs. As such, the setting lent itself to a study which looks at the interplay between selected groupings of residents and staff teams. Specifically, this study sought to determine whether particular patterns of satisfaction, frustration, and/or uncertainty in quality of working life were evident amongst staff teams depending on the diagnostic characteristics of the resident group.

A review of the relevant research and practice literature

In recent years, the argument that 'nothing works' has been shown to be the result of broad generalizations about a very complex area of study. While policy makers in North America have been swayed by these arguments, some practitioners, agency managers, and researchers have continued to press home the point that selected interventions do work with particular groups of offenders under certain conditions (Gendreau and Ross 1979; Jesness 1980; Jesness *et al.* 1972; Palmer 1974, 1976, 1978; Ross and Gendreau 1980; Warren 1983). Many researchers have noted the masking effect which occurs when all youngsters, programs of care and treatment, methods of intervention, staff, and conditions under which services were provided are grouped together for evaluation purposes (Gendreau and Ross 1979; Grant and Grant 1959; Hunt 1971; Jessness 1965, 1971; Lukin 1981; Megargee 1977; Palmer 1978; Quay 1977). Programmes which have used differential methods of assessment and other programme elements have contributed much to our knowledge about what works, with whom, and under what conditions.

Practice wisdom would suggest that in some instances the characteristics of young people placed in a residential centre will impact the functioning of individual staff members and the functioning of teams of care-givers as a whole. Any team of workers who have had to cope with the admission of a resident, whose needs drastically alter the social climate of the centre, would probably agree that this is so. The literature on transference and counter-transference phenomena would suggest that some forms of influence between the characteristics of particular residents and particular staff may be especially subtle and even more enduring. Still the knowledge available about these influences and dynamics is still largely at the level of speculation or assumptive wisdom.

Some researchers who have used differential assessment methods to control for characteristics of both client and service provider have concluded that the inappropriate matching of client and worker is among the most important decisions of all to be faced. That this should be so important a variable is supported by researchers both inside and outside the group care field. When controlling for differences between types of children, style of teaching or counselling, and setting, researchers have demonstrated that such a match can result in important differences in terms of behaviour management, educational achievement, treatment outcomes, and/or cost-effectiveness (Andre and Mahan 1972; Brill 1978; Hunt 1971; Palmer 1976; Warren 1983).

Palmer (1976) found that by matching an 'internally oriented' fieldworker with 'internally conflicted' delinquent young people, it was possible to identify differences in patterns of rearrest, reconviction, and recidivism. These differences could be accounted for up to four years after treatment in community-based projects which had used a variety of residential programs as back-up. While the use of matching was indicated for certain other sub-types, none of the results were quite so spectacular as with those involving 'internally conflicted' young people. Barkwell (1976) replicated this study in a juvenile probation setting in Manitoba, Canada, finding that the more intensive the contact between worker and client, the more important it became to avoid inappropriate matching. Worker style was asserted to be a major variable predicting outcome.

Andre and Mahan (1972) found differences in the performance of students who were matched with the style of their teachers when compared with those who were not matched. The characteristics of preferred teaching plans (including 'atmosphere' of classroom), procedures for motivating students, curriculum content, and behaviour management strategies were defined. Students in the homogeneous classrooms did as well as or outperformed the students in regular classrooms on all measures. In addition, staff satisfaction with teaching assignments was reported as higher in the homogeneous classrooms.

Utility of the Conceptual Level matching model has been demonstrated in a variety of settings including, for example, the classroom (Tomlinson and Hunt 1971), group psychotherapy with alcoholics (McLachlan 1972, 1974), and residential education programs (Hunt and Hardt 1967). In each instance, students or patients were matched with the level of program structure and/or the Conceptual Level of the teacher or therapist. Of particular relevance to practice in residential group care settings is the finding by Brill (1978) that delinquent boys whose Conceptual Levels were 'matched' with that of their 'primary worker' evidenced fewer behaviour problems during their period of placement and for at least six months during follow-up than did a group of mismatched controls. In separate studies where group care and treatment environments were matched to the type of youngster, Palmer (1972) and Jesness (1971) found benefits for particular types of youngsters ranging from reduced recidivism to decreased management problems. In the former, the perceived needs of youngsters were taken into account when one of five group home 'atmospheres' was selected and in the latter, residents were grouped homogeneously according to assessment characteristics. While valuable enough in their own right to beg careful application and further research, these findings are unable to account for a dimension of group care practice thought to have considerable relevance to planning and outcome, that involving the complex dimension of teamwork.

During the course of a 168-hour work week, residents may come into contact with a variety of 'types' of workers, educators, administrators, volunteers, and other auxiliary personnel. They will also be in contact with other residents who are different from themselves. As such, reciprocal influences become more difficult to evaluate, restricting applications of a single-subject research design where interactions between one worker and one resident are investigated. Still the team variable remains something of an enigma. The value of a team approach has become a prominent theme in the group and organizational literature, prompting a plethora of ideas associated with team building, team development, and teamwork, to mention but a few. It has always been assumed that the collective and co-operative actions of staff were of major importance in group care settings where a number of different workers engage youngsters or groups of residents through a variety of mediums (Fulcher 1979). Within the residential centre itself, it has been difficult to evaluate the impact of multiple staff interactions with children around the tasks and meaning of experience in day-to-day living (Maier 1981; Mattingly 1977; Ross 1983; Whittaker 1979).

One way researchers have sought to account for the collective actions of staff has been through attempting to measure the degree of program implementation (Scheirer and Rezmovic 1983). Researchers attempting to control for program design and operation, have found that staff frequently work from program designs and/or job descriptions which are insufficiently detailed to guide staff interventions at the minimum, let alone satisfy requirements for reliability, validity, or accountability (Quay 1977). Johnson (1981) found that programs tend to 'drift' from their intended practices and that 'program drift' tends to occur for a variety of reasons.

The idea of 'team building' is not a new one. The foundations for this idea are to be found in the literature on small group theory and studies of organizational behaviour. The influence of Bales (1950), Homans (1950), Lewin (1952), and others is unmistakable when analysing the daily assumptions made about small groups in the work setting. The concepts of norms, roles, cohesion, interaction, group systems or subsystems, and group activities are all part of the language taken for granted when discussing the collective of individuals we call a team. The metaphor of an athletic team is perhaps the best-known analogy amongst group care workers. Most workers have been introduced to the idea of two or more members executing a series of linked behaviours aimed at a single outcome.

An example of the expectation for 'team performance' is evident in the illustration of a fifteen-year-old girl placed in a short-term emergency care unit. While the initial assessment clearly predicted the girl's propensity for initiating seductive behaviour with male workers, some staff during the initial phase overlooked her suggestive comments when they were alone with her. These escalated into further manipulative behaviour on two or three occasions by 'acting as if something forbidden had been going on' when a female worker entered the room where she and a male worker were alone. After an initial period of hostile reaction when all staff began to challenge her each time she initiated sexual conversation or engaged in inappropriate sexual behaviour, only then did she reveal a history (later confirmed) of family incest which had been concealed up to that time.

In examples like this one and numerous others in the literature on group care, teamwork is easier to define when 'it' does not happen than it is to describe, in a practical way, when found in its optimal state. In attempting to construct a typology of residential environments, Moos (1975) sought to isolate and measure those aspects of social climate which were thought to influence behaviour of staff and residents. Moos argued that the satisfactions of both groups may be related to some indicators of program quality such as reduced absconding. While this is not the only attempt to relate job satisfactions with measures of output, in the main researchers have found little support for this conclusion (Argyle 1972). Perhaps one of Moos's most valuable contributions to the group care field so far has been to link the perception of staff as a group to the residents as a group around a common set of dimensions: relationship, treatment, and system maintenance. As such, Moos's methodology has received support from practitioners because it stimulates focused discussion between staff members, or between staff and residents, about whether or not people are working together towards shared aims.

Hall has argued that while job satisfactions vary, particularly in relation to a member's position in the occupational hierarchy, 'it is the meeting of expectations that contributes most to job satisfactions' (1969: 47). Argyle has contributed the idea that 'job satisfaction is greater among workers who belong to a cohesive group and are accepted by it' (1972: 248). Job dissatisfaction on the other hand appears related to a number of factors such as 'types of work, age, ... sex, ... and minority group membership' (Hall 1969: 53).

In an attempt to control for the collective variable of a team of group care staff, Fulcher (1983) used a measure of self-reported work satisfaction, frustration, and uncertainty (Heimler 1975, 1979) with individual members of work groups attached to residential and day care centres. By extending Hertzberg's (1968) traditional job satisfaction paradigm to include frustration and satisfaction activities on and off the job (Bronfenbrenner 1979a, 1979b), and by studying the functioning of group care teams with a wider 'quality-of-working life' paradigm (Davis and Cherns

1975), Fulcher constructed a 'team functioning dimension'. The most salient influences on team functioning were found to include: siting and physical design of the centre, ratio of female to male workers, percentage of married or co-habiting workers, living in tied accommodation, trade union membership, the degree of predictability encountered in the external organizational environment, and the type of social policy mandate (Fulcher 1983).

A pilot study: sample, measurement, and limitations

In this pilot study, an attempt was made to examine whether the diagnostic composition of resident groups and the functioning of staff teams may impact one another, and if so, to form hypotheses for further examination into this aspect of group care practice. An analysis of correlation is given in relation to pre-selected characteristics about residents in group care services for delinquent youngsters (independent variables) and staff members providing services (dependent variables)[2] (see *Figure 8.1*). Besides including certain demographic data for both groups, two different diagnostic

Figure 8.1 Preselected variables – residents and staff

Resident data – independent variables	Staff data – dependent variables
mean age	length of time in post
median age	mean age
number of residents	percentage of women
number of resident groups	percentage of members
interpersonal maturity	with degrees
level	percentage of unqualified
sub-type	members
conceptual level	percentage never married
	percentage of staff with children of
	their own
	work orientations schedule
	satisfactions
	frustrations
	total outlook

Source: Shawbridge Youth Centres 1978, 1979, 1980

typologies were used with residents to isolate different psychological characteristics and two instruments were used with staff members to measure self-reported change (Holmes and Masuda 1974; Holmes and Rahe 1967) and quality of working life satisfaction and frustrations (Heimler and Fulcher 1981).

A. The sample

Founded in 1907, the Boys Farm and Training School was re-named Shawbridge Youth Centres during a period of rapid growth and expansion in the mid-1970s. The agency provides a continuum of care for acting-out and delinquent boys and girls between the ages of twelve and seventeen using secure units, campus-style institutional cottages, group home and community residence facilities, day care, and fieldwork programmes. All youngsters occupying a residential bed on 5 September 1978, 15 April 1979 and 15 January 1980 were included in the study. Demographic and diagnostic information was taken from files in the assessment division under the direction of the Directors of Treatment and Professional Services. In every case, the most recent assessment or reassessment data on the youngster prior to the calendar date of data collection were selected, and recorded separately for each year.

All child care, supervisory, and auxiliary staff attached to a residential living unit on the calendar dates in question were invited to participate in the study. A team was not included in the sample unless 90 per cent of its membership submitted their questionnaires. A more detailed breakdown of resident group and staff team variables is provided in *Figures 8.2* and *8.3*.

Resident characteristics – see Figure 8.2

1. Demographic data included mean and median ages of residents in each living unit taken separately for each year, the total number of residents, age range, and number of places or beds in the centre.

2. Interpersonal Maturity Classification System: Juvenile (Warren *et al.* 1966). While the seven maturity levels in this classification system are theoretical descriptions of development around perceptual integration levels, the nine behavioural sub-types were empirically derived from data collected on delinquents found at different maturity levels. The system yields three diagnostic possibilities all used in this study:

Figure 8.2 Overall resident data by year

	1978	1979	1980
Total number of residents	100	113	93
Total number of resident groups	10	11	11
Mean age	16.1	16.3	16.3
Median age	16	16.3	16.2
Inter-personal maturity			
No. of Integration Level Three (I3) youths	26	24	23
No. of Conforming youths	17	13	12
No. of Power-oriented youths	9	9	8
No. of Integration Level Four (I4) youths	73	88	69
No. of Conflicted youths	69	81	64
No. of Neurotic Acting-out	29	44	40
No. of Neurotic Anxious	40	37	24
No. of other levels and sub-types	5	10	9
Conceptual level			
No. of Stage A (0.0–1.89)	23	29	28
No. of Stage AB (0.9–1.2)	52	42	39
No. of Stage B (1.21–1.5)	16	26	18
No. of Stage BC (1.51 and up)	9	14	8

Source: Shawbridge Youth Centres 1978, 1979, 1980

– Maturity Level (Warren *et al.* 1966): Studies have shown that the vast majority of delinquents fall into three of the seven maturity levels, with small numbers falling into a fourth. This sample contained only Maturity Level Three (middle maturity) and Maturity Level Four (higher maturity) youths.
– Delinquent sub-type (Warren *et al.* 1966): Of the nine sub-types, only five were found in this sample: the Immature Conformist (CFM), the Anti-social Manipulator (MP), and the Cultural Conformist (CFC) are middle maturity or Level Three (I3) youngsters; and the Neurotic Anxious (Nx) and the Neurotic Acting-out (Na), are higher maturity or Level Four (I4) youngsters. Research has shown that only a small percentage of non-delinquent youth can be described by any of these delinquent sub-types (Harris 1983).
– Delinquent subgroup (Palmer 1974): These three subgroupings collapse certain of the sub-types together because of characteristics they have in common; they are: the Internally Conflicted group (Neurotic Anxious and Neurotic Acting-out sub-types taken together), the Power-oriented group (Anti-social

Manipulator and Cultural Conformist sub-types taken together), and the Passive Conformists (the Immature Conformist group).

3. Each living unit in the study was rank ordered by the percentage of each I-Level classification (maturity level, delinquent sub-type, delinquent subgroup) taken separately, and using the median to divide the resident groups into two subgroups (fewer/more) which could be used for comparative evaluation.

4. Conceptual Level (Hunt *et al.* 1978): This assessment involves a six-item sentence-completion test which provides a measure of cognitive complexity. While two final scores are yielded, the C.L.6 or the combined score for the six items was used for this study. The following scoring ranges were used: Stage A = 0.0–0.89; Stage AB = 0.9–1.2; Stage B = 1.21–1.5; Stage BC = 1.51 and up. Stage AB was determined solely for the purpose of this study. This was done because so many of the youngsters fell below 1.0 and yet were above 0.5 on the measure of conceptual complexity. This particular range is frequently described clinically as a stage of transition, suggesting that the youngster is beginning to show some acceptance of rules which indicates minimal conformity. Three categories of Conceptual Level data were generated for this study:

- Stage: Each living unit in the study was rank ordered by the percentage of youngsters in the group in each Conceptual Level stage taken separately. The median was used to divide the groups into two subgroupings for comparison, done separately for each year.
- Group mean: The mean was calculated for each living unit and rank ordered separately for each year, again using the median to divide the groups into two subgroupings for comparison.
- Group stage: Each group was classified consistent with the lowest Conceptual Level Stage to account for one-third of the population of the living unit. For example, if one-third of the group were Stage A youngsters, the group was classified as a Stage A group and so on in ascending order until a particular stage accounted for one-third of the group.

Staff characteristics – see Figure 8.3

1. Demographic data included number of staff in each unit, mean age of staff, mean length of time in post (months),

Figure 8.3 Staff characteristics by year

	1978	1979	1980
Number of staff	78.0	59.0	96.0
Mean age (years)	30.2	32.6	32.2
Mean length of time in post (months)	15.4	21.6	20.6
Percentage of women	36.8	37.7	36.3
Percentage of members with degrees	51.8	48.9	50.4
Percentage of unqualified members	19.0	23.5	22.6
Percentage never married	33.9	21.5	27.1
Percentage staff with children	30.3	41.5	38.6

Source: Shawbridge Youth Centres 1978, 1979, 1980

percentages of women, members with degrees, unqualified members, those married or single, and those with children of their own.

2. The Schedule of Recent and Anticipated Events (Holmes and Rahe 1967): Four scores were used from this 43-item measure of past and predicted change.

– Past change: Total mean change was calculated for each item separately for each year. Teams were rank ordered and the median was used to divide the teams into two subgroupings for comparison.
– Future change: Same procedure as for past change.
– Past/future change total: Same procedure using the mean for total past/future change.
– Past/future change: Same procedure using the difference between past and future change means for each team.

3. The Work Orientation Schedule (Heimler 1970; amended by Fulcher (Fulcher and Ainsworth 1981)): This 55-item measure of satisfaction and frustration is scored as follows: 'yes' = 4, 'perhaps' = 2, 'no' = 0. Mean scores were aggregated for each team on the following dimensions:

– Total Satisfaction Score (BPS): Sum of all 'yes' answers in 'work', 'finance', 'social life', 'home life', 'personal contract'.
– Total Potential Satisfaction Score (GPS): Same as above including 'perhaps' answers.
– Area Satisfaction Scores: Sum of 'yes' answers taken separately for 'work', 'finance', 'social life', 'home life', 'personal contract'.

- Area Potential Satisfaction Score: Same as Area Satisfaction Scores above including 'perhaps' answers.
- Total Frustration Score (BNS): Sum of all 'yes' answers in 'activity', 'health', 'personal influence', 'moods', 'habits'.
- Total Potential Frustration Score (GNS): Same steps as Total Frustration Score above including 'perhaps' answers.
- Area Frustration Scores: Sum of 'yes' answers taken separately for 'activity', 'health', 'personal influence', 'moods', 'habits'.
- Area Potential Frustration Scores: Same as Area Frustration Scores above including 'perhaps' answers.
  - Outlook total: Mean Average of raw scores for each team.
  - Outlook subscores: Mean Average of raw scores for each team taken separately for: Achieved Ambition, Hope for the Future, Meaning in Life, Opportunity for Self-Expression and Life Worthwhile.
  - Functioning at best score: Ratio of satisfactions to frustrations when potential satisfactions (GPS) are compared with certainty in frustrations (BNS).
  - Functioning at worst score: Ratio of satisfactions to frustrations when certainty in satisfactions (BPS) is compared with potential frustrations (GNS).
  - Positive swing score: The difference between certainty of satisfactions (BPS) and potential satisfactions (GPS). This score indicates the amount of uncertainty reported about satisfactions.
  - Negative swing score: The difference between certainty of frustrations (BNS) and potential frustrations (GNS). This score indicates the amount of uncertainty reported about frustrations.
  - Average frustration: The mean of the overall frustrations (MNS) compared with the overall satisfactions (MPS) scores.

B. Measurement

A Pearson Product–Moment analysis of correlation was selected to analyse the relationship between the independent variables (resident characteristics and data) and the dependent variables (staff characteristics and data) separately for each year. The pre-selected level of acceptance was set at $r > .05$ and $r2 > .7$ (Knapp 1978).

C. Limitations

The results of this study suffer from all of the flaws associated with research which comes about as an afterthought to practice. Such limitations render the findings somewhat unpredictable in so far as they can be interpreted beyond the particular setting in which they were obtained.

First, the diagnostic criteria used with residents in this study is very specific to the two assessment typologies in question. For example, the young people classified as Neurotic by the I-Level system may or may not be viewed that way by other systems of diagnosis and classification. Generalizations of this kind must be left to rigorous cross-classification studies. The same would appear to be true for the Conceptual Level model. While there may be some temptation to generalize to other cognitive models, Conceptual Level would appear to be a very specific measure.

Second, no attempt was made to actually observe or record in any rigorous way the behaviours or expressions of attitude relative to what satisfied and what frustrated the staff. A measure of staff perception of quality of working life satisfactions and frustrations was used instead.

A third limitation means that the data cannot be generalized over time since some team members and residents were present during more than one of the years in which the samples were drawn. For the same reason, the data cannot be lumped together to form an aggregate sample. While other kinds of statistical analysis might have been used to reduce the suspected bias in this regard, other sources of bias would have been introduced if this were done because of the type of data collected in the study. For example, the Work Orientation Schedule permits only three possible answers: 'yes', 'perhaps', or 'no'. By itself, this is certainly not interval or ratio level data which would permit the use of more sophisticated analytic procedures. By taking the average scores for each team and rank ordering these, it was suggested that data could be yielded of the higher order necessary. However, several researchers, consulted on this point, disagreed.

Finally, the youngsters and the staff were not randomly assigned to living units. They were assigned on the basis of clinical and professional hunch, as well as the frequently occurring need to put a resident in a vacant bed and a staff member in a vacant position. In spite of these limitations, the data still lend themselves – in their present form – to some objective interpretations within the framework outlined above.

Analysis of the findings

The relationships between resident group composition and patterns of team functioning at Shawbridge Youth Centres between 1978 and 1980 are summarized below.

Figure 8.4 Resident data (IV) *v.* staff data (DV) 1978 (Pearson r²)

| | Satisfactions | | | | |
	B work	G work	B home	G home	B soc. life
Conform			0.71	0.81	
			(0.016)	(0.004)	
NXs					−0.72
					(0.015)
CL stage	0.71	0.71			
	(0.017)	(0.016)			
Stage A*					

| | Frustrations | | | |
	B habits	G habits	Worst	Av. frust.
Conform				
Nxs				
CL stage	−0.75	−0.79	−0.75	−0.72
	(0.010)	(0.005)	(0.010)	(0.014)
Stage A*	0.72	0.75		
	(0.015)	(0.010)		

Source: Shawbridge Youth Centres
Notes: B active, B–G Health, G Moods all 0.62 or better (0.033, 0.037, 0.025, 0.033)

1978 – *see* Figure 8.4

1. The teams of employees working in living units with higher percentages of Passive Conforming youngsters reported higher average satisfaction and higher potential satisfaction in the Home Life Area.

2. The teams of employees working in living units with higher percentages of Neurotic Anxious youngsters reported fewer average satisfactions in the Social Life Area.

3. The teams of employees working in living units with groups of higher Conceptual Level 'stage' reported higher satisfactions in the Work Area; less frustrations in the Habits Area; and less frustration overall.

4. The teams of employees working in living units with groups that had a higher percentage of 'Stage A' (Conceptual Level) youngsters reported more frustrations in the Habits Area.

1979 — see Figure 8.5

Figure 8.5a Resident data (IV) *v.* staff data (DV) 1979 (Pearson r²)

		Satisfactions					
	GS	B soc. life	G soc. life	B home	G home	BPS	PO swing
I3s*		0.80	0.84				−0.86
		(0.008)	(0.005)				(0.003)
Power							
Conform		0.88	0.93			0.70	−0.87
		(0.002)	(0.000)			(0.026)	(0.002)
I4s		−0.80	−0.83			−0.72	0.92
		(0.008)	(0.006)			(0.023)	(0.001)
Conflicted		−0.77	−0.82			−0.78	0.93
		(0.012)	(0.007)			(0.011)	(0.000)
NAs				−0.80	−0.81		
				(0.009)	(0.007)		
NXs	−0.70						
	(0.028)						
Sub-types		0.72	0.72			0.75	−0.88
		(0.023)	(0.022)			(0.016)	(0.002)

Note: BPS .6919 (0.29)

1. The teams of employees working in living units with higher percentages of Maturity Level Three (I3 or middle maturity) youngsters reported higher satisfactions and less uncertainty about satisfactions.

2. The teams of employees working in living units with higher percentages of Power-oriented youngsters reported fewer potential frustrations in the Habits Area. These teams reported much less uncertainty in the Habits Area although they reported about the same overall amount of frustration as other teams.

3. The teams of employees working in living units with higher percentages of Passive Conforming youngsters reported higher

Figure 8.5b Resident data (IV) v. staff data (DV) 1979 (Pearson r²)

	G active	G health	B influ.	G moods	G habits	Neg. swing	BNS	GNS	Best	Worst	X̄ frust.
					Frustrations						
I3s Power					−0.73 (0.021)						
Conform											
I4s Conflicted			0.70 (0.028)			0.70 (0.028)					
NAs											
NXs	0.74 (0.018)	0.72 (0.022)		0.87 (0.002)	0.97 (0.000)		0.85 (0.003)	0.85 (0.003)	0.84 (0.004)	0.74 (0.018)	0.80 (0.009)
Sub-types			−0.71 (0.023)								

Source: Shawbridge Youth Centres

satisfactions in the Social Life Area; greater overall satisfactions; and less overall uncertainty about satisfactions.

4. The teams of employees working in living units with higher percentages of Maturity Level Four (higher maturity) youngsters reported fewer satisfactions in the Social Life Area; fewer overall satisfactions; and greater overall uncertainty about satisfactions.

5. The teams of employees working in living units with higher percentages of Conflicted youngsters reported fewer satisfactions in the Social Life Area; fewer satisfactions overall and greater uncertainty about satisfactions; greater frustrations in the Personal Influence Area; and greater uncertainty about frustrations overall.

6. The teams of employees working in living units with higher percentages of Neurotic Acting-out youngsters reported fewer satisfactions in the Home Life Area.

7. The teams of employees working in living units with higher percentages of Neurotic Anxious youngsters reported fewer potential satisfactions in the Finance Area, and more potential frustrations in the Activity Area; greater frustration in the Health, Moods, and Habits areas; more frustrations overall; a higher 'Functioning at Best' score, a lower 'Functioning at Worst' score, and the highest average frustration scores.

1980 – see Figure 8.6

1. The teams of employees working in living units with higher percentages of Maturity Level Three (I3 or middle maturity) youngsters reported fewer frustrations in the Personal Influence Area.

2. The teams of employees working in living units with higher percentages of Passive Conforming youngsters reported less uncertainty about overall satisfactions; less potential frustration in the Personal Influence Area; and fewer frustrations overall.

3. The teams of employees working in living units with higher percentages of Power-oriented youngsters reported more potential frustrations in the Moods area.

4. The teams of staff working in living units with higher percentages of Neurotic Acting-out youngsters reported less certainty of satisfaction in the Home Life Area.

5. The teams of staff working in living units with higher 'Stage'

Figure 8.6 Resident data (IV) *v.* staff data (DV) 1980 (Pearson r^2)

| | Satisfactions | |
	PO swing	B home
I3s		
Conform*	−0.76	
	(0.003)	
Power		
NAs		−0.82
		(0.001)
Conceptual level		0.72
stage		(0.006)

| | Frustrations | | | | |
	B influence	G influence	B moods	G moods	BNS
I3s	−0.73	−0.74			
	(0.006)	(0.005)			
Conform*	−0.83	−0.83			−0.71
	(0.001)	(0.001)			(0.007)
Power			0.78	0.81	
			(0.002)	(0.001)	
NAs					
Competence level					
Stage					

Source: Shawbridge Youth Centres
Note: * + BPS, − GNS 0.68 or better (0.011, 0.009)

Conceptual Level resident groups reported greater certainty of satisfaction in the Home Life Area.

Maturity level

Percentage of I-Level Three (I3) residents was predictive of higher satisfaction (Social Life, 1979), lower frustration (Influence, 1980), and greater certainty about satisfactions (Positive Swing, 1979). Percentage of I-Level Four (I4) residents was predictive of lower satisfaction (Social Life and Overall Satisfactions, 1979) and greater uncertainty about satisfactions (Social Life and Positive Swing, 1979) amongst the staff teams investigated.

Delinquent sub-type

The Neurotic Acting-out Sub-type youngsters accounted for lower satisfaction (Home Life, 1979 and 1980) and lower certainty about satisfaction (Home Life, 1979) amongst staff teams.

The Neurotic Anxious Sub-type youngsters accounted for lower satisfaction (Social Life, 1978) and higher uncertainty about satisfaction (Finance, 1979); higher frustration (Health, Moods, Habits, Overall Frustrations, and Average Frustrations, 1979) and more uncertainty about frustration (Activity, Health, Moods, Habits, Potential Frustrations, 1979); and highest ratio of frustration to satisfaction (Functioning at Best and Functioning at Worst, 1979).

The Immature Conformist Sub-type youngsters accounted for higher satisfactions (Home Life, 1978; Social Life and Overall Satisfactions, 1979) and greater certainty about satisfactions (Home Life, 1978; Social Life, 1979; and Positive Swing, 1979); lower frustration (Personal Influence, 1980) and greater certainty about frustrations (Personal Influence, 1980).

Because of the comparatively small numbers of Cultural Conformist and Manipulator Sub-type youngsters in the study, the two groups were evaluated together under the 'Power Oriented' heading for 'Delinquent Subgroups'.

Delinquent subgroup

The Conflicted subgroup accounted for lower satisfaction (Social Life and Overall Satisfactions, 1979) and greater uncertainty about satisfaction (Social Life and Positive Swing, 1979). The Passive Conforming subgroup findings were the same as for the Immature Conformist Sub-type.

The Power-oriented subgroup accounted for higher frustration and uncertainty about some frustrations (Moods, 1980) and less uncertainty about other frustrations (Habits, 1979).

Conceptual level stage

Low Conceptual Level, Stage A youngsters accounted for higher frustration (Habits, 1978) and greater uncertainty about frustration (Habits, 1978).

Conceptual level group mean

Accounted for nothing.

Conceptual level group stage

Higher Conceptual Level Stage groups accounted for higher satisfaction (Work, 1978; Home Life, 1980), less uncertainty about satisfactions (Work, 1978); less frustration (Habits and Average Frustrations, 1978), less uncertainty about frustrations (Habits, 1978) and a higher ratio of satisfaction to frustrations (Functioning at Worst, 1978).

Discussion

Resident characteristics

The diagnostic characteristics of residents based on the Interpersonal Maturity Classification System: Juvenile, and the Conceptual Level Matching Model, appear to interact differentially with the team functioning dimension. While it has already been established that these characteristics are important considerations when making individual assignments of worker and teacher, they also appear to have relevance for work with teams in group care practice.

Conforming youngsters   The pattern of higher satisfaction, lower frustration, and greater certainty in teams working with more of these young people is not surprising based on clinical impressions that such youngsters are oriented towards rules and compliance towards rules. These youths are said to gain in feelings of security when the structure around them is clear and definite, when relationships are perceived by them to be safe and fair, and when they gain the approval of persons whom they perceive to be powerful. One staff member with experience of work with conforming youngsters acknowledged that 'they need a firm, stable parent figure with whom they feel protected and who can also educate them to stand up and take care of themselves'.

Power-oriented youngsters   The pattern of higher frustration in teams working with more of these youngsters is not surprising, although the levels of frustration might have been expected to be even higher. The amount of manipulation and anger so frequently evidenced by this group, coupled with their superficial ability to relate to others on the basis of power, render other residents and many staff wary of their variable and hostile behaviour patterns. Other studies show that staff who get along with these youngsters best are those who can keep 'one step ahead of them' and not be easily misled by superficial acquiescence to authority (Palmer and Grenny 1971). Practice wisdom came from one worker who declared that: 'They have to know that I can and will control them but they also need fair play.'

Neurotic sub-types Again the variable patterns of lower satisfaction, greater frustration, and greater uncertainty are not surprising given the clinical descriptions associated with these youngsters. It probably comes as no surprise to experienced group care workers that the teams working with these youths became emotionally involved in such a way that their social and home life satisfactions were reduced and levels of frustration and uncertainty were increased. However, there is an absence of documentation of this phenomenon except in descriptive or anecdotal accounts. What is even more interesting to the authors is the apparent 'contagion' with which this may occur in the 'off duty' (home/social life) areas for teams who work with higher proportions of neurotic residents. It is as if staff teams periodically internalize, in some way, the tortured self-concepts which these youths are said to manifest and carry this over into their relationships outside the centre. One experienced group care worker is quoted: 'You can't just supervise these kids, you have to develop a relationship with them and talk about the things which are important to them.'

Conceptual level Once again the patterns which emerge come as little surprise in light of the characteristics described by Conceptual Level. The low Conceptual Level youngster is described as being the most concrete in his/her thinking, is extremely egocentric, and is said to take a negative anti-authority stance towards others. In addition, there is an absence of internalized, culturally accepted beliefs and values. While this type of young person has the potential to present high frustration to staff at all times, this would probably be greatest, according to Conceptual Level theory, when structure is too low or when expectations are perceived by them as ambiguous (Reitsma-Street 1982). Higher Conceptual Level residents are thought to be more comfortable with some uncertainty, for example in a 'discovery' approach to learning where they must take some initiative (Brill 1978).

Staff characteristics

The demographic variables   The social background information collected from staff teams did not correlate significantly with any of the resident group characteristics. This is somewhat difficult to understand since variables such as sex and marital status have played so prominent a role in other studies of job satisfaction and in Fulcher's (1983) wider study of team functioning with a large international sample. It is possible that these variables were masked because of the small numbers in the sample or that they become less influential in mediating the differences between characteristics of residents. Perhaps the intensity of involvement between neurotic youths and staff in residential group care is at times such a powerful element in staff team functioning that almost everyone is affected.

The life events measure   Variables derived from the Schedule of Recent and Anticipated Experiences (Holmes and Rahe 1967) did not correlate with any of the resident characteristics. This is not surprising in the light of recent findings which suggest that many life measures appear to mask subjective interpretations of events by individuals, the complex associations between events, sex differences, and a number of methodological problems (Kale and Stenmark 1983; Lester, Leitner, and Posner 1983; Monroe 1982; Zimmerman 1983).

The work orientation measures   Variables derived from the Work Orientation Schedule (Heimler and Fulcher 1981) were highly correlated with many of the resident group characteristics under investigation. As such, this instrument would seem to provide an unobtrusive measure of quality of working life which offers distinct advantages over the more traditional job satisfaction measures. A variety of themes can be identified through the use of the Work Orientation Schedule, illuminating satisfactions, frustrations, and uncertainties in working life. These themes appear to be influential for individual workers and for group care centres as a whole, since they are instrumental in shaping patterns of team functioning and performance over time. While developmental research with this instrument has, to date, focused on groups of workers in teams, there would seem to be considerable scope for the use of the Work Orientation Schedule in staff supervision, personnel management, and employment counselling in the group care field (Fulcher 1983).

Conclusions

Support was obtained for the practice-oriented impression that there is important interplay between diagnostic characteristics of the residents and staff team functioning in group care centres. That this interplay is not always present or dominant, lends further credibility to the idea that factors which affect quality of working life satisfactions and frustrations are variable over time. These factors may be unique to individual staff members yet at any given time particular events or issues come into focus which have at least symbolic value for most members of a group care team. This is consistent with the notion of culture in organizations (Smircich 1983; Wilkins and Ouchi 1983) and supports the notion of resource dependency (White 1974). Whether these influences originate within the team, the resident group, the organization, or the social policy environment in which the group care centre is situated, the result may draw team members together or promote destructive levels of turbulence or maladaptation. Based on the results of this study, it would appear that an awareness of patterns of frustration and satisfaction in the staff team, coupled with increased understanding of the diagnostic characteristics of residents, could be used to further team cohesion, promote mutual support of staff members, and increase the level of purposeful activity directed towards the residents by the 'team'.

A note of caution is indicated. Teamwork is an ongoing process intimately related, as has been shown, to patterns of satisfaction and frustration in staff. It is not something which happens in a single training session. Regression or fade-out, particularly after off-site team building sessions, is well known to researchers and students of organizational and management behaviour (Boss 1983). A combination of staff development and training, involving management and supervisory structures as well as carefully identified consultative supports and follow-up, is fundamental.

With this in mind, the following suggestions can be made about team supervision in group care.

1 Teams working with neurotic young people are likely to require psychodynamic supervision geared towards helping workers clarify what is happening in the resident group and sharing their own feelings about residents, particularly when these feelings begin to interfere with 'off duty' time.

2 Teams working with power-oriented residents may become stalemated over how best to deal with the behaviour presented by this type of youth. As a result, workers may be inclined to over-emphasize immediate control measures and will need support to ensure that longer-range attention is given to growth and development needs.

3 Teams working with conforming youngsters may need to be stimulated to ensure that this type of resident does not become too dependent. Both workers and residents may settle into a comfortable and relaxed collaboration with one another which can very easily become surrogate parenting. The relatively poor showing on recidivism measures for conforming youngsters who have been in treatment-oriented programs suggests that many are still highly vulnerable to conformity with delinquent and criminal peers once they leave care.

Perhaps the most significant outcome of this study is that the measure of team functioning is sensitive (if not yet fully understood) to differences among residents in group care practice. These findings are consistent with those of Eisner (1982) who employed similar measures to those used in this study. This conclusion is based on assessment typologies which have been reliably identified with the use of appropriate classification methods. The assessment typologies are also valid to the extent that they have demonstrated their relevance with a host of differential outcome measures, including behavioural management, academic-vocational gains, and reduced recidivism. Further refinement of the team functioning dimension is indicated in the development of group care research and practice.

Notes

1 One view of the situation in the English-speaking sector of services for children in Montreal leading up to the admission of girls to Shawbridge can be found in Carinol (1979).
2 Thanks to Michael Holosko PhD for assistance in data analysis.

References

Andre, C. R. and Mahan, J. A. (1972) *Final Report on the Differential Education Project.* Educational Research Series, No. 11 Sacramento: California Youth Authority.

Argyle, M. (1972) *The Social Psychology of Work.* New York: Penguin Books.

Bales, R. F. (1950) *Interaction Process Analysis.* Cambridge, Mass.: Addison-Wesley.

Barkwell, L. (1976) Differential Treatment of Juveniles on Probation. *Canadian Journal of Criminology and Corrections* 18 (4): 363–78.

Boss, R. W. (1983) Team Building and the Problem of Regression: The Personal Management Interview as an Intervention. *The Journal of Applied Behavioral Science* 19 (1): 67–83.

Brill, R. W. (1978) Implications of the Conceptual Level Matching Model for Treatment of Delinquents. *Journal of Research in Crime and Delinquency* 12: 229–46.

Bronfenbrenner, U. (1979a) *The Ecology of Human Development.* Cambridge, Mass.: D. C. Heath.

—— (1979b) Contexts of Child Rearing: Problems and Prospects. *American Psychologist* 34 (10): 844–50.

Carinol, B. (1979) Children's Rights: Social Action to Change Conditions in Juvenile Detention Centers. In B. Wharf (ed.) *Community Work in Canada.* Toronto: McClelland & Stewart.

Davis, L. E. and Cherns, A. B. (eds) (1975) *The Quality of Working Life,* vols. I and II. New York: Free Press.

Eisner, S. (1982) The Interplay Between the Heimler Scale of Social Functioning and the Interpersonal Maturity Level Classification System. MA Dissertation, Université de Montreal, Montreal, Quebec.

Fulcher, L. C. (1979) Keeping Staff Sane to Accomplish Treatment. *Residential and Community Child Care Administration* 1 (1): 69–85.

—— (1983) Who Cares for the Caregivers? A Comparative Study of Residential and Day Care Teams Working with Children. PhD Thesis, University of Stirling, Stirling, Scotland.

Fulcher, L. C. and Ainsworth, F. (1981) Planned Care and Treatment: The Notion of Programme. In F. Ainsworth and L. C. Fulcher (eds) *Group Care for Children: Concept and Issues.* London: Tavistock.

Gendreau, P. and Ross, R. (1979) Effective Correctional Treatment: Bibliotherapy for Cynics. *Crime and Delinquency* October 1979: 463–89.

Grant, J. D. and Grant, M. Q. (1959) A Group Dynamics Approach to the Treatment of Non-Conformists in the Navy, *The Annals of the Academy of Political and Social Science* 3 (22): 126–35.

Hall. R. H. (1969) *Occupations and the Social Structure.* Englewood Cliffs, NJ: Prentice-Hall.

Harris, P. (1983) The Interpersonal Maturity of Delinquents and Non-Delinquents. In W. L. Laufer and J. M. Day (eds) *Personality Theory, Moral Development and Criminal Behavior.* Toronto: Lexington Books.

Heimler, E. (1970) The Scale of Organizational Functioning. Unpublished.

—— (1975) *Survival in Society.* New York: Halsted Press.

—— (1979) On the Emotional Significance of Work: An Audio-taped Interview (27 September). Department of Sociology, University of Stirling, Scotland.

Heimler, E. and Fulcher, L. C. (1981) *The Work Orientation Schedule*. In L. C. Fulcher (1983) Who Cares for the Caregivers? A Comparative Study of Residential and Day Care Teams Working with Children. PhD Thesis, University of Stirling, Scotland.

Hertzberg, F. (1968) *Work and the Nature of Man*. London: Staples Press.

Holmes, T. H. and Masuda, M. (1974) Life Change and Illness Susceptibility. In B. S. Dohrenwend and B. P. Dohrenwend (eds) *Stressful Life Events: Their Nature and Effects*. New York: John Wiley.

Holmes, T. H. and Rahe, R. H. (1967) The Social Readjustment Rating Scale. *Journal of Psychosomatic Research* 11: 213–18.

Homans, G. C. (1950) *The Human Group*. New York: Harcourt-Brace.

Hunt, D. (1971) *Matching Models in Education: The Coordination of Teaching Methods with Student Characteristics*. Toronto: Ontario Institute for Studies in Education.

Hunt, D. and Hardt, R. (1967) The Role of Conceptual Level and Program Structure in Summer Upward-Bound Programs. Paper presented at Eastern Psychological Association Meeting, Boston, April. From Brill, R. (1977) Implications of the Conceptual Level Matching Model for the Treatment of Delinquents. *Journal of Research in Crime and Delinquency* 12: 229–46.

Hunt, D., Butler, L., Noy, J., and Rosse, M. (1978) *Assessing Conceptual Level by the Paragraph Completion Method*. Toronto: Ontario Institute for Studies in Education.

Jesness, C. (1965) *The Fricto Ranch Study: Outcomes with Small vs. Large Living Groups in the Rehabilitation of Delinquents*. Sacramento: California Youth Authority, Research Report No. 47.

—— (1971) The Preston Typology Study: An Experiment with Differential Treatment in an Institution. *Journal of Research in Crime and Delinquency* 8: 38–52.

—— (1980) Was the Close-Holton Project a 'Bummer'? In R. Ross and P. Gendreau (eds) *Effective Correctional Treatment*. Toronto: Butterworth.

Jesness, C., Derisi, W., McCormick, P., and Wedge, R. (1972) *The Youth Center Research Project: Final Report*. Sacramento: California Youth Authority and American Justice Institute.

Johnson, V. S. (1981) Staff Drift: A Problem in Program Integrity. *Criminal Justice and Behavior* 8 (2) (June): 223–32.

Kale, W. L. and Stenmark, D. E. (1983) A Comparison of Four Life Event Scales. *American Journal of Community Psychology* 11 (4): 441–58.

Knapp, R. G. (1978) *Basic Statistics for Nurses*. Toronto: John Wiley.

Lester, D., Leitner, L., and Posner, I. (1983) Recent Life Events and Stress Scores: An Examination of the Holmes and Rahe Scale. *Psychological Reports*: 53–70.

Lewin, K. (1952) *Field Theory in Social Sciences*. London: Tavistock.

Lukin, P. (1981) Recidivism and Changes made by Delinquents During Residential Treatment. *Journal of Research in Crime and Delinquency* January: 101–12.

McLachlan, J. (1972) Benefit from Group Therapy as a Function of Patient–Therapist Match on Conceptual Level. *Psychotherapy: Theory, Research and Practice* 9: 317–23.

—— (1974) Therapy Strategies, Personality Orientation and Recovery from Alcoholism. *Canadian Psychiatric Association Journal* 19: 25–30.

Maier, H. (1981) Essential Components in Care and Treatment Environments for Children. In F. Ainsworth and L. C. Fulcher (eds) *Group Care for Children: Concept and Issues.* London: Tavistock.

Mattingly, M. A. (1977) Sources of Stress and Burn-out in Professional Child Care Work. *Child Care Quarterly* 6 (2): 127–37.

Megargee, E. (1977) The Need for a New Classification System. *Criminal Justice and Behavior* 4: 107–14.

Monroe, S. M. (1982) Life Events Assessment: Current Practices, Emerging Trends. *Clinical Psychology Review* 2: 435–53.

Moos, R. (1975) *Evaluating Community and Correctional Settings* New York: John Wiley.

Palmer, T. (1972) *Differential Placement of Delinquents in Group Homes, Final Report.* Sacramento: California Youth Authority and National Institute of Mental Health.

—— (1974) The Youth Authority's Community Treatment Project. *Federal Probation* March: 3–14.

—— (1976) *Final Report of the Community Treatment Project, Phases 1, 2 and 3.* Sacramento: California Youth Authority and National Institute of Mental Health.

—— (1978) *Correctional Intervention and Research: Current Issues and Future Prospects.* Lexington, Mass.: D. C. Heath.

Palmer, T. and Grenny, C. (1971) Stance and Techniques of Matched Nx, Na, MP-CFC and 12 Workers. California Youth Authority. Mimeographed paper.

Quay, H. (1977) The Three Faces of Evaluation: What Can Be Expected to Work. *Criminal Justice and Behavior* 4: 341–54.

Reitsma-Street, M. (1982) A Critical Review of the Conceptual Level Matching Model and Its Relevance for the Treatment of Maladjusted Youth. *The Differential View*: A Publication of The International Differential Treatment Association – Sixth Annual Conference Proceedings. Issue 12, September.

Ross. A. L. (1983) Mitigating Turnover of Child Care Staff in Group Care Facilities. *Child Welfare* 62 (Jan.–Feb.): 63–7.

Ross, R. and Gendreau, P. (1980) *Effective Correctional Treatment.* Toronto: Butterworth.

Scheirer, M. A. and Rezmovic, E. L. (1983) Measuring the Degree of Program Implementation: A Methodological Review. *Evaluation Review* 7 (5) October: 599–633.

Smircich, L. (1983) Concepts of Culture and Organizational Analysis. *Administrative Science Quarterly* 28 September: 339–58.

Tomlinson, P. and Hunt, D. (1971) Differential Effects of Rule-Example Order as a Function of Learner Conceptual Level. *Canadian Journal of Behavior Science*: 235–7.

Warren, M. Q. (1983) Application of Interpersonal Maturity to Offender Populations. In W. L. Laufer and J. M. Day (eds) *Personality Theory, Moral Development and Criminal Behavior.* Toronto: Lexington Books.

Warren, M. Q. et al. (1966) *Interpersonal Maturity Classification System: Juvenile,*

Diagnosis of Low, Middle and High Maturity Delinquents. Sacramento: California Youth Authority.

White, P. E. (1974) Resources as Determinants of Organisational Behavior. *Administrative Science Quarterly,* September: 366–79.

Whittaker, J. (1979) *Caring for Troubled Children.* San Francisco: Jossey-Bass.

Wilkins, A. L. and Ouchi, W. G. (1983) Efficient Cultures: Exploring the Relationship Between Culture and Organizational Performance. *Administrative Science Quarterly* 28 September: 468–81.

Zimmerman, M. (1983) Methodological Issues in the Assessment of Life Events: A Review of Issues and Research. *Clinical Psychology Review* 3: 339–70.

9 Working across boundaries in group care practice[1]

Angela Hopkinson[2]

Introduction: a weekly review meeting

The weekly review meeting in a child psychiatric unit is taking place. About twenty people are present, mainly nursing staff who are the direct care providers in this setting. They are discussing Tommy whose difficult behaviour has been disrupting the unit all week. The plumber has had to be called three times to unblock the toilets after Tommy had put things down them – mostly other children's possessions. The staff now have to watch him all the time, even in the toilet. As there are usually two staff on duty with Tommy's group, this means one is with Tommy while the remaining worker is with the other five boys – provided Tommy's behaviour is not requiring two staff to deal with it, and as long as neither of them needs to take a tea break, answer the phone, or see to visitors! The staff are angry that the other children are getting little or no attention beyond basic care. They are also frustrated at being unable to get beyond supervision of Tommy to do any more positive work with him.

Staff also find Tommy's parents most peculiar and difficult to deal with. The staff are not making any progress at getting to know Tommy's parents and do not know if the social worker is making progress either. They are certain that Tommy's behaviour will not improve unless there is also some change in his parents.

Tommy is the responsibility of a consultant psychiatrist who requested his admission to the unit. A social worker sees his family and a psychologist is devising a treatment programme for him. None of these three people is present at the meeting. Care staff do not feel they can make any plans for coping with the situation without the agreement of one or more of the 'outside' professionals. Debate about what can be done to help Tommy gets mixed up with what can be done about the 'outside' workers. Will they agree with any plans made? Will they come to the next meeting? Should the care staff send a 'deputation'?

Feelings of desperation and despondency settle on the meeting. Some are saying keeping Tommy in the unit is not doing him any good, and the other children are being prevented from making the progress of which they are thought capable. Though not said explicitly, discharge is definitely in people's minds (discharge in this unit is the only decision that care staff are empowered to take unilaterally). Nothing is settled but time is running out. The other children are discussed hurriedly in the remaining time.

Later in the week a case conference is held on Tommy. This is one of a series of regular meetings to review progress and make plans. The care staff repeatedly answer the door to admit people who have come for the conference. Most are people they do not know well and some they have never seen before. Most of the care staff will not be able to attend because they are minding the children. One of the care staff, Mrs Forbes, gives a report about Tommy's behaviour in the unit since the last meeting. In the formal atmosphere this report is phrased in the neutral terms of professional jargon. Tommy is said to have been 'acting out' and 'needing limits to be set'. There is no flavour of the chaos that Tommy has been causing, the staff's exasperation or the other children's outrage about their lost belongings (the other children are not mentioned because the meeting is only about Tommy). With so many strangers present, Mrs Forbes feels overawed and unable to assert her point of view. The discussion gets very theoretical as people suggest psychodynamic reasons for Tommy's behaviour. No attempt is made to discuss the practical difficulties of coping with Tommy *and* five other children. The psychiatrist suggests that the care staff should try talking to Tommy when he is being difficult. He does not explain how they are to do this while separating a roomful of fighting boys. Mrs

Forbes feels insulted: does the psychiatrist really think that care staff do not talk to the children?

Let us consider these two meetings in terms of the obstacles and difficulties that prevent those involved from working together more effectively. The most obvious problem concerns the number of people involved with this one child, both within the agency and from other agencies. In any residential setting many staff are needed to give 168 hours per week coverage. In many units like this one, the staff can never meet together all at the same time because of shift working and because the children must be supervised. All too often agency roles are clearly distinguished by profession and status within each profession, so that the tasks to be done are allocated to a number of different people. For instance, care of the child and decision-making may become separated, with the latter resting with workers who are 'attached' to the unit but whose main working base lies outside. In addition to tasks that are directly concerned with the child, there are also tasks related to management of the unit and supervision of staff which may involve yet more people.

A child like Tommy, whose behaviour causes chaos wherever he goes, has already attracted the attention of a number of other agencies before arriving at this unit. These other agencies may include school, special educational services, the local social work department, the juvenile court system, the school health service, and others. They all have a legitimate continuing interest, and need to be kept involved if the best use is to be made of available resources for Tommy's future. Therefore their representatives may also be invited to meetings.

These 'outsiders' and also some of the attached workers from within the agency, may only come to the unit to attend meetings. The geographical separation of the unit from the rest of the agency is partly responsible for this. Thus, there may be no informal contact between 'outsiders' and unit staff. Any difficulties which arise have to be dealt with via the formal machinery of the organization, and this can be very cumbersome and ineffective at times.

Systems and Boundaries

One can see that many of the difficulties described above have to do with the organizational structure of the agency, as noted earlier in this volume by Maier, particularly those difficulties related to processes of planning and decision-making. Others are associated with role differentiation and the nature of communications between workers.

In order to analyse the nature of problems encountered and to suggest ways of tackling them, it is helpful to view the unit, its parent agency, and its contacts with the outside from a systems perspective (Miller and Rice 1967). This perspective incorporates ideas about individuals as organisms interacting with their environment. Studies on the functioning of groups have shown that groups have characteristics which are more than the sum of the individuals that form it, and in this respect a group may be seen as a living organism (Monane 1967). Systems perspectives have been used to examine natural groupings in society including families, peer groups, institutions, neighbourhoods, and communities (Emery 1969).

A systems orientation seeks to make explicit the idea that groups or systems have boundaries and that there are interactions across boundaries with the external environment or the world outside. No change can take place within a living system without exchanges taking place with its environment. A system may, therefore, be examined in terms of its inputs, its conversion process, and its outputs. The larger organization of which it is a part may be evaluated as a system also. Every system is, from this perspective, part of a larger system, and every system has smaller groups within it which are sub-systems. Every system except the largest *has* an environment and every system except the smallest *is* an environment (Hearn 1969).

Perhaps the real value of systems thinking is that it highlights ways in which, to understand or change an individual's behaviour or attitudes, one must take account of their environment. This involves the relationships, stresses, and expectations that influence behaviour. Such a notion applies to ourselves as workers, our colleagues, and our work organizations, as much as to the children with whom we work.

If we regard a group care unit as a system, as suggested by Polsky and Claster (1968), then we need to examine the dynamics within it, the functioning of the staff group as a team (Fulcher 1981); and interactions with the outside world, which may be referred to as transactions across the boundary. The important boundaries are those around the unit and around the agency. Some staff are clearly inside the unit and others outside it, but some may have an ambiguous position. They may be seen as inside or outside depending on the viewpoint of the observer. For instance, an outside agency or the child's parents may regard a social worker as being a member of the unit, and thereby inside the boundary. On the other hand, unit care staff and the children may regard this person as a visitor or an outsider.

In reality there is a multitude of boundaries that have differing degrees of permeability to different people. Many of the staff both inside and outside the unit become involved in tasks which mean crossing boundaries. The allocation of these boundary tasks to particular workers depends on the organizational structure of the agency, and assumptions about the roles appropriate to particular professions and ranks. The need for particular tasks and their relative importance will also depend on these, as well as on the individual needs of each child and family.

What are the tasks of a boundary worker?

One task is improving patterns of communication: to assist the sharing of information about work undertaken by the team with or on behalf of the child, and to ensure that decisions and plans are known to all affected by them. In addition to just passing on information in various directions, there is a process of co-ordinating and drawing together the different views. Another important element is that of support for staff, particularly those working in the somewhat enclosed and often intensive atmosphere of the living unit.

This sounds all very purposeful and organized! In reality, of course, such situations are so beset with opportunities for failure of communication and conflict over decisions, that a large part of the work of the boundary worker involves trying to patch up the gaps. It involves providing an outlet for the frustration, anger, and sadness of care staff who may feel that their opinions go unheard as well as supporting decision-makers who find resources inadequate to meet a particular child's needs. In an inter-disciplinary setting, it is also unlikely that the many workers with different training backgrounds, experience, and methods of practice will find themselves in total agreement. Boundary workers may often find it necessary to balance conflicting views or wishes, and carry the resulting confusion and uncertainty. Several other boundary tasks will be discussed in more detail later, but firstly consideration of the relationship between organizational structures and the need for boundary workers is necessary.

The hospital child psychiatric setting is perhaps the ultimate illustration of organizational complexity and division of labour. Not only are many professions involved in the inter-disciplinary department, but fairly rigid hierarchies also exist within some of these professions, notably nursing. Isobel Menzies's classic study (1970), for example, showed how the nursing profession's hierarchical structure serves to reduce the anxiety of basic care staff by passing responsibility to a higher level in that structure. The tradition of training and the nature of the work in general nursing has not in the main encouraged care staff who come from that background to use personal initiative or step outside their assigned physical care tasks. Certainly in some in-patient units where nurses are the care workers, the tradition still exists that care involves physical needs only and that the daily or weekly clinical session with a 'therapist' is the major agent for change. This is in spite of evidence to the contrary (Polsky 1962; Trieschman, Whittaker, and Brendtro 1969).

In such a setting it is invariably easier (although not desirable) for individual workers if they keep to their established territory: nurses provide physical care, psychologists make assessments, teachers teach, doctors provide therapy, and social workers give support to the family. In this way of working it is of course traditionally the medical consultant who co-ordinates all the various efforts.

However, increasingly things are changing and all disciplines are more ready to share or exchange tasks as the common basis of work with children is understood. This helps workers to see the links between all the separate tasks and to view the child, family, and social environment as a total system. The increased understanding of each other's work that this promotes also helps to improve staff relationships and offers a firm base for further inter-disciplinary co-operation. It provides for more flexibility in the provision of services to children, and also offers greater opportunities for professional development amongst all the workers. Yet at the same time, such role sharing must be carefully managed if confusion is to be avoided.

In the psychiatric hospital setting, some boundary tasks are normally tackled by use of formal structures. For example, out-patient team meetings and group meetings within disciplines offer opportunities for co-ordination as well as professional support, even though this latter issue may not be an overt aim. In the in-patient unit, Kardex meetings and case conferences are also set up to facilitate communication and provide arenas for decision-making.

The 'within-profession' structure referred to above does of course pre-date the coming together of the different professions in the inter-disciplinary setting of a hospital. In many cases, however, the cross-profession structure that true inter-disciplinary work implies has yet to evolve. The stages in creating such an inter-disciplinary team are, however, usefully described by VanderVen (1979). Fortunately, collaborative practice generally moves ahead of the formal structures needed to contain this. As a consequence, in many hospital settings, the authority remains clearly defined in regard to each professional group. Competing professional hierarchies continue to cloud the issue of team accountability and the degree of individual autonomy as exercised by key professions in inter-disciplinary teams.

In many public service areas, attempts have been made to deal with this kind of difficulty by structural re-organization with the ultimate idea of developing corporate management approaches. Thus local government in Britain underwent changes between 1957 and 1974, which re-organized the tiers and boundaries of local government and the management system operating within them (Cockburn 1977). A particular example is seen in the re-organization of social services in Scotland in 1968, in which the previously separate, specialist services for different client groups were integrated into one Social Work Department. In the Health Service, similar ideas were less fully implemented. The overall structure of the services has been re-organized, with the separate General Practitioners, Hospitals, and Community Services being brought together under one Area Health Board. However, the power held by some clinicians has made it difficult to move towards principles of corporate management, principles which are viewed as antipathetic to the exercise of individual clinical judgements. Moreover within a health care setting some workers (for instance social workers and teachers) are employed by a different system altogether, being seconded to hospital settings and lacking accountability to any corporately structured management group.

The formal system of management is then very diffuse, and it is not surprising that contradictions and difficulties often emerge. It is indeed remarkable that the system works at all! As stated clearly by Whittaker:

> 'The structural implications of the infusion of psychoanalytic treatment into the therapeutic milieu have been particularly unfortunate.... Since the therapist was isolated from the actual behaviour in the ward, his view of the child was derived from information collected in the artificial environment of the 50-minute therapy hour. To compound the problem, the individual therapist was often the person responsible for directing the child's total treatment plan.... Small wonder that the forces actually governing the course of a child's progress in residential treatment often had less to do with the formal structure of treatment authority and more to do with informal, covert systems.'   (1981: 100)

In spite of this situation the formal system of management does provide a framework within which the overall work of any child psychiatric unit takes place. The smooth running of the system and the effectiveness of the work may however depend upon informal systems that workers create and boundary workers are frequently key people in making these systems work. The balance between formal and informal structures will of course vary with the size and complexity of the organization. Roberts (1982) has noted how theoretical approaches to understanding organizations emphasize structure or personal interactions to differing degrees.

Where formally prescribed tasks can be delineated in job descriptions, and where specific actions are performed by someone under the direct supervision of a line manager, then the informal aspects of work depend upon close personal relationships, the development of trust, and a mutual working out of tasks. Strangers cannot work an informal system. Group care, with its demand for constant care and close involvement in the life in the unit, leaves little time to cultivate contacts with all the outsiders concerned. One can see, therefore, the importance of a boundary worker who can bridge the gap, getting to know as far as possible both insiders and outsiders.

Various tasks that a boundary worker may take on as part of the informal system are discussed below. The possibilities are extensive, and obviously no one worker can attempt to cover more than a few of the tasks involved. Each worker will select according to the needs of his or her particular situation: the kind of formal structure in operation and the needs it creates; the tasks taken on by other workers; and the particular skills and preferences found amongst the members of an inter-disciplinary team.

Some boundary tasks in group care practice

Management

In an inter-disciplinary hospital setting the formal management system normally lies within the different professional organizations. In Britain, for instance, junior doctors are accountable to a consultant; nurses have a hierarchical system whose upper strata may be outside a particular unit and located in another part of the main hospital; domestic staff have their own supervisory hierarchy within the hospital but one that is separate from the nurses; social workers are accountable through their departmental organization to a Local Government Regional Authority; teachers are the responsibility of another department in the same authority; clinical psychologists have their own department and hierarchy within the Health Board.

The decisions that individual workers can take are clearly laid out in regard to the different professions. In practice, individuals may feel they can make all but major decisions themselves, particularly where they have good relationships within their own department's supervisory system and that they can expect that sensible decisions will be backed. Where this expectation does not exist, and where workers are inexperienced, they may feel they have to defer decisions to others higher up in the departmental structure. Workers who have the support of colleagues and a chance to make use of others' ideas and experience in joint discussion are likely to have more confidence in making their own decisions. They are less likely to feel free to make decisions in situations where there is distrust or disagreement with other workers.

Though the formal hospital structure may be clear, it is not always easy to resolve difficult issues, particularly where there is conflict between professional groups that have separate systems of accountability. Equally, the medical profession may claim that theirs is the overall responsibility in a hospital setting, and in any question of treatment for individual children, it usually is. Yet few doctors have managed to influence a determined nursing hierarchy that persists, for example, in the view that nurses in a psychiatric unit must wear uniforms, including caps! Equally if a child is suspected of being the victim of non-accidental injury, a social worker may argue that the legal duty to take action is more important than a doctor's view that this would be detrimental to the treatment plan.

The informal aspects of management, then, are divorced from the power and authority to make decisions for others. These informal aspects involve creating working situations and relationships wherein individual staff can feel supported in making their own decisions at an appropriate level. Obviously no one person can do this, but each person can contribute. The boundary worker, or 'outsider' in the context of the unit, has a special contribution to make in validating the right of 'inside' workers to make decisions about those issues which are primarily 'inside' concerns. The boundary worker may be the person best placed to bring 'outside' issues into the unit; to try and balance discussion about details of daily life in the unit with reminders of the situation outside, so that these issues are also given due consideration. This applies to general issues of policy, working methods and such like, as well as to work with individual children.

Staff support
The formal system for staff support is generally found within professional groups, and varies considerably from one group to another. Some support systems exist across professional boundaries, as found within the inter-disciplinary team. At its best and most trusting, such a team offers a very supportive environment in which members can learn from each other, share tasks, and expand their own views within the wider perspective of different approaches. However, many inter-disciplinary teams are such in

name only. As VanderVen points out, some teams are merely collections of people from separate departments, and, because the power balance is unequal, some impose the views of one or more professions on the others (VanderVen 1979). It is most commonly the care staff whose views are discounted. Working in a living situation with disturbed and difficult children produces a tremendous amount of stress. Add to this the frustration of not being in a position to make decisions about plans for the children, other than on a superficial level associated with daily routines, and the dissatisfactions can be overwhelming. The need for support is therefore immense.

In a hierarchical system such as health care, it is flying in the face of tradition and training for senior staff to accept or look for support from junior staff or even from peers. A boundary worker who is outside this hierarchy may be in a good position to give support to senior personnel, who cannot ask for support from below, nor get it from above. Support from above may not be available because the higher ranks are removed from the unit, have no relevant training or experience, and because they are not felt to be in touch with the nature of the difficulties. The boundary worker can also help in staff support groups, by bringing in a rather more detached viewpoint to problems arising from intensive involvement, or by bringing in an expectation that difficulties can be shared with mutual benefit – perhaps by bringing his or her own difficulties to the group.

The most important aspect of support is availability. This is not always as easy as it sounds! In addition to the practical difficulties of finding sufficient time in the midst of a busy working schedule, there is the difficulty of establishing reasons for being in a unit and overcoming the suspicion of inside staff towards all outsiders. Initially when visiting an unfamiliar unit, it helps to have a specific task in mind as a focus for the visit. Just 'dropping in' raises all sorts of anxieties when the visitor is an unknown quantity. As time passes and friendliness and interest are established, it becomes possible to extend visits beyond the ostensible task, and then to visit without a task at all. Finding out when staff take a coffee break is a great help in this, especially as much useful communication takes place over coffee! Flexibility is needed, along with the ability to respond when someone wants to talk about something that is bothering them. Too tight a schedule, with just time for an interview or meeting, does not help. In this middle stage, staff can speak with an available person, but will not actively seek someone out, perhaps because they are not sure that their needs are valid. Later on workers may become able to initiate contact, asking when the boundary worker would have time, or phoning up for a chat. Depending on other factors – the general atmosphere in a unit or the training and experience of staff – it may also be possible to set aside times specifically for support purposes for individuals or groups with or without a boundary worker or outsider as third party.

As well as establishing one's presence, one has to establish some credibility as a worker, and also indicate some sort of allegiance to the unit. Support can be offered by anyone, but it may only be taken up from certain people. Credibility can be difficult to establish as a boundary worker, since it usually depends on work done, and seen to be done. The boundary worker is not often involved in direct work in a unit, or at least not in the 'real' work of caring for children. If boundary workers are directly involved, as therapist or as key worker, then they obviously have a means of establishing their credibility, provided their influence is seen as positive, and as long as they can steer clear of rivalries. The worker who is seeing a family may also display the results of his/her efforts for inspection, but here there are possible difficulties when staff see the parents as causing the child's problems, and the worker as allied with the parents. A boundary worker whose involvement is via teaching or supervising students has a further difficulty, since practice teaching is usually not considered to be real work! Other ways of establishing credibility are through assiduously following procedures, for instance in relation to recording in the notes what the worker has been doing, or by making sure that everyone who should be is provided with all relevant information and consulted about decisions. Those who enter purely as consultants, with no working links with the unit, will depend for credibility on their work elsewhere and their reputation. Hopefully, such people will have been invited in the first place because their credibility is good.

Allegiance to the unit is both difficult to define and difficult to establish. It may have something to do with valuing the aims of and the work done in the unit, and seeing the positive aspects of group care and treatment. Those who think any group care setting is institutional and should be avoided at all costs, or used only as a last resort, will not find it easy to give positive messages to care staff. Any group care setting that caters for disturbed children is likely to be an uncomfortable place at times. A worker must be able to accept the less agreeable aspects of the place without fearing the worst, and remain able to see that stress and crisis are often an accompaniment to growth and change. Indeed these influences may be a necessary part of development for some people!

Allegiance is also about valuing the staff who work in the unit. Indeed valuing other workers is often the most important element in being a boundary worker. This includes those who work both inside and outside of a unit, are members of various professional groups in a multi-disciplinary department, or workers from separate agencies. Each group has its own tasks to perform and its own skills to contribute, and each is needed to achieve a total service. Even within one professional group, individuals have their different personalities and interests, and the total service is richer for this variety. If some allegiance is felt on both sides, then mistakes and omissions on the part of a boundary worker are likely to be viewed as such, and can then be mentioned to the person concerned, dealt with, and forgiven. Otherwise, deficiencies may be viewed as being either signs of incompetence in the worker or deliberate insults.

Another aspect of staff support for the boundary worker is in sharing the burden of responsibility and holding some of the anxiety that goes with it. This is achieved primarily by listening to staff when they express worries and frustrations. Sometimes worries such as these are not so much about whether actions were appropriate or effective, but whether others will approve. The boundary worker may need to stand alongside the inside worker to defend a decision or to negotiate with outsiders. Quite often the best response is to do nothing, thereby giving implicit approval and permission for inside workers to take the initiative. Doing nothing can be very difficult since it goes against all our expectations of how to be helpful. When staff come with worries about the way things are going, the immediate response may well be to offer advice or directions. But often the staff member knows how to handle the situation, and merely wants to share the anxiety and frustration about how to manage it. It may be precisely because the boundary worker is *not* part of the chain of authority that these anxieties are brought to him or her, since advice or action are not wanted.

Anxieties and frustration may be dealt with as we have seen, either by passing responsibility for decisions up the professional hierarchy, or by sharing within a supportive group or with particular individuals. Another way such feelings are dealt with is to put blame for failure or difficulties onto a scapegoat. Because staff in a group care unit develop close inward-looking relationships and tend to be suspicious of relatively unknown outsiders, and because it is much more comfortable to place such blame outside the unit, the chosen scapegoat is usually someone with peripheral contact with the unit. Boundary workers may well find themselves in this position, particularly in the early stages when they have a formal role but have not yet developed informal links. It is an uncomfortable position, and one that makes it difficult to achieve any of the other, more positive tasks of a boundary role. It is also a position that tends to be self-perpetuating, because of the mutual distrust and anger that is engendered. Frequently, such a worker can do nothing right: action is seen as interference and inaction as disinterest or worse. For all of these reasons, the boundary worker will need to have his or her own source of support to help hold these anxieties. For similar reasons, this may need to be outside both the care system in which they arise and outside the system of responsibility for decisions.

Co-ordination of work with individual children
Work with a child in group care may well be split up into a number of small specialized contributions, making it easy to forget that the child is a whole person. It is important when planning for a child to be aware of all the influences which impinge on him within his environment. If this is not done, then it may be that some factors are working to maintain the *status quo*, however hard one tries to achieve changes in a particular area. In deciding how to intervene, it is important to assess what changes would be possible within the child's total situation, or what changes to other aspects of that situation would also need consideration. This said, it is common practice to work in fairly limited areas, and very often small changes in one aspect will create a knock-on effect to create wider changes in the situation.

In a group care centre, and particularly in a hospital setting where there are workers from different professions and specialities, a child's problems are approached on a number of different fronts. One worker may be helping the child to improve social skills, another may be setting limits on his behaviour, while a third may be encouraging him to consider difficult relationships at home. In addition, the child himself will select, from among the staff available, particular relationships which will be used to meet his needs.

There are some who think that the only way a number of people can work efficiently together is if they share the same philosophy and method of working. This may be possible in a small, close-knit unit dealing with a limited range of difficulties and where external resources are not required. It is not always possible in settings that are part of large bureaucratic organizations and is particularly difficult in a multi-disciplinary hospital setting. Children are rarely confused by the differences in people; it is after all something that we all have to cope with in daily life! Sheltering children from obstacles or inconsistencies may be unhelpful in the long run. Helping children cope with activities or people that they dislike or find difficult may also be part of the whole therapeutic process.

A boundary worker needs to be able to accept and value every contribution without feeling a need to improve on it, or fit it into a neat pigeon hole. This comes perhaps with a basic acceptance of one's own particular skills and limitations. One of the great satisfactions of boundary work comes from seeing effective work being done without having to feel responsibility for doing it all! Results are possible that one worker could never hope to achieve alone.

The training of social workers may particularly fit them for boundary tasks in that such training has traditionally covered a wide view of society and of different working ideologies. The social worker is encouraged to be aware of social and economic conditions, cultural influences, family and group dynamics, community institutions and resources, as well as intra-psychic processes. This background may help social workers in taking on liaison tasks. However, social workers do not have a monopoly on boundary tasks and many do not wish to act in this role, feeling their interests and skills lie elsewhere. Many colleagues in other professions will, from interest and experience, have an equal ability to see a wider perspective. In any one setting, it would be an enormous expectation for a single worker to perform the boundary tasks in respect of all children in the unit. The need to share these tasks is no doubt one reason for the growing practice of allocating a key worker to each child.

In many group care settings the key worker is one of the care staff, that is she/he is working directly with the child.[3] The primary task of a key worker is to be a special person in the eyes of a child and to be responsible for liaison with others on behalf of that child. As the person who has most information about the child and his situation, she/he will be responsible for overall plans and will therefore need to have authority to make decisions.

In a setting where decision-making lies outside the immediate living situation, this role of co-ordination may fall on a boundary worker rather than a member of the unit staff. In the particular instance of a hospital psychiatric setting, the responsibility for long-term plans for a child is likely to rest with the medical consultant and the out-patient team. Every member of this team is potentially a boundary worker, in the sense of coming between the in-patient unit and the outside world. As therapist for the child or worker with the family, she/he also carries the out-patient team's authority to take decisions, into the in-patient unit. Many team members find this a difficult task, for the reasons outlined at the end of the previous section: they readily fall into the trap of becoming a scapegoat. Their boundary role is allocated on the basis of membership in an outside group and not on the basis of their attachment to the inside setting. Thus, their allegiance is suspect. They easily become the focus for all the frustrations engendered by a system that removes authority from the care workers.

Even in a setting where the formal structure is less complex and the care workers are directly involved in planning, there is still a need for some one person to take the role of co-ordinator. If the psychiatric hospital setting is at one end of the spectrum of organizational size and complexity, then one might find at the other extreme the example of a small hostel for young adults working their way from institutional care towards independence. Sponsored by a voluntary agency, and staffed by five or six workers, this hostel operated according to a democratic philosophy.

All the workers were of the same profession and status, and a clear division of labour was not much in evidence. Indeed the absence of other kinds of worker (cook or secretary) and the absence of hierarchy resulted in a certain amount of inefficiency when it came to carrying out some tasks. There was always some uncertainty about who would cook dinner, and what would happen to telephone messages! Task sharing was based more on time (shifts) than on individual roles, and any worker could be expected to perform a range of tasks when they were on duty. Such an arrangement required a close-knit group of staff, where information and work was shared closely. However, it soon became apparent that some kind of key worker system was necessary, since every staff member could not maintain a special interest in every resident nor keep a hold on the large amount of information available about all the residents. If the five or six workers found it confusing to try and be all things to all residents, then the confusion was further compounded in communications across the boundary with families, other workers, and agencies.

Communication
In some ways communication is simply an aspect of the co-ordination required in group care practice since it provides the means through which service co-ordination takes place. It merits separate consideration, however, because of its importance to all who are involved with children, and because the manner (as opposed to the content) of communication is not always given sufficient attention. Boundary workers may be used as channels of communication even when they have little or no involvement with a particular child, simply because they happen to be present. This means passing information in two or more directions, and not just collecting it for oneself. Such a go-between role is difficult to fulfil in that it is not always easy to pass on the full flavour of a communication at second hand. A significant part of any communication is implicit, that is non-verbal, and – though recognized – may not be sufficiently clear as to be passed on to others.

In such cases communication is clearly different from co-ordination since it is entirely separate from responsibility for work or decisions. This type of communication without authority is **particularly evident in working on the boundary between separate** agencies, since each agency will be autonomous in decision-making within their own sphere. It may also apply between different professional groups, particularly where professional roles are clearly and rigidly demarcated.

The formal communication system consists largely of meetings and written reports. In any group care setting there are likely to be daily change-of-shift meetings, and regular review meetings for longer-term planning, to which outsiders may be invited. Written records may also be organized for daily, weekly, and longer-term reports, and for inside and outside use. It is difficult, however, to ensure that the formal system meets all communication needs. People miss meetings (perhaps because they are minding the children!) and fail to read reports. Reports tend to be factual and often do not contain impressions or 'intuitive' understanding. Moreover, communication is not just about information, it is about relationships, trust, and support. When emotional aspects of communication are blocked, workers are left feeling unheard or misunderstood and a frequent result is that distrust arises. Any lapse in factual communication is then magnified, and attempts may be made to change the formal system to ensure fuller discussion and agreement. What is more often needed are better informal opportunities for talk in a relaxed atmosphere where feelings can be more freely expressed.

Communication is about understanding. If the formal content of communication is divorced from the relationship between communicators, then misunderstandings are all too frequent. To an extent, one hears what one expects to hear. Expectations are set up by one's attitude towards the other person, by one's previous experiences of working with him or her, and by the pressures one is under at the time. Words are an inadequate medium to convey the richness and complexity of our thoughts and feelings. Understanding is only achieved through the medium of non-verbal signals, openness, freedom from anxiety, and shared experience. Otherwise what one says may reach the other person with a changed meaning. The story is told of an old lady who played the bugle. Her favourite saying, when accused of playing out-of-tune, was that 'it was all right when it left me'. Perhaps the lesson to be learned from this is that if one wishes to be understood, one needs to have, as well as an idea of what one wants to say, an awareness of the other's point of view.

Working with families

In some group care settings, particularly those provided by social services, children may be there because they have no effective home base, and contact with parents may be minimal or non-existent. In a psychiatric setting children are likely to have their own or substitute families, who have frequent contact with their children while in the unit, and usually these children return home afterwards. In this case the work being done with the families outside the unit parallels that done with the child inside the unit, and is likely to be just as important to the eventual outcome.

The boundary worker's role with a family includes of course keeping unit staff informed about what is happening within the family, and the family informed about what is happening with their child in the unit. More important is the process of engaging the family to work alongside the staff towards mutual goals. Initially the parents may feel a lot of anger and guilt towards care staff, at having failed to cope with their own child and because the staff seem able to cope so much better. Parents need to be reassured that the staff also find their child difficult at times. Staff have the added advantage of having other people available to help, of having a time-limited commitment with the certainty of leaving at the end of a shift, and are able to work with no other distracting tasks which must be carried out simultaneously, such as housework. Given such reassurances, staff may then be able to help parents observe and try out alternative ways of managing their child's difficult behaviour, as suggested by Conte elsewhere in this volume.

Group care staff may also come to feel quite angry towards parents, because the parents are seen as being the root cause of the child's problems. This is particularly the case with parents who seem rejecting, who fail to visit or keep promises, or who criticize and undermine their child when they do visit. Staff see the effect of this behaviour on the child, and it often stirs up deep-rooted fears and anxieties of their own. The family's worker is likely to suffer the same emotional reaction, but being less closely involved with the child, she/he may be able to remain detached enough as to try and understand the reasons for the parents' difficulties.

Teaching

Many boundary workers may also have a formal teaching role with staff in a group care unit, since most in-service training tends to be provided within professional groups. Boundary workers may sometimes have a role supervising students who are working temporarily in or around a unit. Informal teaching occurs through a process of mutual learning which is one of the great benefits found in working closely with members of different professions. A liaison worker's contribution to the unit team is to bring in information about a child's family, environment, and contributions of workers outside the unit, so that the child's behaviour can be better understood. The worker may also be able to promote sharing of tasks and the emergence of inside workers into the outside arena. Many group care staff are becoming more and more involved with, for instance, work with families, and are beginning to participate in family therapy and home visits. Since work of this nature involves the blurring of roles and the taking on of tasks previously regarded as belonging to other professions, performance is initially accompanied by diffidence and uncertainty.

Care staff in particular may feel ill-equipped for such work because of the narrowness or inappropriateness of their earlier training. Nurses working in psychiatric settings, for example, may not have had any suitable specialist training. For instance in Scotland there is no training course for nurses in child psychiatry, and elsewhere such courses are usually limited to a few centres. It is therefore not unusual for nurses to have a weighting of general training, with its emphasis on physical care, regular routines, and close supervision from senior staff. Inevitably, therefore, nurses working in child psychiatric in-patient settings have to learn many of the skills they need on the job, by observing others at work, by working alongside a more experienced staff member, and by 'trial and error'. As well as senior nurses, members of all the other professions involved have a useful part to play in this. Where the other professions are organizationally separated from the group care unit, then such involvement becomes a boundary task.

Public relations
Group care is one of a range of services and facilities available for helping troubled children. It is often seen as undesirable, harmful, to be avoided at all costs, and only used when other measures have failed. This is particularly the case at present given the drive away from institutional care towards community-based

services. Group care offers an experience that is different from other forms of professional intervention because of its intensity and its all-embracing nature. At its best, group care provides considerable impetus for change in a setting which is safe and controlled, and which offers a choice and flexibility of means through the number and varied skills of a staff team. It also provides opportunities for the development of a much more comprehensive picture of a child and his or her problems. Group care can also have a considerable influence on children and their problems because of the close relationships which can be formed there.

One of the most important tasks of a boundary worker is to 'sell' this more positive view of the potential of residential treatment to those outside. 'Outside' includes colleagues working in, say, the out-patient department of a hospital as well as those from other agencies, since acquaintance with and responsibility for a unit does not necessarily mean that it is favourably regarded. Indeed influencing the views of colleagues on an out-patient team or in an external agency can be paramount, since it is they who decide whether to ask for admission to a unit for any particular child. The group care unit may refuse admission on the grounds of inability to cope with a particular child or because of an unbalanced mix of children currently in the group, but they cannot make a positive choice. And yet successful outcomes, and consequently work satisfaction for the staff, depend upon the suitability of children referred to a unit and their ability to respond to the experiences which can be offered to them there.

Conclusions

It has been argued throughout this chapter that much of the role of a boundary worker consists of establishing and encouraging informal mechanisms to carry out the tasks of communication, co-ordination of work, and so on; and that the need for this informal system arises from the complexity and inbuilt conflicts contained in the formal system of management operating in many group care centres. The smaller the organization and the less cumbersome its formal structure, the less need there is for some boundary roles. There will always be a need for communication and liaison with the community and agencies outside the group care setting. But tasks inside the setting, in particular support and sharing of anxiety and frustration, may be minimized if the formal structure is one in which authority is clearly delegated, where there is frequent and open discussion of work, and where relationships are characterized by trust and valuation between members of staff.

Two questions can be said to have arisen out of direct experience of work in a boundary role. The first question involves whether it is possible to sit right in the middle of the boundary without moving to one side or the other. It can be a very uncomfortable place, attracting maximum blame and minimum satisfaction. One is not closely enough involved in the direct work of the unit to share the pleasure of seeing children improve and one can sometimes feel loaded with all the problems. One alternative is to look for satisfaction in work outside the unit (for example, with families) and see the boundary tasks as a necessary but onerous duty. The other is to become more involved with the staff and children in the unit, and see oneself as something of an ambassador, rather than a neutral negotiator.

The second question is whether it is necessary to have actually practised as a care worker, inside a group care unit, in order to perform boundary tasks adequately. It is very helpful in relating to care staff to have some idea of the kind of stresses their work imposes. Group care practice is non-stop and can be exhausting. The pace is quite different from that of planned appointments, and much of the time it is a matter of responding to the constant demands of others. There may only be a small number of children, but relationships with them are likely to be close and sometimes intensive. The world 'outside' can seem far away and not very relevant to the task at hand. It is thus easy to develop a certain distrust of strangers and outsiders. One is dealing with a group of children, not just one individual, and this can multiply any problems. If a boundary worker is not aware of all this, she/he may not hear when staff complain of feeling stressed and thereby not respond helpfully. It is of course possible to understand what group care work is like without having direct experience of it. However, without the experience, it is not possible to know whether one could cope oneself in that situation! Descriptions of a day in the life of a unit can sometimes sound quite horrendous. The inexperienced boundary worker may react with panic measures: suggest discharging a child or send in the experts. Such a reaction is not necessarily helpful to staff and may have disastrous consequences for children. Helping staff to tolerate crises and even to use such experiences is far more convincing if one has been able to do the same oneself on previous occasions.

Notes

1 This chapter is written from the point of view of group care practice in the Health Care System. There it is commonplace to find a highly differentiated division of labour between different categories of worker. In smaller, community-based group care centres, some workers – especially senior staff – carry several of the boundary roles outlined in this chapter.
2 Angela Hopkinson is a social worker at the Royal Hospital for Sick Children in Edinburgh, Scotland.
3 The notion of a 'key worker' has its origins in the Social Welfare System in Britain. A number of other terms can be found, such as 'primary worker', 'prime care agent', or 'assigned worker', depending on which side of the Atlantic the reader engages in practice. In Britain, the term 'key worker' can be traced to a report published in 1976 by a joint working party set up by the Residential Care Association and the British Association of Social Workers (*Social Work Today* September 1976). While there are strong beliefs held in support of the 'key worker' idea, no general agreement is to be found as to the specific tasks carried out by such a person. For this reason, application of the 'key worker' principle in direct practice is extremely variable.

References

Cockburn, C. (1977) *The Local State: Management of Cities and People*. London: Pluto Press.
Emery, F. E. (ed.) (1969) *Systems Thinking*. Harmondsworth, England: Penguin.
Fulcher, L. C. (1981) Team Functioning in Group Care. In F. Ainsworth and L. C. Fulcher (eds) *Group Care for Children: Concept and Issues*. London: Tavistock.
Hearn, G. (1969) Progress Toward an Holistic Conception of Social Work. In G. Hearn (ed.) *The General System Approach: Contributions Toward an Holistic Conception of Social Work*. New York: Council of Social Work Education.
Menzies, I. E. P. (1970) *The Functioning of Social Systems as a Defence Against Anxiety*. London: Tavistock.
Miller, E. J. and Rice, A. K. (1967) *Systems of Organization*. London: Tavistock.
Monane, J. H. (1967) *A Sociology of Human Systems*. New York: Appleton-Century-Crofts.
Polsky, H. W. (1962) *Cottage Six*. New York: Russell Sage.
Polsky, H. W. and Claster, D. S. (1968) *The Dynamics of Residential Treatment: A Social Systems Analysis*. Chapel Hill, North Carolina: University of North Carolina Press.
Roberts, E. (1982) A Presentation of Perspectives of Organisational Theory

Relevant to Social Work. In J. Lishman (ed.) *Research Highlights No. 4: Social Work Departments as Organisations.* Aberdeen: University of Aberdeen, Department of Social Work.

Trieschman, A. E., Whittaker, J. K., and Brendtro, L. K. (1969) *The Other 23 Hours: Child Care in a Therapeutic Milieu.* Chicago: Aldine.

VanderVen, K. D. (1979) Towards Maximum Effectiveness of the Unit Team Approach in Residential Care: An Agenda for Team Development. *Child Care Administration* 1 (3): 287–98.

Whittaker, J. K. (1981) Major Approaches to Residential Treatment. In F. Ainsworth and L. C. Fulcher, (eds) *Group Care for Children: Concept and Issues.* London: Tavistock.

10 The group care worker as a teacher of parents[1]

Jon R. Conte[2]

Introduction

The relationship between a child's natural parents and the group care workers who care for and treat the child is often tenuous. These relationships vary, depending on a variety of factors which include the theoretical orientation used in the group care setting, the degree of comfort group care workers feel in having a child's parents 'about' the setting, the degree to which the workers see their role as 'rescuing the child' from bad parents, or frequently, some ambiguity surrounding what exactly to do with and for a child's natural parents. This chapter will provide an introductory overview to a relatively new practice method which we believe has a great deal to offer the group care worker who wishes to work with a child's natural parents or parent surrogates. This method is generally referred to as *parent training*. The reader is cautioned that, as an introduction to parent training, this chapter aims to suggest the potentials of parent training for group care practice and is not intended to represent a thorough review of the literature on teaching parents. For a review of the literature, see Conte (1979), Gordon and Davidson (1981), and O'Dell (1974).

In recent years there has been a significant increase in approaches to teaching or training parents. These approaches have included parent education, parent discussion groups, 'toddler classes', parenting groups of a wide variety of models, and parent training. Although there is no clear consensus on what the various terms 'teaching', 'training', 'parenting groups', etc. mean, it is important in order to accomplish the task of this chapter to think of these terms distinctly. Auerbach (1968) identified the goals of *parent education* as: (1) helping parents to become familiar with basic concepts of child growth and development; (2) helping them clarify their own role and that of their children; and (3) increasing parental understanding of the complexities of everyday situations, to enable them to make better management decisions. These goals emphasize education and understanding as essential ingredients. Another kind of group parenting experience is summarized by Tavormina (1974) who summarized the goals of the *reflective counselling* model as: (1) understanding the child's needs at various stages of growth; (2) examination of what group members expect of themselves as parents; (3) a focus on feelings within the parent–child relationship; and (4) recognition of children as reacting and feeling individuals (1974: 828).

Parent training involves a very different orientation from the preceding models and emphasizes training parents in specification child management (behaviour-changing) skills. Parents are taught how to use behaviour-modification skills with their own children. Emphasis in parent training is clearly on skill development, rather than understanding or feelings alone, although both of these are important aspects of training.

There are at least two major approaches to training parents to modify the behaviour of their own children. One involves direct manipulation of parent behaviour in the home or in a clinic laboratory by direction from a parent trainer/therapist. Such direction may be in the form of direct verbal instructions in which the trainer tells the parent what to do. For example, a parent might be told to ignore the child's inappropriate behaviour or to restate the parent's instructions to the child in a more concise manner. Directions from the trainer to the parent might also involve the use of hand signals. Much training in clinical laboratories has involved placing the child and parent in a play room equipped with a one-way mirror behind which the trainer/therapist observes parent–child interaction and communicates with the parent through a small receiver ('bug-in-the-ear', Farrell instrument) worn by the parent (Forehand and King 1977). The other major approach to parent training involves didactic instruction of material (behaviour-change techniques and social learning theory) and the application of this content by the parent(s) in their own environment. This type of training has been conducted with parents either individually or in groups.

It is generally believed by parent trainers that parents of older children (approximately fourteen years or older) should be involved in a training programme which recognizes the particular problems of parent–adolescent relationships. Behaviour change with older children has many of the characteristics of behaviour change with adults and requires the ability to communicate about problems, to negotiate for behaviour change, and to solve problems. This chapter will emphasize training parents of younger children. Because the training approaches for direct manipulation of parent behaviour and for training parents of older children involve clearly separate techniques and bodies of literature, these methods will not be covered here.

Assumptions about parent training

Professional interest in the training of parents whose children are young began for a number of reasons. One reason involved the concern that there were insufficient helping professionals available to meet the needs of problem children and their families. There was also a concern which speaks directly to the feelings of many group care workers, that changes produced in the clinic, office, or out-of-home placement were not maintained when the child returned to her/his natural home. It is a common lament among group care workers that they work for a period of time to get children 'into shape' only to have them return to their home and within the space of a relatively short period of time to find the children functioning just as they were prior to entering group care. This kind of problem led developers of parent training to search for ways to reach out of the clinic, office, or group care facility into the child's natural environment.

One means of reaching out into the child's natural environment is to train a child's parents to carry out certain change-producing and change-maintaining tasks with their child in her/his natural environment. Parent training, then, rests on a number of propositions. Some of these propositions have to date been empirically verified; others have not. Taken as a whole, their propositions communicate an orientation which is at the heart of parent training. These propositions and their implications will be presented below.

Those most directly involved in a child's environment are often in the best position to change the child's behaviour. Although it depends in part on the type of behaviour and the specific child under discussion, generally it is assumed that children behave differently in different environments (Conway and Bucher 1976). Therapeutically, it is necessary either to prepare the child to go back to that environment and maintain changes produced in the clinic or group care facility (e.g. through self-control procedures) or to find means to produce change in the home environment. Parent training assumes the latter strategy by working with the child's parents. Although there have been reports where the child has been trained to produce changes in her/his home (Benassi and Larson 1976), generally it is believed that training parents is a more direct means of producing change in the home environment. There are a number of reasons for this, but to a great extent this assumption is made because parents are in positions of greater decision-making power within families and presumably have *greater control* (but not total control) over reinforcers and punishers in families than do their children. This assumption should not be understood to suggest that parents are solely responsible for their children's behaviour. On the contrary, there is increasing evidence to support the notion that parents and children teach each other both appropriate and inappropriate behaviour (Patterson 1976).

One of the implications of this first proposition is that training tends to focus on child behaviours which take place in environments under direct parent influence (especially the home). It is more difficult and requires different techniques for the parent to change child behaviour which takes place outside of the home. For example, in order for parents to help alter a child's behaviour at school, it is necessary to develop procedures for the parent to obtain reports from the teacher on child performance and to reinforce or punish such performance at home (Barth 1979). So while it is not impossible for the parent to change behaviour which takes place outside of her/his immediate influence, training parents to produce such change does require special procedures. These include either a means for the parent to obtain accurate information on the child's behaviour in other environments, so that reinforcement may be given by the parent, or for the parent to teach the child self-control procedures which can be used in other environments when the parent is absent.

Parents can learn and appropriately apply behaviour-change technology. A number of research studies have shown that parents can conceptually learn behaviour-change technology and can successfully apply this technology in reducing the problematic behaviour of their own children (see the section on 'The effects of parent training' which follows). This proposition causes concern for some helping professionals, even in the light of the research evidence supporting it. Although this concern has not been formally developed, it gives voice to a distrust of behaviour-modification approaches to parenting. In part, such distrust is based either on ignorance about what behaviour modification actually entails, or on a relatively few highly publicized accounts of grossly unethical applications of supposedly behavioural interventions such as entrapping children in plywood boxes as a form of punishment.

Although there have been clearly inhumane applications of techniques by workers who are supposedly trained in behaviour modification, the point which the group care worker should consider is that these violations of sound clinical practice are not inherent in behaviour modification. Nor is there any reason to assume that there have been more inappropriate or unethical applications of behavioural principles than with any other theoretical orientation to practice. More importantly, the procedures which parents are taught and the behaviour change undertaken by parents are a direct result of: first, what the trainer teaches parents; and second, that with which the parent feels comfortable. For example, this writer has trained a number of parents who had strong objections to one or another form of reinforcement, such as food, money, or television. In each of these cases parents were able to select a number of reinforcers which they felt more comfortable using with their child. Occasionally there are parents for whom behavioural techniques become another means of expressing basic anger towards or dislike of their child. Although these parents are rare, when the trainer becomes aware that a parent is using behaviour techniques in aversive or inhumane ways, then this usage should become the focus of clinical intervention.

It is often believed erroneously that parent training is practised as a unique intervention. In fact it is the case that in many settings parent training is used in conjunction with any number of other methods as the clinical needs of the case indicate. For example, the parent training literature describes a number of training approaches which include humanistic elements (Sadler *et al.* 1976) or training parents to modify the behaviour of their children and to use coping skills, relaxation techniques, problem solving, and self-observation (Wells, Griest, and Forehand 1980; Wolfe, Sandler, and Kaufman 1981). There is no reason why parent training cannot be used in conjunction with other therapeutic interventions with a child or parent, as clinically indicated. Indeed, this is one of the advantages of parent training as a clinical method.

Parent training teaches parents to change their children's behaviour. As a necessary step in this process, the parent changes her/his own behaviour. In training parents to be behaviour modifiers, they are taught a behaviour-change process which requires that they alter their own behaviour. It is largely impossible for them to change their children's behaviour without altering their own behaviour. For example, in the most simplistic situation a parent identifies some behaviour which their child is not exhibiting (such as complying with requests). In such a case, a parent might be taught to provide some kind of reinforcement (verbal praise or a token) contingent on the child's complying with a request. The parent's use of reinforcement requires a change in parent behaviour. Indeed, in many homes where parents and children have been involved in long histories of painful interactions, the introduction of reinforcement into those relationships can be clinically important, although to do so requires pairing some more powerful reinforcement initially with the parent's social reinforcement. It is important to keep in mind that the goal of parent training is to produce change in a child's behaviour by producing change in parent's behaviour. Part of the challenge of parent training is to undertake training efforts at a group care facility or training site and then finding these successful in modifying parents' behaviour in the home which is removed in time and place from the actual training. In part, the identification of which parent behaviour should be modified is a decision made by the trainer in conjunction with the parent and such decisions should be informed by a thorough clinical assessment of the case. Reports describing parent behaviour which has been modified through parent training efforts have included: parental anger, coping, depression, and assertiveness. There is no reason, however, to rule out any behaviour amenable to change.

It is also important to note that in some situations it is not the child's behaviour at all which may require modification. For example, Lobitz and Johnson (1975) in a study of two groups of children, where one group had been referred to a clinic and the other had not, found that parent attitude towards child behaviour carried a greater weight in discriminating between the two groups than did child behaviour. These authors noted that children who come to the attention of helping professionals may fall into one of two groups. One group involves children who actually exhibit deviant behaviour, and the other involves children who do not exhibit deviant behaviour but whose parents report that they do. For these children, efforts to change their parent's perception becomes the major clinical goal. In part, this process takes place as parents are taught to be more accurate observers of their children's behaviour while at the same time designing and implementing a behaviour-change project. Parents who are unable to observe and accurately monitor their children's behaviour present a more significant clinical problem. Special interventions may be planned to address the needs of these parents (Wahler, Dumas, and Gordon 1981).

Clinical intervention proceeds in response to information from ongoing empirical feedback. Parent training provides an excellent example of an empirically based clinical method. In a number of ways, parent training has developed in direct response to research efforts to validate certain procedures or to understand certain clinical problems (e.g. the aggressive child). Much of this chapter on parent training is based on research studies which have addressed various training issues. Of equal importance is the central role which empirical methods play in assessment, monitoring progress through treatment, and determining the effects of treatment. Parents are taught to keep a record of behaviour which they seek to change in their child and occasionally of their own behaviour as well. Trainer-collected data are also an essential component of parent training, as they provide the trainer with information about whether parents are acquiring the desired knowledge or skills, whether they are successfully implementing the behaviour-change techniques, or whether the parents are having unintended problems during the course of training. While data collection is dependent upon the procedures which a trainer initially establishes, and there is variation in what information trainers believe is important, there is widespread recognition that detailed records are fundamentally important for decision-making in parent training.

Training content and approach

There are a number of dimensions with which to measure parent training activities. One of these dimensions is *length of training,* although generally speaking, parent training may be thought of as a brief, time-limited intervention. For example, Eyeberg and Johnson (1974) reported eleven one-hour sessions and Patterson (1974) reported an average of 31.4 hours per case. Most training procedures seem to run from eight to twelve weeks. However, there is no reason why they could not run for a longer period, as needed. Indeed Mathis (1971) reported on a single case where it took thirty weeks to reduce extreme child behaviour problems. The severity of the child and parent problems are one variable which may be helpful in determining the length of parent training.

Another variable which distinguishes between parent training approaches is whether parents are trained *individually or in groups.* Although there has been some attention paid to this variable, much of this research attention has focused on the difference in cost or staff time required by the two approaches, and the results are inconclusive (Mira 1970; Kovitz 1976). Training parents individually provides an opportunity for the trainer to focus exclusively on one parent or couple. Frequently, training efforts can take up a small proportion of any client–worker contact with the remainder of the time being devoted to other clinical issues (e.g. marital counselling). However, group training provides a number of distinct, although as yet unproven, advantages. These include: an opportunity for parents to see that other parents have similar problems and consequently that they are not alone and a 'failure'; social contact with other adults; and the possibility of learning behaviour change methods from other parents. Group trainers also believe that the small group can have an important influence on parent behaviour as it reinforces the parent for attendance, participation, and sincere attempts at changing behaviour. One disadvantage of group training is that it takes more time to run a training group than it does to train individual parents, and the actual time any specific parent receives is a small proportion of the time they spend in the group. Research, such as is currently available, is not helpful in determining whether to train parents individually or in groups. Practical issues, such as how experienced the new trainer is or how many parents are available at a particular point in time, may influence such a decision.

Another variable affecting the length of training is the *amount of content* which is the focus of training. There are two major approaches to selecting content. The limited focus or limited technique approach provides parents with a pre-designed behaviour-change method for a specific behaviour (e.g. child non-compliance) or trains parents in the use of one behaviour-change method (e.g. the use of reinforcement). In the limited-focus approach, the behaviour-change method is frequently designed by the trainer, and the parent is trained to implement the programme (Johnson 1971; Tams and Eyeberg 1976). In the comprehensive approach to selecting content, the parent is trained in the use of a wide number of behaviour-change techniques (e.g. reinforcement and time out) and frequently is given some education in the principles upon which the techniques are based.

Research addressing this issue is contradictory. Herbert and Baer (1972) reported adverse effects of training parents in the use of differential parent attention alone, noting that rates of deviant child behaviour increased in some cases as a function of training parents in the use of this technique. Glogower and Sloop (1976) compared a general approach plus a specific-problem-behaviour focus (combination group) with a specific-problem-focus-only training procedure. On non-observational measures they found that both groups learned principles equally well and were successful in implementing behaviour change with their child. On a behaviour analogue measure and observation of parent–child interaction in structured laboratory situations, they found significant improvement for the combination group. McMahon, Forehand, and Griest (1981) compared training in techniques alone (no theory) and techniques with social learning principles in a training format which focused on direct manipulation of parent–child interaction in a laboratory through a 'bug in the parent's ear' listening device. They found that the social learning group had significantly greater knowledge gains, perceived their children as more adjusted, and reported greater satisfactions than the technique-alone group. In contrast to these findings, O'Dell, Flynn, and Benlolo (1977) compared three kinds of pre-training experiences: (1) behaviour theory; (2) placebo attention but with content not likely to increase parent knowledge; and (3) no theory. All groups were trained in a workshop during which they were helped to carry out a behaviour modification plan. On measures of parent knowledge, in-class demonstrations of behavioural skills, levels of involvement in the class, and attitudes towards training, there were no group differences.

Until additional research becomes available, the decision about how much and what specific content should be made available to parents will have to rest on practice hypotheses. In part, this decision may rest on the particular goals of the training procedure. If reduction in a specific child problem is the focus, then training which emphasizes trainer-designed behaviour-modification plans may be appropriate. However, if it is thought desirable to place greater responsibility with the parents, either because there are a large number of problem behaviours or because greater involvement in the plan will help ensure the parent's continued use of the training material, then training parents to use a number of techniques seems desirable.

Another dimension distinguishing one parent training programme from another is what *materials* they employ. Most training procedures which provide parents with a more comprehensive set of behaviour-change techniques also present some theory. There is an impressive array of resources available for parents including written materials and audio or visual aides. (Although no single bibliography covers the variety of materials available to train parents, the review by Bernal and North (1978) and the latest catalogue from Research Press in Champaign, Illinois, should be helpful. The 'how-to-do-it' manuals by Miller (1975) and Patterson *et al.* (1975) are also useful to the beginning parent trainer.) Unfortunately, as Bernal and North (1978) noted in their survey of parent training manuals, few of these materials have been evaluated to determine their effectiveness, or the problems that parents encounter in using them. Arkell, Kubo, and Neunier (1976) as well as Bernal and North (1978) reported on the reading level of the major parent training texts, and their findings may help in the selection of materials which a special group of parents are likely to be able to read. Other than reading level, the selection of materials for training parents currently rests on the trainer's personal judgement.

Most comprehensive texts cover more or less the same material. Patterson (1976) presented material on social reinforcement, punishment, accidental training, how to use reinforcement to change behaviour, and steps in the behaviour-change process including: observation, baseline, intervention, types of reinforcement, time out, and application of these principles to typical child-management problems, such as whining, temper tantrums, and non-compliance. Other texts, such as those by Becker (1971), Madsen and Madsen (1972), and Rettig (1973) cover much of the same material.

Several issues are involved in the use of written materials in training parents. First, for many parents who found their own schooling difficult or who failed to complete school, the apparent similarity between training and schooling – books, homework, and knowledge tests – is initially frightening. It is often a good idea to prepare parents for this initial reaction and to provide reassurance that they will in fact be able to complete the training procedures. Second, the issue of how technical the content needs to be for parents to successfully change behaviour has not been fully addressed in parent training research. Many trainers feel that ideas behind concepts are important and that some technical language is necessary in order to achieve precision of communication around certain crucial areas of family life and the behaviour-change process. However, once again, this remains a matter of personal judgement.

The training process

Although parent training procedures may vary in the ordering of content, the actual number of training sessions, or in which issues are emphasized, most procedures include more or less the same ingredients. Parents are asked to complete reading assignments which review the principles of behaviour change and describe the techniques used in modifying behaviour. They carry out a series of homework assignments which help them pinpoint behaviour(s) to be modified, establish a baseline for that behaviour, and implement a behaviour-modification plan. In some training programmes parents maintain major responsibility for designing the modification plan (Kovitz 1976), while in others the therapist trainer provides them with a pre-designed modification plan for a predetermined behaviour (Tams and Eyeberg 1976). Other training procedures involve the use first of a therapist-designed plan which is used both to train the parents and to demonstrate the utility of the approach and is subsequently followed by a parent-designed programme (Wiltz and Patterson 1974).

In the process of developing new child-management skills, parents are exposed to a number of other training methods. These include role playing or behavioural rehearsal and observing someone performing the skills. Several research studies point to the importance of providing parents with an opportunity to either observe someone performing the skill or to observe and rehearse the skill themselves. Nay (1975) compared written, lecture, video-taped, modelling, modelling plus role playing presentation of training material, and a no-treatment control and found no difference between groups in terms of knowledge gained. However, a significant difference was observed for parents' responses on an audio-taped simulated situations measure, with modelling and role playing superior to written and lecture formats. The modelling-alone group was not highlighted in the same manner. O'Dell *et al.* (1980), in a study of methods used to teach parents about time out, compared written take-home materials, a film plus written manual, individual modelling and rehearsal plus written manual, and a no-treatment control. On measures of time-out knowledge, role playing with a child actor, and in-home observations, all the methods were superior to no training at all, but no differences were noted between the various training methods. In contrast, Flanagan, Adams, and Forehand (1979) reported results indicating that video modelling is significantly more effective than written presentation of training materials, with lecture and role play falling in between modelling and written presentations. O'Dell *et al.* (1980) also reported that video and a brief individual contact with parents was superior to written manual presentation of materials. These findings tend to confirm the standard training format which includes a number of training methods. Written presentation of training content with the use of rehearsal and modelling of training content appears necessary to ensure that parents actually acquire the new child-management skills.

The important thing to bear in mind about the methods used in training is that their ultimate goal is to change parent behaviour. For example, it is believed that teaching parents the principles of behaviour change is a necessary foundation to the parents being able to go back to their home and effectively modify their child's, and hence their own, behaviour. The difficulty for the trainer is that she/he is attempting to change behaviour which takes place in the family's home removed in time and space from the trainer. The primary task during training is to develop exercises, homework, and other experiences which can be used to successfully modify behaviour that takes place outside the training sessions. Having the parents rehearse the new skills in a training session increases the likelihood that they actually understand what the skill entails and will exhibit the skill in their own home.

Several studies describe more direct influences over parent behaviour. Mira (1970) reported a training requirement that parents complete a baseline of target behaviours before keeping their actual training appointment. Eyeberg and Johnson (1974) and Rinn, Vernon, and Wise (1975) examined the influence of reimbursement and the use of weighted consequences upon parent behaviour. These studies found that direct attempts to influence parent behaviour were associated with the amount of time required to complete the programs and treating fewer behaviour problems. Weighted consequences did have a positive effect on attendance, punctuality, and assignment completion. Peine and Munro (1973) presented results from two experiments dealing with behaviour contracts and token reinforcement with parent groups. In one experiment they found that direct influence produced greater attendance, punctuality at meetings, and assignment completion. In the other experiment they found no differences between groups of parents whose behaviour was subjected to direct influences as compared with those not so exposed. These findings tend to suggest that direct influences, especially in the form of reinforcement, can be helpful in affecting parent behaviour.

However, there is no reason to expect that they should be used, nor that they are necessary in every situation. The potential trainer should keep in mind, however, that influencing parent behaviour is a clear goal of parent training. This holds whether behaviour change takes place as a result of the homework assignments, of direct influences on parent behaviour (such as opportunities for participation or reinforcement for assignment completion), or through a number of less direct influences which are an inherent feature of training, especially group training of parents.

Non-specific influences which result from parent training may include any reinforcement parents receive from social interaction or attention from other group members or the parent trainer. Parents may gain an appreciation that their child's behaviour is no worse than the behaviour of other children, as described by parents in the group. Hopefully, parents come to recognize that their child's behaviour reflects both positive and negative behaviours and that the actual frequency of negative behaviour is less than their memory suggests. To make full use of these potential influences on parent behaviour, it is necessary to facilitate the creation of a positive group atmosphere. This group atmosphere must be sufficiently reinforcing to compensate for any initial punishment which parents may experience from others in their natural environments not involved in the training. A positive group atmosphere can also support parents as they encounter potentially aversive aspects of the training itself, such as reading or homework assignments.

In part, a positive group atmosphere is created through the selective use of reinforcement for parent behaviour by the trainer. For example, verbal behaviour should be monitored and positive statements about a parent's ability to influence their home life should be reinforced. The training process itself helps to structure parent behaviour in a number of ways. For example, in the early stages of training, parent participation is kept to a minimum as initial assessment and didactic instruction take place. At the point at which parent in-group participation increases, parents have been provided with new conceptual skills which they can use to describe family life. This kind of situation helps control both parent negativism and a sharing among parents of inappropriate child-management techniques, such as the way to stop cursing is to wash a child's mouth out with soap. Parent behaviour within the group can also be influenced by parents having to present the results of each week's homework assignments to the group. The undivided attention of a group of adults, as parents present their weekly homework assignments, can be a powerful reinforcer for adults who have problematic interpersonal relationships.

Characteristics of children and parents

A wide range of child behaviours have been changed by parents who receive child-management training. These include: socially aggressive children (Wiltz and Patterson 1974); aggressive, disobedient, hyperactive, temper tantrums, or high-rate activity (Eyeberg and Johnson 1974); hyperactive, autistic, schizophrenic children (Herbert and Baer 1972); children who were extremely difficult to manage and control (Hawkins *et al.* 1966); screaming, fighting, disobedience, and bossing behaviour (Zeilberger, Sampen, and Sloane 1968); children who were hyperactive (Schaefer, Palkes, and Stewart 1974); disruptive (Wahler 1969); encropretic (Balson 1973); fire setting (Holland 1969); asthmatic (Neisworth and Moore 1972); and enuretic (Tough, Howkins, McArthur and Swaay 1971). There has been very little research examining the influence of different child behaviours on the outcome of training efforts. Eyeberg and Johnson (1974) examined two groups of parents, one who treated difficult behaviour problems and one treating less difficult problems. They found no significant difference in terms of the time required by the parent to treat the problem or the number of successfully treated problems. In an earlier single case report, Mathis (1971) indicated that one parent required thirty weeks to treat an extreme behaviour problem child. These studies are so limited that the question of what influence child behaviour has on the effectiveness of parent training remains open.

There has been more attention devoted to research describing how various parent characteristics influence the outcome of training. However, the conclusions drawn from these studies are contradictory. Some studies have found that higher educational level, higher socio-economic status, and greater reading level are associated with better outcome (O'Dell *et al.* 1979; Salzinger, Feldman, and Portnoy, 1970). Rinn, Vernon, and Wise (1975) found that lower-income parents attend fewer classes and were less successful than middle-class parents in a large lecture training class, whereas Patterson (1974) found that lower social class was inversely related with poor outcome. Other studies have failed to document a relationship between socio-economic class and outcome in parent training (Fleischman 1981; Rose 1974; Mira 1970). Some investigators have reported that maternal depression is a significant factor affecting outcome or that mothers who report marital difficulties at the time of training are less able to transfer the effects of parent training to other settings than mothers who do not report marital problems at the time of training (Reisinger, Frangia, and Hoffman 1976). In a recent review, O'Dell (1982) identified a number of variables which potentially influence outcome in parent training. These include: the parent's life situation and demographic factors; knowledge, attitudes, or beliefs of the parent which have the impossibility of change as a theme; parent personality traits (e.g. external locus of control or lack of energy) and profound psychological and family problems (e.g. depression or marital conflict).

A number of issues are raised by the conflicting results of research on parent characteristics. To begin with, it is only recently that parent trainers have begun to address the question of differential results by type of parent. In a recent survey of parent training centres in the United States, Hargis and Blechman (1979) found that the lower socio-economic groups are underrepresented among clients in training centres. In the developmental stages of parent training, it is not surprising that potential clients would include people who were likely to come into contact with parent training research centres operated largely out of psychology clinics at universities. However, there is increasing evidence in the literature to suggest that parent trainers are addressing the parenting needs of abusive parents (Crozier and Katz 1979) and lower-income families (Wahler 1980). It appears that parent trainers are confronting the problems which most professional helpers face in providing services to multi-problem, low-income families (Lorion 1978). Indeed, one major parent training research centre has taken on this problem as a major research focus. Wahler and colleagues (Wahler 1980; Wahler, Dumas, and Gordon 1981; Wahler, Hughey, and Gordon 1981) have identified a group of mothers who, in spite of initial positive effects from involvement in parent training, had difficulty maintaining these effects over time. These 'insular mothers' lived in social environments characterized by insularity, poverty, lack of education, high-crime neighbourhoods, and aversive inter-personal relationships. Relationships with their children, marital partners, and community (especially professional helpers) are highly aversive. These mothers have been shown to respond to events that are peripheral to their child's behaviour as if they were responding only to child behaviour. Efforts in parent training with such mothers must first be directed towards changing the way in which they pay attention to specific behaviour patterns, so that they may respond more accurately.

Findings on the relationship between parent characteristics and effectiveness of parent training seems to support several practice notions in working with parents, especially low-income and multi-problem parents. First, the kind of service that attracts middle-class, more educated parents will not attract other types of parents. A parent training class offered at a university psychology clinic or in a mental health agency may be too threatening or be seen as irrelevant by some parents. Offering classes in community centres, day care centres, churches, or schools may be indicated. Second, active outreach efforts to identify and recruit parents in low-income areas may be essential. Gabel *et al.* (1977), reporting on parent discussion groups, indicated that the number of phone contacts between a parent and teacher was positively linked to the parent's attendance at parent meetings. This tends to support the importance of active, especially relationship-building, outreach contacts. Third, it is extremely difficult to get even highly motivated parents to attend to their children's problems when they are preoccupied with personal problems. Wahler, Hughey, and Gordon (1981) have given empirical support to this clinical wisdom and have extended it by suggesting that the problem is not one of self-centred preoccupation. Rather, some parents living in highly stressful environments are unable to accurately attend to their children. Wahler's findings support the notion that parent training is only one of a number of needed social services for multi-problem families (others include income and housing supports, job training, and counselling for adult problems).

Most parent trainers will refrain from training parents who are so out of touch with reality and preoccupied with their own intra-

or inter-personal problems that they lack the attentional and personal resources to benefit from training. For the present, these appear to be sound guidelines. These guidelines do not, however, preclude work with multi-problem, low-income families. What is necessary is a clear recognition of the difficulties which these families face and an appreciation of how life-style influences parenting. For these parents, training should be only one of a number of services.

The effects of parent training

In large part, because parent training has developed as an interest within behaviour modification, concern has always been expressed within the literature regarding the effectiveness of parent training. Early studies reporting the results of training parents tended to be single case or small sample studies, such as that of Johnson and Brown (1969) with two families. More recent research has reported results obtained from larger samples, frequently using more complex methodology, as illustrated by Fleischman (1981) with twenty families, and Baum and Forehand (1980) with thirty-four mother–child pairs. There are at least five types of outcome questions which should be asked of any parent training intervention:

1 What are the immediate effects of intervention?
2 Do these effects maintain for some follow-up period?
3 Do the effects of intervention generalize to other settings, behaviours, or situations?
4 What are the unintended effects of intervention?
5 What is the effectiveness of this approach as compared with other approaches?

Although it is still early in the development of parent training to expect a great deal of evidence addressing these questions, there are research findings which begin to answer some of these questions. As will be seen, these findings suggest a range of positive and negative answers to the various evaluative questions.

Findings which describe the immediate effects of parent training seem to suggest that training can be successful in changing the behaviour of parents and children as well as parents' attitude towards their children. For example, Wiltz and Patterson (1974) reported results indicating that deviant behaviour, identified by the parent for change, can be successfully reduced. Patterson (1974) presented findings on twenty-seven conduct problem boys which indicated that two out of every three cases reflected a reduction of 30 per cent or better in problem behaviour. At a twelve-month follow-up, problem behaviour amongst these boys was found to be within the range exhibited by normal children. Patterson, Cobb, and Ray (1973) described results with thirteen aggressive children indicating significant reductions in deviant behaviour identified for change by parents, as compared with other behaviour, and these effects were maintained for six cases seen at follow-up. These and other results indicate that training is successful in reducing negative behaviour on the part of children and parents and increasing some appropriate behaviour. Moreover, these effects would seem to maintained over time (Baum and Forehand 1980; Conger, Lahey, and Smith 1981; Fleischman 1981; Johnson and Christenson 1975).

A methodological issue dealing with reliability of measurement should be noted when thinking about outcome results. The number of cases which any study reports as successful depends in part on the type of information used to make a determination of success. Parent-collected data tends to indicate a higher number of successful cases than does information obtained from independent observers. For example, in the research reported by Johnson and Christenson (1975) on twenty-two parent training cases, 95 per cent of the cases obtained a 30 per cent or better reduction in deviant child behaviour based on parent-collected data. Information collected by observers in the families' homes showed a *non-significant* reduction in deviant child behaviour. Generally speaking, parent-collected data has been shown to disagree with the findings of independent observers (Rinn, Vernon, and Wise 1975; Tavormina 1975) or to indicate improvement in child behaviour while independent observers recorded deterioration (Walter and Gilmore 1973). In contrast to these findings, Reid (1975) reported on parent training efforts where agreement was found between parents and observers.

These findings on the reliability of parental reports of child behaviour, and information generated in a series of studies on the relationship between child behaviour and parent perception, suggest a complex role for parent-reported data in evaluating the

immediate effects of parent training. For example, Griest *et al.*
(1980) indicated that parent-completed measures in clinically
referred cases were influenced by parental adjustment and child
behaviour, whereas in non-clinical cases they were influenced by
child behaviour alone. Similarly, Lobitz and Johnson (1975)
demonstrated that a parent's attitude towards a child is a better
indicator for distinguishing between groups of clinic and nonclinic cases than is child behaviour. These studies, as well as those
conducted by Wahler, Dumas, and Gordon (1981), seem to
indicate that parental reports of child behaviour may be a central
feature of parent training for some parents as well as being an
important measure of outcome. Notwithstanding this methodological concern, the evidence collected by independent observers does
seem to suggest that training parents can be successful in: changing
parent and child behaviour (Baum and Forehand 1980; Fleischman
1981; Patterson 1974); changing parents' attitudes towards children
(Peed, Roberts, and Forehand 1977); and changing parental
perceptions of the home environment (Karoly and Rosenthal
1977).

   Research evidence which addresses the question of whether
these effects can be generalized to different settings, behaviours,
or situations is less positive. A number of studies have shown
how behaviour change in children is not easily transferred from
one setting to another (Forehand *et al.* 1979; Wahler 1969; Miller
and Sloane 1976). These results confirm the behaviour-modification
concept that change in one environment is not accompanied by
change in other environments unless specific interventions are
carried out in both environments.

   Several studies have reported on changes in the behaviour of
siblings of deviant children. In a study of the siblings of twenty-
seven aggressive children, Arnold, Levine, and Patterson (1975)
reported that training the parents of these children was associated
with change in sibling behaviour as well as the designated
'problem' child, although changes in the behaviour of siblings
were less dramatic than for the aggressive child. The authors
noted that two-thirds of the families received trainer supervision
for behaviour change efforts with these siblings. Consequently
these findings do not reflect a no-treatment generalization effect.
In another study, Resnick, Forehand, and McWhorter (1976)
reported mixed results for an identified deviant boy and his non-

deviant brother. When the identified boy's problem behaviours were similar to and took place at the same time as the sibling's behaviour, treatment was associated with an immediate effect in the other child's behaviour. When behaviours were different in content and place, the effects were neither immediate nor long lasting. In their review of evidence on the generalization of treatment effects, Forehand and Atkeson (1977) suggested that there is little evidence for generalization across settings, from targeted to non-targeted behaviours or to siblings not targeted by the parents for intervention. They also noted that the more rigorous the research, the less positive the results tended to be.

There has been very little research addressing questions about unintended effects of parent training. Adverse effects or deterioration as a function of clinical interventions are receiving increasing attention (Gurman and Kniskern 1978). There are several early studies which reported adverse effects as a function of training parents (Herbert *et al.* 1973; Herbert and Baer 1972). However, since these studies reported on adverse effects of training parents in a single technique, such as differential parent attention, they do not seem to address the issue directly about whether more comprehensive training may be associated with adverse effects. Since training is not successful with all parents, careful attention should be given to the possibility that for some people involvement in training may produce negative effects.

Ultimately, an approach to clinical intervention should be compared with alternative approaches to determine which approaches offer the most effective and efficient problem-solving strategy. To date, there has been very little comparison between parent training and other parenting interventions. Such studies as are available offer conflicting findings. Tavormina (1975), in a study of fifty-one mothers of mentally retarded children, examined the effects of assignment into one of three groups: a reflective counselling approach; behavioural parent training; and a waiting list control. Although the two intervention groups were found to be superior to the waiting list control group, on both parent report and observational findings about mother–child interaction in a laboratory, the behavioural group was found to show improvement on a larger number of measures. Hampson and Tavormina (1980) examined the effects of treating foster parents in either reflective or behaviour-modification parenting groups and found that reflective-trained mothers had the most significant change in attitudes, while the behaviourally trained mothers showed the most change in behaviours (increase in appropriate behaviour and decrease in problem behaviour). In contrast, Anchor and Thomason (1977) examined the differential effectiveness of a behavioural parent training group and a *Parent Effectiveness Training* (PET) group (Gordon 1970), where no group differences were found on measures of communication, parent report of child behaviour, parent self-concept, and parent verbal behaviour in class. The authors did note that the parents in this study were 'highly educated'; consequently they would not seem to be typical clients. Ambiguous results were reported by Bernal, Klinnert, and Schultz (1980) in a study of thirty-six families treated in behavioural, client-centred, or assigned to a waiting list control group. While data from the behaviourally trained group alone indicated significant reductions in problem behaviour and improved parent attitudes towards their child's aggressive behaviour, other measures indicated no difference between groups. At six- and twelve-month follow-up contact, test data from parents in both groups showed improvement, whereas observational data showed no group differences.

Parent training in group care

Although to date there has been little written about the use of parent training in group care facilities, contact with a variety of centres suggests that it does occur. There are a number of reasons why more group care settings should consider parent training. First, and perhaps most importantly, the available research suggests that it is a promising clinical intervention. Although additional research is needed and evidence tends to suggest that the effects of training will vary from parent to parent, it is nevertheless the case that research results seem to warrant further development in the use of parent training. For a large number of family problems, parent training would appear to be an effective and efficient way of reducing many of the problems which brought the family into contact with a group care centre in the first place.

Second, parent training offers a number of distinct advantages over other clinical interventions which group care workers might employ. Some of these benefits include the following: (1) parent training can be a non-threatening way to involve families in the group care service; (2) parent training can be used in conjunction with a number of other clinical interventions, taking up as much or as little time as necessary and extending over as long a period as parents and group care workers determine to be appropriate; and (3) training provides parents with skills they can use to manage their own and their child's behaviour, an empowering process which affects parents and families in a number of ways.

A third reason why group care programmes should consider parent training is that it represents an economical, potentially change producing, and ethical intervention. It can help parents acquire skills which may be used to alleviate the conditions that originally required removal of a child from the home, resulting in placement in a group care centre. Professionals are becoming more and more aware that once children are removed from their homes, they tend to remain in out-of-home placements – most typically in one placement after another (Knitzer, Allen, and McGowan 1979). This realization is forcing group care centres to rethink the services provided for or, more frequently, not provided for parents. Parent training would appear to be one of a number of new service arrangements which could reach out to parents and actively engage them in remedial efforts so that child and parent may be reunited.

There are a number of obstacles or issues group care workers will need to confront when implementing parent training procedures in group care settings. One major issue is that parent training requires that a parent have ongoing contact with their child. This ongoing contact in the family home provides the context in which parents practise their new parenting (behaviour-changing) skills, and carry out the behaviour-change process through which positive changes in family interaction are facilitated. When parent–child contact is missing, the need for parent–child contact in the home will require that group care programmes experiment with different ways in which to allow this contact to take place. This should not be so difficult to achieve, since it is common for a child nearing the end of a group care placement gradually to increase the amount of time spent at home. Weekend or once-a-week visits, although less than ideal, do provide some contact during which the family can begin to learn new ways of changing each other's behaviour.

A second issue for the group care worker wishing to begin training parents is a complex one and has to do with ensuring that clients receive the highest quality of care. Damage has been done to children and parents by workers who have been inadequately trained to apply what they wrongly believe to be 'behavioural principles'. It is a great error to believe that behaviour modification is the simplistic application of reinforcement and punishment to some behaviour. Competent parent training would seem to require – at a minimum – both theoretical and practical learning about behaviour, behaviour change, family functioning, and therapeutic processes. As this chapter should illustrate, the research findings which inform the training of parents are diverse and extensive. A group care worker who keeps abreast of developments, who practises under clear ethical guidelines, and who is careful to evaluate what she/he is doing with parents can be expected to provide quality parent training.

Finally, parent training raises a challenge for many group care workers. This challenge confronts the theoretical provincialism of single model group care settings. Parent training poses the very real question of whether such settings will consider a clinical intervention which appears to be helpful to children and families, even if it is different from the orientation in current use. In an age when the ineffectiveness of service is a major indictment against many group care programmes, and at a time when the public is discovering children 'adrift' in a system of out-of-home placements, the challenge that parent training presents will be difficult to ignore. The expanding professional literature on parent training and the popularity of workshops on the topic of parent effectiveness training would seem to suggest that this challenge is being addressed. For the group care worker, training parents represents an effective means of addressing the age-old dilemma of how to work meaningfully with a child's parent(s).

Notes

1 Planned involvement with the parents of children in group care is a new and developing area of practice for direct care workers. It has been carried out traditionally by social workers, psychologists, and others working in association with group care centres. The editors are not aware of any substantial material on this subject which provides more than interesting descriptions of local initiatives. This chapter summarizes the research literature

in an attempt to give workers a sound conceptual basis for developing practice in this area.
2 Jon Conte is an Assistant Professor at the School of Social Service Administration, University of Chicago, Chicago, Illinois, USA.

References

Anchor, K. N. and Thomason, T. C. (1977) A Comparison of Two Parent-training Models with Educated Parents. *Journal of Community Psychology* 5 (20): 134–41.

Arkell, R. N., Kubo, H. R., and Neunier, C. P. (1976) Readaptability and Parental Behavior Following Family Intervention. *Behavior Therapy* 7: 265–66.

Arnold, J. E., Levine, A. G., and Patterson, G. R. (1975) Changes in Sibling Behavior Following Family Intervention. *Journal of Consulting and Clinical Psychology* 43 (5): 683–88.

Auerbach, A. B. (1968) *Parents Learn Through Discussion.* New York: John Wiley.

Balson, P. M. (1973) Encopresis: A Case Study of Symptom Substitution. *Behavior Therapy* 4: 134–36.

Barth, R. (1979) Home-based Reinforcement of School Behavior: A Review and Analysis. *Review of Educational Research* 49 (3): 436–58.

Baum, D. G. and Forehand, R. (November 1980) Long Term Follow-up Assessment of Parent Training by Use of Multiple Outcome Measures. Paper presented at the Association for Advancement of Behavior Therapy, San Francisco.

Becker, W. C. (1971) *Parents are Teachers.* Champaign, Ill.: Research Press.

Benassi, V. A. and Larson, K. M. (1976) Modification of Family Interactions With the Child as the Behavior-change Agent. In E. J. Mash, L. A. Hammerlynch and L. C. Handy (eds) *Behavior Modification and Families.* New York: Brunner/Mazel.

Bernal, M. E. and North, J. A. (1978) A Survey of Parent Training Manuals. *Journal of Applied Behavior Analysis* 11 (4): 533–44.

Bernal, M. E., Klinnert, M. D., and Schultz, L. A. (1980) Outcome Evaluation of Behavioral Parent Training and Client-centered Parent Counseling for Children with Conduct Problems. *Journal of Applied Behavior Analysis* 13 (4): 677–91.

Conger, R. D., Lahey, B. B., and Smith, S. S. (July 1981) An Intervention Program for Child Abuse: Modifying Maternal Depression and Behavior. Paper presented at the Family Violence Research Conference, University of New Hampshire, Durham, New Hampshire.

Conte, J. R. (1979) Helping Groups of Parents Change Their Children's Behavior. *Child and Youth Services* 2 (3): 1, 3–13.

Conway, J. B. and Bucher, B. D. (1976) Generalization and Maintenance of Behavior Change in Children: A Review and Suggestions. In E. J. Mash, L. A. Hammerlynch, and L. C. Handy (eds) *Behavior Modification and Families.* New York: Brunner/Mazel.

Crozier, J. and Katz, R. C. (1979) Social Learning Treatment of Child Abuse. *Journal of Behavior Therapy and Psychiatry* 10 (3): 213–20.

Eyeberg, S. and Johnson, S. M. (1974) Multiple Assessment of Behavior Modification with Families: Effects of Contingency Contracting and Order of Treated Problems. *Journal of Consulting and Clinical Psychology* 42 (4): 594–606.

Flanagan, S., Adams, H., and Forehand, R. (1979) A Comparison of Four Instructional Techniques for Teaching Parents the Use of Time Out. *Behavior Therapy* 10: 94–102.

Fleischman, M. J. (1981) A replication of Patterson's 'Intervention for Boys with Conduct Problems'. *Journal of Consulting and Clinical Psychology* 49: 342–51.

Forehand, R. and Atkeson, B. M. (1977) Generality of Treatment Effects with Parents as Therapists: A Review of Assessment and Implementation Procedures. *Behavior Therapy* 8 (4): 575–93.

Forehand, R. and King, H. E. (1977) Noncompliant children. *Behavior Modification* 1 (1): 93–108.

Forehand, R., Sturgis, E. T., McMahon, R. J., Aguar, D., Green, K., Wells, K. C., and Breiner, J. (1979) Parental Behavioral Training to Modify Child Noncompliance. *Behavior Modification* 3 (1): 3–25.

Gabel, H., Graybill, D., DeMott, S., Wood, L., and Johnston, L. E. (1977) Correlates of Participation in Parent Group Discussion Among Parents of Learning Disabled Children. *Journal of Community Psychology* 5 (3): 275–77.

Glogower, R. and Sloop, E. W. (1976) Two Strategies of Group Training of Parents as Effective Behavior Modifiers. *Behavior Therapy* 7: 177–84.

Gordon, S. B. and Davidson, N. (1981) Behavioral Parent Training. In A. S. Gurman and D. P. Kniskern (eds) *Handbook of Family Therapy*. New York: Brunner/Mazel.

Gordon, T. (1970) *P.E.T. Parent Effectiveness Training*. New York: Peter H. Wyden.

Graziano, A. M. (1977) Parents as Behavior Therapists. In M. Hersen, R. Eisler, and R. Miller (eds) *Progress in Behavior Modification*. New York: Academic Press.

Griest, D. L., Forehand, R., Well, K. D., and McMahon, R. J. (1980) An Examination of Differences Between Nonclinic and Behavior-Problem Clinic-referred Children and Their Mothers. *Journal of Abnormal Psychology* 89 (3): 497–500.

Gurman, A. S. and Kniskern, D. P. (1978) Deterioration in Marital and Family Therapy: Empirical, Clinical and Conceptual Issues. *Family Process* 17 (1): 3–20.

Hampson, R. B. and Tavormina, J. B. (1980) Relative Effectiveness of Behavioral and Reflective Group Training with Foster Mothers. *Journal of Consulting and Clinical Psychology* 18 (2): 294–95.

Hargis, K. and Blechman, E. A. (1979) Social Class and Training of Parents as Behavior Change Agents. *Child Behavior Therapy* 1 (1): 69–73.

Hawkins, R. P., Peterson, R. F., Schweld, B., and Bijou, S. (1966) Behavior Therapy in the Home: Amelioration of Problem Parent–child Relations with the Parent in the Therapeutic Role. *Journal of Experimental Child Psychology* 4: 99–107.

Herbert, E. and Baer, D. M. (1972) Training Parents as Behavior Modifiers: Self-recording of Contingent Attention. *Journal of Applied Behavior Analysis* 5 (2): 139–49.

Herbert, E. W., Pinkson, E. M., Hayden, M. L., Sajwau, T. E., Pinkston, S., Cordua, G., and Jackson, C. (1973) Adverse Effects of Differential Parental Attention. *Journal of Applied Behavior Analysis* 6 (1): 15–30.

Holland, C. J. (1969) Elimination by Parents of Fire-setting in Seven Year Old Boys. *Behavior Research and Therapy* 7 (1): 135–37.

Johnson, J. M. (1971) Using Parents as Contingency Managers. *Psychological Reports* 28: 703–10.

Johnson, S. M. and Brown, R. A. (1969) Producing Change in Parents of Disturbed Children. *Journal of Child Psychiatry* 10: 101–21.

Johnson, S. M. and Christensen, A. (1975) Multiple Criteria Follow-up of Behavior Modification with Families. *Journal of Abnormal Child Psychology* 3 (2): 135–54.

Karoly, P. and Rosenthal, M. (1977) Training Parents in Behavior Modification: Effects on Perceptions of Family Interaction and Deviant Child Behavior. *Behavior Therapy* 8: 406–10.

Knitzer, J., Allen, M. L., and McGowan, B. (1979) *Children Without Homes.* Washington, DC: Children's Defense Fund.

Kovitz, K. E. (1976) Comparing Group and Individual Methods for Training Parents in Child Management Techniques. In E. J. Mash, L. C. Handy, and L. A. Hammerlynch (eds) *Behavior Modification Approaches to Parenting.* New York: Brunner/Mazel.

Lobitz, G. K. and Johnson, S. M. (1975) Normal versus Deviant Children: A Multimethod Comparison. *Journal of Abnormal Child Psychology* 3 (4): 353–74.

Lorion, R. (1978) Research on Psychotherapy and Behavior Change with the Disadvantaged. In S. Garfield and A. Bergin (eds) *Handbook of Psychotherapy and Behavior Change.* New York: John Wiley.

McMahon, R. J., Forehand, R., and Griest, C. L. (1981) Effects of Knowledge of Social Learning Principles on Enhancing Treatment Outcome and Generalization in a Parent Training Program. *Journal of Consulting and Clinical Psychology* 49 (4): 526–32.

Madsen, C. K. and Madsen, Jr., C. H. (1972) *Parents Children Discipline.* Boston: Allyn & Bacon.

Mathis, H. I. (1971) Training a 'Disturbed' Boy, Using the Mother as Therapist: A Case Study. *Behavior Therapy* 2: 567–74.

Miller, S. J. and Sloane, H. W. (1976) The Generalization Effects of Parent Training Across Stimulus Settings. *Journal of Applied Behavior Analysis* 9 (3): 355–70.

Miller, W. H. (1975) *Systematic Parent Training.* Champaign, Ill.: Research Press.

Mira, M. (1970) Results of a Behavior Modification Training Program for Parents and Teachers. *Behavior Research Therapy* 8: 309–11.

Nay, W. R. (1975) A Systematic Comparison of Instructional Techniques for Parents. *Behavior Therapy* 6: 14–21.

Neisworth, J. T. and Moore, F. (1972) Operant Treatment of Asthmatic Responding with the Parent as Therapist. *Behavior Therapy* 2: 567–74.

O'Dell, S. L. (1974) Training Parents in Behavior Modification: A Review. *Psychological Bulletin* 81: 418–33.

—— (1982) Enhancing Parent Involvement in Training: A Discussion. *The Behavior Therapist* 5 (1): 9–13.

O'Dell, S. L., Flynn, J., and Benlolo, L. (1977) A Comparison of Parent Training Techniques in Child Behavior Modification. *Journal of Behavior Therapy and Experimental Psychiatry* 8 (3): 261–68.

O'Dell, S. L., Krug, W. W., O'Quin, J., and Kasnetz, M. (1980) Media-assisted Parent Training – A Further Analysis. *The Behavior Therapist* 3: 19–21.

O'Dell, S. L., Krug, W. W., Patterson, J. N., and Faustman, W. O. (1980) An Assessment of Methods for Training Parents in the Use of Time Out. *Journal of Behavior Therapy and Experimental Psychiatry* 11 (1): 21–5.

O'Dell, S. L., O'Quin, J., Alford, B. A., O'Briant, A. L., Bradlyn, A. S., and Giebenhain, J. E. (1979) Predicting the Acquisition of Parenting Skills via Four Training Methods. Unpublished manuscript, University of Mississippi.

Patterson, G. R. (1974) Interventions for Boys with Conduct Problems, Multiple Settings, Treatment and Criteria. *Journal of Consulting and Clinical Psychology* 4 (2): 471–91.

—— (1976) *Families: Applications of Social Learning to Family Life.* Champaign, Ill.: Research Press.

Patterson, G. R., Cobb, J. A., and Ray, R. S. (1973) A Social Engineering Technology for Retraining the Families of Aggressive Boys. In H. E. Adams and I. P. Unikel (eds) *Issues and Trends in Behavior Therapy.* Springfield, Ill.: Charles C. Thomas.

Patterson, G. R., Reid, J. B., Jones, R. R., and Conger, R. E. (1975) *A Social Learning Approach to Family Intervention,* vol. 2. Champaign, Ill.: Research Press.

Peed, S., Roberts, M., and Forehand, R. (1977) Evaluation of the Effectiveness of a Standardized Parent Training Program in Altering the Interaction of Mothers and Their Noncompliant Children. *Behavior Modification* 1 (3): 323–49.

Peine, H. A. and Munro, P. C. (1973) Behavior Management of Parent Training Programs. *The Psychological Record* 23: 459–66.

Reid, J. B. (1975) A Social Learning Approach to Family Therapy: Outcome and Process Data. Paper presented at the Symposium on Behavior Modification: Methodology and Psychotherapy, Monterrey, Mexico.

Reisinger, J. J., Frangia, G. W., and Hoffman, E. H. (1976) Toddler Management Training: Generalization and Marital Status. *Journal of Behavior Therapy and Experimental Psychiatry* 7: 335–40.

Resnick, P. A., Forehand, R., and McWhorter, A. Q. (1976) Case Reports and Studies: The Effect of Parental Treatment with One Child on an Untreated Sibling. *Behavior Therapy* 7: 544–48.

Rettig, E. B. (1973) *ABC's for Parents.* Associates for Behavior Change.

Rinn, R. C., Vernon, J. C., and Wise, M. J. (1975) Training Parents of Behaviorally Disordered Children in Groups: A Three Year Program Evaluation. *Behavior Therapy* 6: 378–87.

Rose, S. D. (1974) Group Training of Parents as Behavior Modifers. *Social Work* 19 (2): 156–62.

Sadler, O. W., Seyden, T., Howe, B., and Kaminsky, T. (1976) An Evaluation of 'Groups for Parents': A Standardized Format Encompassing Both Behavior Modification and Humanistic Methods. *Journal of Community Psychology* 4 (2): 157–63.

Salzinger, K. R., Feldman, S., and Portnoy, S. (1970) Training Parents of Brain-injured Children in the Use of Operant Conditioning Procedures. *Behavior Therapy* 1 (1): 4–32.

Schaefer, J., Palkes, H. S., and Stewart, M. A. (1974) Group Counseling for Parents of Hyperactive Children. *Child Psychiatry and Human Development* 5 (2): 89–95.

Tams, V. and Eyeberg, S. (1976) A Group Treatment Program for Parents. In E. J. Mash, L. C. Handy, and L. A. Hammerlynch (eds) *Behavior Modification Approaches to Parenting*. Chicago: Brunner/Mazel.

Tavormina, J. B. (1974) Basic Models of Parent Counseling: A Critical Review. *Psychological Bulletin* 81 (11): 827–35.

—— (1975) Relative Effectiveness of Behavioral and Reflective Group Counseling with Parents of Mentally Retarded Children. *Journal of Consulting and Clinical Psychology* 43 (1): 22–31.

Tough, J. H., Howkins, R. P., McArthur, M. M., and Swaay, S. V. (1971) Modification of Eneuretic Behavior by Punishment: A New Use for an Old Device. *Behavior Therapy* 2 (4): 567–74.

Wahler, R. G. (1969) Oppositional Children: A Quest for Parental Reinforcement Control. *Journal of Applied Behavior Analysis* 2: 239–46.

—— (1980) The Insular Mother: Her Problems in Parent–child Treatment. *Journal of Applied Behavior Analysis* 13 (2): 207–19.

Wahler, R. G., Dumas, J. E., and Gordon, J. S. (November 1981) Improving the Attentional Tracking of Insular Mothers: Discriminative Restructuring. Paper presented at the Association for Advancement of Behavior Therapy, Toronto, Canada.

Wahler, R. G., Hughey, J. B., and Gordon, J. S. (1981) Chronic Patterns of Mother–child Cohesion: Some Differences Between Insular and Non-insular Families. *Analysis and Intervention in Developmental Disabilities* 1: 145–56.

Walter, H. I. and Gilmore, S. R. (1973) Placebo versus Social Learning Effects in Parent Training Procedures Designed to Alter the Behavior of Aggressive Boys. *Behavior Therapy* 4: 361–77.

Wells, K. C., Griest, D. L., and Forehand, R. (1980) The Use of a Self-control Package to Enhance Temporal Generality of a Parent Training Program. *Behavior Research and Therapy* 18: 347–53.

Wiltz, N. A. and Patterson, G. R. (1974) An Evaluation of Training Procedures Designed to Alter Inappropriate Aggressive Behavior of Boys. *Behavior Therapy* 6: 215–21.

Wolfe, D. A., Sandler, J., and Kaufman, K. (1981) A Competency-based Parent Training Program for Child Abusers. *Journal of Consulting and Clinical Psychology* 49 (5): 633–40.

Zeilberger, J. S., Sampen, S., and Sloane, H. W. (1968) Modification of a Child's Problem Behavior in the Home with the Mother as Therapist. *Journal of Applied Behavior Analysis* 1: 47–53.

Section IV

Conclusion

11 Directions for the future

Frank Ainsworth and
Leon C. Fulcher

A comparative perspective

In conclusion, we would like to call attention to some of the
practice and training issues that seem now – more than ever –
to require urgent attention. In a recent review (Ainsworth and
Fulcher 1984a) our considered view was offered on various aspects
of practitioner education for residential services in the group care
field. This review attempted to summarize findings from more
than a decade of travel, throughout Britain, the United States and
Canada, many of the European countries, Israel, and Australia.
Several major conclusions were drawn from this review, which
seem to hold true for the group care field as a whole:

- With few exceptions, residential child care workers remain
  world-wide a significantly undertrained occupational group, a
  position which is ironic, given the complexity of tasks they
  are asked to perform.
- In some countries, training efforts for residential child care workers
  are now well established, but often these are not free-standing
  educational programmes. In some countries they are linked with
  education, whilst elsewhere they are aligned with social work.
  Each approach has merit, but also distinctive limitations. The
  emergence of independent educational programmes for child care

personnel may be viewed as a further, or possibly final, stage of professional development. Such a position is beginning to find support in a few places, but as yet on a very fragmented basis.

– More broadly based and free-standing educational programmes may be necessary, if a more refined response to the training needs of child care professionals is to be achieved. Such programmes will require an emphasis on knowledge of child development as well as technical skills in providing educational, recreational, counselling, physical, and social care services for children and families.

– It follows that urgent priority needs to be given to curriculum development initiatives that relate to all of the areas referred to above.

– Specific centres for the study of group care practice may also be needed, where personnel with a proven track record of academic and practice achievements could offer in-service training, qualifying studies, and consultancy services to agencies, along with providing an organizational base for practice research.

– In keeping with the efforts referred to above, concerning practitioner training, the service systems which sponsor child care provisions will need to offer a diversified range of programmes (rather than a limited number of institutional options) for children who enter residential care, education, or treatment.

It is clear, however, that much of the difficulty experienced throughout the world in developing training programmes for group care practitioners stems from two distinct sources. The first of these concerns the limited way in which the field has been conceptualized, namely around residential programmes or client groups. Hopefully our earlier volume (Ainsworth and Fulcher 1981) as well as this one will go some way towards addressing this issue, by calling attention to the field of group care, which includes institutional services, residential group living, and day care within its domain of practice. The second difficulty involves the absence of any clear model of practice which identifies the areas of knowledge and skills required of group care practitioners in each of the three types of service referred to above. It is hoped that our continuing work on this issue and the practice curriculum for group care published elsewhere (CCETSW 1983) will have gone some way towards responding to the second deficiency. The broader field of study and the practice curriculum it offers can be said to give potential impetus for the continuing development of services on a wider front.

Applications in practice

If these ideas are to be accepted and endorsed, however, they will have to be shown to be valid in practice. Whenever they have been tested, practitioners have regularly endorsed these ideas for their validity and versatility in addressing the complexities of group care work. Elsewhere (Ainsworth and Fulcher 1984b) we have proposed the development of educational units for teaching group care practice. Four practice teaching models were proposed, taking account of particular types of personnel who require training and different aspects of practice which need development. Practice teaching units such as these would undoubtedly advance the development of practice expertise in the future, and therefore warrant careful consideration.

Allied to this proposal is the work which has already been undertaken by the Group Care Training Project, mounted jointly in 1979 by Dr Barnardo's and the University of Stirling in Scotland (Kinloch and Fulcher 1984). This project has demonstrated ways in which the concept of group care and many of the features identified in our earlier volume can be developed into a curriculum for the training of group care practitioners. This project has also identified the range of training patterns required, including: training for newly recruited workers without qualifications; training for staff *en route* to qualification; training for experienced staff with particular educational needs; and training for senior staff with advanced training needs.

An agenda for the future

Further work is required in all the areas referred to above. The field of group care warrants a more detailed evaluation and mapping. Further definition and refinement are needed in relation to the practice curriculum for group care. The structural features of practice, along with the content and skills areas, will need to be developed further. Relevant teaching aids and materials will also need to be constructed.

Whilst, to date, our efforts have concentrated on developing ideas in relation to children's services, we are convinced that the central notions are viable with respect to services for handicapped adults and elderly people. This holds, regardless of the type of handicap, wherever institutional care, residential group living, and day care are used with the population. Those of our readers who pursue the references given in this final chapter will find frequent illustrations which relate to services for populations other than children. Further work across 'the life cycle of care' seems desirable, especially when one discovers that even greater limitations are to be found in relation to group care practice and training for work with handicapped adults and elderly people.

References

Ainsworth, F. and Fulcher, L. C. (eds) (1981) *Group Care for Children: Concept and Issues*. London: Tavistock.
—— (1984a) Aspects of Residential Child Care Services and Practitioner Education. *Canadian Journal of Child Care* 1 (6): 1–9.
—— (1984b) Student Units for Practice Teaching in Group Care. *Social Work Education* 3 (2): 30–4.
Central Council for Education and Training in Social Work (1983) *A Practice Curriculum for Group Care*. London: Paper 14.2.
Kinloch, H. and Fulcher, L. C. (1984) *The Group Care Training Project: 1979–1982*. Hertford, Herts., England: Barnardo's/University of Stirling.

Name index

Rice, A. K. 69, 218
Rinn, R. C. 251, 257
Rivlin, L. G. 60–1
Roberts, E. 222
Roberts, M. 258
Robinson, J. 127
Romig, D. 127
Rose, S. D. 254
Rosenthal, M. 258
Roses, S. 56–7
Ross, A. L. 159, 166, 191
Ross, R. 109–12, 188

Sabatino, D. 135
Sadler, O. W. 244
Salancik, G. R. 56
Salzinger, K. R. 254
Sampen, S. 253
Sandler, J. 244
Sapir, S. 110
Savicki, V. 172, 174
Schaefer, J. 253
Scheirer, M. A. 191
Schroder, H. M. 87
Schultz, L. A. 260
Scott, T. 64
Silberman, C. 135
Sinclair, I. 99
Slater, R. 61
Sloop, E. W. 247
Sloane, H. W. 253, 258
Small, R. 15, 135, 153, 159
Smilansky, S. 157–58, 176
Smircich, L. 209
Smith, G. 127
Smith, S. S. 257
Snowdon, L. R. 9
Sommer, R. 60
Spivak, G. 136
Stenmark, D. E. 208
Stewart, M. A. 253
Stipek, D. 158, 175
Stocking, S. M. 23
Strauss, A. L. 4
Sullivan, E. D. 88
Sundberg, N. D. 9

Swaay, S. V. 253
Swift, M. 136
Szelenyi, I. 30

Tams, V. 247, 250
Tavormina, J. B. 240, 257, 259–60
Taylor, D. A. 98, 109
Thomason, T. C. 260
Toch, H. 113
Tomlinson, P. 190
Tough, J. H. 253
Trieschman, A. E. 174, 220
Tugginer, H. 155

VanderVen, K. 16, 135, 151, 156–59,
    162, 168–79, 221, 225
VanScoy, H. 159
Vernon, J. C. 251, 257
Vorath, H. H. 94

Wahler, R. G. 245, 253–55, 258
Walter, H. I. 257
Warren, M. Q. 89, 110, 115–23, 126–
    27, 188–89, 194–95
Washington, R. O. 41
Weihs, T. J. 135
Weissman, H. W. 59
Wells, K. C. 244
White, P. E. 209
Whittaker, J. K. 54, 98, 113, 156, 159,
    171–76, 191, 220, 222
Wilkins, A. L. 209
Wilks, J. 109–11, 127
Wilson, T. 159
Wiltz, N. A. 250, 253, 257
Wineman, D. 60, 155, 171
Wise, M. J. 251, 257
Wolf, M. M. 46
Wolfe, D. A. 244
Wolfe, M. 61
Wolfensberger, W. 53, 173
Wolins, M. 32, 38, 51
Wozner, Y. 32, 38, 51

Zeilberger, J. S. 253
Zimmerman, M. 208

Subject index

'Acorn People' 179
Action Plan for group care practice
86–104; child development 93–8;
evaluation 102; key worker
responsibilities 101–02; links with
family, peers, etc. 98–9; policy and
philosophy 90–3; programme
development and evaluation 102–
04; staffing and staff development
99–101
activities 155–79; analysis of 171–74;
climate of involvement 166–68;
goal-setting 169–71; as
intervention 156–58; involving
children in 174–77; and passivity
161–62; process and product 162–
64; programming 158–74;
structure, creativity and freedom
164–66; universal adaptation 159–
61
adaptation of activities 159–61
administration see organization;
secondary care
affect: emotional demands on workers
31–2, 38–40; teaching competence
142–44
after-care 99
aggression 77, 121, 253
allegiance, staff 226–27
analysis: of activities 171–74; systems
29–31, 218

art activities 164–66, 178
assessment of residents: competence
148–49; effects on staff teamwork
193–210; presentation of 127–29;
typologies of 86–9, 113–16, 127–
130, 118–93
attitudes towards child behaviour:
parents' 245, 258; staff 94–6
auditory perception 139–40
autism 167–68, 253
availability of boundary workers 225–
26

behaviour of children: attitudes
towards 94–6, 245, 258;
management of 108–09, 117–18,
135–36; types of 253; see also
parent training
boundaries in care systems 54, 217–
19; working across 215–37
boundary work 219–23;
communication 219, 231–32;
coordination 228–31; in group care
223–35; management 223–24;
public relations 234–35; role of
235–37; staff support 224–28; tasks
219–23; teaching 233–34; work
with families 233
British Association of Social Workers
90, 237
buildings for care centres 60–3